D0725196

GiViNG

STUDENTS

a

SAy

ASCD MEMBER BOOK

Many ASCD members received this book
as a member benefit upon its initial release.

Learn more at **www.ascd.org/memberbooks**

ALSO BY THE AUTHOR

*Grading Smarter, Not Harder: Assessment Strategies
That Motivate Kids and Help Them Learn*

MYRON
DUECK

GIVING

STUDENTS

a

SAY

Smarter
Assessment
Practices to
Empower
and Engage

Alexandria, Virginia USA

ASCD®

1703 N. Beauregard St. • Alexandria, VA 22311-1714 USA
Phone: 800-933-2723 or 703-578-9600 • Fax: 703-575-5400
Website: www.ascd.org • E-mail: member@ascd.org
Author guidelines: www.ascd.org/write

Ranjit Sidhu, *CEO & Executive Director*; Stefani Roth, *Publisher*; Genny Ostertag, *Director, Content Acquisitions*; Julie Houtz, *Director, Book Editing & Production*; Miriam Calderone, *Editor*; Thomas Lytle, *Creative Director*; Donald Ely, *Art Director*; Masie Chong, *Graphic Designer*; Valerie Younkin, *Senior Production Designer*; Kelly Marshall, *Manager, Project Management*; Trinay Blake, *E-Publishing Specialist*

Copyright © 2021 ASCD. All rights reserved. It is illegal to reproduce copies of this work in print or electronic format (including reproductions displayed on a secure intranet or stored in a retrieval system or other electronic storage device from which copies can be made or displayed) without the prior written permission of the publisher. By purchasing only authorized electronic or print editions and not participating in or encouraging piracy of copyrighted materials, you support the rights of authors and publishers. Readers who wish to reproduce or republish excerpts of this work in print or electronic format may do so for a small fee by contacting the Copyright Clearance Center (CCC), 222 Rosewood Dr., Danvers, MA 01923, USA (phone: 978-750-8400; fax: 978-646-8600; web: www.copyright.com). To inquire about site licensing options or any other reuse, contact ASCD Permissions at www.ascd.org/permissions or permissions@ascd.org. For a list of vendors authorized to license ASCD e-books to institutions, see www.ascd.org/epubs. Send translation inquiries to translations@ascd.org.

ASCD® and ASCD LEARN. TEACH. LEAD.® are registered trademarks of ASCD. All other trademarks contained in this book are the property of, and reserved by, their respective owners, and are used for editorial and informational purposes only. No such use should be construed to imply sponsorship or endorsement of the book by the respective owners.

All web links in this book are correct as of the publication date below but may have become inactive or otherwise modified since that time. If you notice a deactivated or changed link, please e-mail books@ascd.org with the words "Link Update" in the subject line. In your message, please specify the web link, the book title, and the page number on which the link appears.

PAPERBACK ISBN: 978-1-4166-2980-1   ASCD product #119013

PDF E-BOOK ISBN: 978-1-4166-2981-8; see Books in Print for other formats.

Quantity discounts are available: e-mail programteam@ascd.org or call 800-933-2723, ext. 5773, or 703-575-5773. For desk copies, go to www.ascd.org/deskcopy.

ASCD Member Book No. FY21-4A (Jan. 2021 PSI+). ASCD Member Books mail to Premium (P), Select (S), and Institutional Plus (I+) members on this schedule: Jan, PSI+; Feb, P; Apr, PSI+; May, P; Jul, PSI+; Aug, P; Sep, PSI+; Nov, PSI+; Dec, P. For current details on membership, see www.ascd.org/membership.

Library of Congress Cataloging-in-Publication Data
Names: Dueck, Myron, author.
Title: Giving students a say : smarter assessment practices to empower and engage / Myron Dueck.
Description: Alexandria, Virginia USA : ASCD, 2021. | Includes bibliographical references and index.
Identifiers: LCCN 2020040094 (print) | LCCN 2020040095 (ebook) | ISBN 9781416629801 (Paperback) | ISBN 9781416629818 (PDF)
Subjects: LCSH: Educational tests and measurements—United States. | Grading and marking (Students)—United States. | Educational evaluation—United States.
Classification: LCC LB3051 .D6679 2021 (print) | LCC LB3051 (ebook) | DDC 371.260973—dc23
LC record available at https://lccn.loc.gov/2020040094
LC ebook record available at https://lccn.loc.gov/2020040095

29 28 27 26 25 24 23 22 21   1 2 3 4 5 6 7 8 9 10 11 12

To all the students I've learned from:
Your voices, opinions, and honesty
made me a better educator.

FOREWORD

Come into the elevator.

Some years ago, I led a team to develop the assessment scheme for New Zealand elementary and high schools (https://e-asttle.tki.org.nz), and New York City was interested in adopting it. My bosses told me that in business and politics, it is critical to get the elevator pitch perfect, since you often have only one chance to get the message across. My business developer worked on the pitch and trained me with religious zeal in delivering it before we went off to New York. Once there, we just happened to enter an elevator at the same time as Joel Klein, then-chancellor of the New York City Department of Education. Somehow my perfectly prepared elevator pitch went by the wayside, and we talked about… *sheep*.

I now have the chance to deliver another elevator pitch, so here goes: "Assessment is something we have done *to* students rather than *with* them." Pause and reread this message. If one sentence sums up the reason this book was written, this is it. This book's aim is for educators to work *with* students for a most just cause: to help students become confident learners who can interpret assessment information, use it to improve their learning outcomes, and be better prepared for the various challenges they encounter. The importance of this pitch is why I was honored to be asked to write this foreword.

I have worked in assessment for most of my career, and within the assessment community, we moved from seeing tests as valid *if they measure what they intended* to seeing tests as valid *if the interpretations are defensible.* In other words, if a test doesn't result in any consequential reflection, interpretation, decision making, or action, then it doesn't matter if it has all the lovely measurement properties that we psychometricians love. This shift, beginning in the 1990s, has allowed the measurement community to come into closer contact with classroom teachers to help them reliably interpret assessment data, make decisions based on the data, and act on those decisions. These skills are precisely the ones we also need to teach students. We should see the score as but the starting point.

But for too many students, the score is the end point, and the number screams to them that the work is now over. They know how to interpret the score relative to the scores of their peers, and they know that 100 percent is perfect (although in reality, 100 percent usually means that the work was too easy). Such a narrow interpretation of the score won't tell them about their gaps, strengths, and misunderstandings or help them decide what to do next.

I'd like to invite you to carry out two simple tasks. First, ask your students to grade their own performance on the next test *before* they start it. Second, after you have graded the test and written thorough comments, ask your students to write a short list of statements describing what they have learned about their learning and where they need to move next in light of your grade and comments. The results of this experiment will likely bear out what research suggests: that from about age 8 onward, students are quite accurate in determining their place in the achievement equation and predicting their scores—and that teacher grades and comments do little to help students understand what they've learned and where they need to go next.

After students complete a test, we should be asking ourselves what *we* learned—about what we taught well, whom we taught well, and the magnitude of growth that students have made from the beginning of the learning period to this point. Asking these questions will result in more informative tests both for teachers and for students.

Throughout this book, the notion of assessing *with* students is termed as a *student-centered* approach to assessment. With this approach, assessments do not dominate students' radar (as revealed by the eternal question "Will this be on the test?") but, rather, are seen as a supportive interpretive method to enhance student learning. This approach ensures that learning targets, instruction, learning tasks, success criteria, and rubrics are aligned *with* assessment. What is valued should be ever-present and aligned; therefore, the test does not dominate but becomes part of the learning process.

Assessment applies to so much more than achievement; it can be an invaluable tool to help us understand and effectively use learning strategies. Myron explores such notions as retrieval versus storage strength, desirable difficulties, solution generation effects, how to persist and enjoy challenges, spaced versus massed practice, and interleaving rather than blocking—ideas that have been known for decades in learning theory but rarely are practiced by those most empowered to influence learning. One fascinating idea is that rubrics can be powerful learning aids. I disagree with the common belief that rubrics' main purpose is to assess performance: of course they do that, but they also help students dive deeper and spread their wings of knowing, and they guide students' progression to a lesson's success criteria. Myron's exploration of rubrics as learning tools is just one of the powerful applications of ideas that make this book so practical for teachers and bring to life the goal of assessing with students.

Myron ends the book back in the elevator. If it were me in this elevator, I would ponder all my missed opportunities to talk about something other than sheep: *If only I had thought of presenting these great assessment ideas, if only I had the richness of experience and practice that is evident throughout this book, if only I had focused on conducting assessment* with *students rather than administering it to students.* Never mind. Myron is here, and he has done it for us.

John Hattie

ACKNOWLEDGMENTS

Students

I'll speak generally for teachers by saying that we like schools: the classrooms, labs, hallways, theaters, and gymnasiums conjure good memories. Many of us gravitated back to school for our careers based on these positive experiences. I have come to realize, however, that many students' feelings about school range from passive disinterest to abject fear. For these kids, coming to school is a struggle. So I first want to acknowledge all students: without you, this book simply wouldn't exist. Thank you for your honesty, courage, and feedback. Thank you for teaching me to listen.

I also want to acknowledge a few specific students. Malaina, thank you for providing the quote that in many ways encapsulates the theme of this book: "No one knows me like I know me." Xavier, thank you for digging into your school experience and providing a candid appraisal. Rayman, thank you for raising a valid concern about assessment and being willing to engage in conversation about it. I wish many more students would do the same.

Educators

To the thousands of educators I've met since starting this journey into assessment, thank you for your curiosity, passion, and willingness to learn. Your questions and our conversations have pushed my thinking and caused me valuable discomfort. I want to especially thank the teachers who contributed their voices, resources, experiences, and opinions to this book: Josh Almoite, Shona Becker, Helen Carelse, Josh Eastwood, Melanie Henning, Joelle Hernandez, Sydney Jensen, Nick Kast, Nicola Korvin, Scott McIntosh, Marnie Mennell, Tristan Mennell, Barry Morhart, Paige Mullins, Mark Osborn, Russ Reid, Elizabeth Salinas, Kari Straube, Rachel Stubbert, Troy Stubbert, Dave Van Bergeyk, and Tim Van Ness. To Scott McIntosh, Paige Mullins, and Russ Reid in particular, thank you for allowing me to spend extended periods of time with your students, delving deep into how we can assess *with* them. You are remarkable educators.

Thank you to the school and district leaders who provided opinions and opportunity: Brandon Blom, Judith King, Don MacIntyre, Todd Manuel, Naryn Searcy, and Alan Stel.

Chris Van Bergeyk, I think you were right when you said, "Our years at Summerland Secondary might just turn out to be some of the best years ever." Thank you for modeling leadership, compassion, and vision. Your thoughts, suggestions, and diversions had an incredible impact on my work, and this book in particular. Your feedback of "Myron, that's surprisingly good" offered measured support while keeping my ego in check.

Tom Guskey, not only have you been an incredible source of knowledge, but also, more important, you model honesty, selflessness, and authenticity. Ken O'Connor, there's no way I'd have put a dent in this thing called assessment without your influence, direction, and support. (Sloane says hi.)

To Sherry Bennett, recently retired from the Alberta Assessment Consortium (AAC): seldom do I come back from delivering professional development feeling as though *I* did the bulk of the learning. Your work with the AAC is amazing, and the conversation around rubrics in this book owes much to you. Celeste Kidd, thank you for the enlightening conversations surrounding your experiences and research. You provided an invaluable perspective.

John Hattie, thank you for writing the thoughtful foreword to this book. What I am even more grateful for, however, is what I gleaned from our conversation in Melbourne in 2019. I was well into writing my second book when you asked me about it. After I gave a brief description, you gave your candid appraisal: "That sounds kind of boring." When you asked if I had anything else in mind, I commented that I'd considered writing about "giving students a say" in assessment, and you immediately responded, "Write about that!" Your polite yet pointedly honest redirect resulted in this book. I agree that my original plan was boring. (Elijah says hi.)

Other contributors

Carter Bryant, Leslie Hasselbach Adams, and Dan Laak, thank you for providing your sports expertise and perspective at key points in this book. You demonstrate that we can learn so much from our desire to compete.

Genny Ostertag, Miriam Calderone, Ken Cornwell, and the rest of the team at ASCD, you have provided me with a voice on a much larger stage than I ever could have imagined. Your professionalism and direction have been invaluable.

Garth and Tammy Larson and all the people at First Educational Resources, thank you for taking a chance on me many years back and giving me my first major keynote opportunities. As well, thanks for letting me explore a range of topics with the educators who attend your fantastic events.

Friends and family

Lorne Siemens, thank you for that feed mill job I mention on page 111. I learned so much during my time there, and your impact proves that some of our best teachers are not found in schools. Paul Girard, thank you for helping me coach our sons in volleyball. Your insights and opinions have led me to look at situations through the invaluable "noneducator" lens. Oh, and your adage "I'm trying to be less wrong every day" is as funny as it is apt. Jeremy Hiebert, since elementary school, you've been a sounding board, voice of reason, and constructive critic. In recent years, our mountain bike climb conversations have helped shape my thinking about learning and life. Ben Arcuri, somehow we've melded the joys and challenges of building projects, parenting, surfing, and just about everything else with our assessment chats. A special thanks to you and Jessa for serving as backup when needed—especially for Elijah and Sloane.

To Tracey, Elijah, and Sloane: I couldn't imagine tackling a project like this without your patience, understanding, and unconditional support. I know I've taken liberties sharing our stories, images, and experiences when they illustrate a point or serve as real-life examples; thank you for granting me this license. Finally, some of the hundreds of hours spent writing this book were carved out of precious family time. I've never understood how you three navigate these challenges without a hint of frustration or judgment. Thank you.

THE ELEVATOR PITCH

How can we make the case for student-centered assessment—and why is it important to do so?

Terry O'Reilly's book *This I Know* (2017) is a must-read for anyone with the slightest interest in marketing. And if you couldn't care less about marketing, you might just enjoy the background stories to the multitude of ads and products that've shaped our lives. O'Reilly bases much of the book on stories and lessons from his popular podcast *Under the Influence*. One of my favorite tales is that of Steve Jobs attempting to entice John Sculley to leave Pepsi and join Apple. In 1982, Sculley was at the top of his game and firmly entrenched as president of PepsiCo. Starting as a truck driver for the soft drink giant, Sculley had been climbing the Pepsi ladder for 16 years (Mazarakis & Shontell, 2017), though none of his work involved tech (Pollack, 1983). As president of PepsiCo, Sculley was the marketing genius behind the "Pepsi Challenge," which pitted Pepsi against Coca-Cola in a series of blind tastings, and he was considered a strong candidate to become CEO of the entire Pepsi brand. Seeing the effectiveness with which Sculley carved away market share from Coca-Cola—and the inescapable comparison to Apple taking on Microsoft—Jobs was obsessed with poaching Sculley. Unfortunately for Jobs, Sculley wasn't interested in the Apple scene. Although Jobs offered Sculley a huge salary and lucrative stock options, he couldn't be swayed. After months of campaigning by Jobs, Sculley attempted to put the matter to rest in a face-to-face meeting with Jobs:

> I've been thinking about it a lot and I'm not coming to Apple. I'm going to stay here in the East Coast doing what I'm doing. I'll be an adviser for free. Let's just be friends, but I'm not coming to Apple. (Mazarakis & Shontell, 2017, para. 41)

Most people would probably have left it at that, but Steve Jobs wasn't like "most people." Upon hearing that seemingly final rejection, Jobs walked up to Sculley and, 20 inches from his face, uttered his now famous line: "Do you want to sell sugar water for the rest of your life? Or do you want to come with me and change the world?" (Mazarakis & Shontell, 2017).

A week later, Sculley was employed at Apple. Ten years later, Apple was the most profitable computer company in the world.

O'Reilly cited this story to highlight the power and importance of the "elevator pitch"—the succinct encapsulation of an idea that takes no more than 20 seconds to convey. In his campaign against the formidable Jimmy Carter, Ronald Reagan had a simple, successful elevator pitch he posed to voters: "Are you better off now than you were four years ago?" (O'Reilly, 2017, p. 29). Any product you've purchased, movie you've watched, or book you've read likely came to fruition because it had an elevator pitch that convinced someone that it was worth producing.

According to O'Reilly, a good elevator pitch has a few fundamental qualities. It needs to be concise and captivating and reflect the essence of the organization or brand. "Pitches are an exercise in clarity," writes O'Reilly (p. 20), and they reflect the adage "Less is more." O'Reilly encourages organizations to distill their mission into an immediately digestible and compelling hook. Warning against our desire to elaborate, O'Reilly states, "If [your elevator pitch] takes a paragraph, it's not ready yet" (p. 24).

Steve Jobs may have understood the power of a good elevator pitch more than anyone. He described Apple as follows: "Apple has always had the ability to take really complex technology and make it easy to understand and use by the end user" (Arthur, 2014).

That's compelling—and likely the main reason why I am typing this on a Mac, own an iPhone and an Apple Watch, subscribe to Apple TV, and stop to admire a vintage Apple IIc whenever I pass one.

I've often wondered what responses you might get from a room of teachers if you asked them to produce an elevator pitch for their subject, class, or school. What about an elevator pitch for teaching in the 21st century? How might educators summarize their entire reason for being into a single sentence or two? While

I was attending a conference in Australia, John Hattie shared with me his simple quest: *Know thy impact* (personal communication, May 2018). I liked it. It was simple, powerful, and inextricably tied to feedback—for the teacher!

Based on the experiences of businesses such as Apple and authors such as Hattie, we will want to start with *why we are* in education, not *what we do* in education. In his book *Start with Why*, Simon Sinek (2009) encourages us to imagine we sell Apple computers, and he predicts that our sales pitch might start with this: "We make great computers. They're beautifully designed, simple to use and user-friendly" (p. 40). Although this may seem logical and describe the essence of our product, this pitch is related to *what* the computer is, not *why* we produce it.

O'Reilly (2017) argues that in crafting really compelling elevator pitches, the most successful companies have a clear understanding of the business they are in, and some examples might surprise us. Nike isn't in the shoe business; it's in the *motivation* business. Michelin doesn't sell tires, it sells *safety*. The marketing geniuses at Heineken no longer flog beer as much as they sell *inclusion, tolerance,* and *moderation*.

Following the lead of these top brands, perhaps educators need to clarify the business they're in, and I'm not sure it's education. I think we would transform our schools if we rebranded ourselves as being in the *empowerment* and *engagement* business. As U.S. representative and civil rights leader Barbara Jordan declared, "Education remains the key to both economic and political empowerment" (quoted in Newman, 1998, p. 124). If you think about it, throughout history, education is inextricably tied to empowerment.

We explored elevator pitches with our faculty at Summerland Secondary School (SSS) in British Columbia, Canada. Principal Alan Stel and I devoted a significant portion of our staff meetings to crafting individual elevator pitches to answer the question "Why attend Summerland Secondary?" It was an interesting and challenging activity, and the results were as fascinating as they were varied. Here are a few examples:

> SSS helps to build students' skills and confidence so that they can be successful in whatever path they choose.

> We are small enough and big enough to create amazing opportunities for our students and staff. Our opportunities reflect modern realities and valued traditions to balance all areas of learning and to prepare our students for challenges known and unknown.

> Small, Supportive, Innovative, Creative, Flexible... Like *Cheers,* where everybody knows your name.

I've been working on my own *education* elevator pitch, and a while back I arrived at this:

> I empower my students through authentic learning experiences and engaging assessment practices. In all that I do, I develop meaningful relationships with students so that they become confident learners—better prepared for whatever they might encounter.

I've edited versions of this more than a dozen times, and I'm sure it'll live in continuous development. With each iteration, however, the word *assessment* seems to remain a constant. As much as I've tried, I can't separate my educational elevator pitch from the topic of assessment and why it must be student-centered.

Assessment is the language of learning. From establishing our purpose and defining the learning objectives, to evaluating student progress and reporting on it, assessment is, in the words of Dylan Wiliam, "the bridge between teaching and learning" (2018, p. 56). I recall teaching my own kids to ice skate, ride a bike, back up an ATV with a trailer in tow, and countless other things. Each experience dripped with assessment components: objectives, success criteria, evaluation, and feedback. In the case of skating, my back never really recovered, and the ATV trailer sessions had me periodically walking away out of sheer frustration. However, eventually both of my kids *learned* how to skate and back up a vehicle with a trailer—thanks largely to assessment and their part in it.

The word *assessment* originates from the Latin *assidere*, meaning "to sit beside" ("Assess," n.d.). Let that reverberate through your mind. To sit beside. When looking at assessment practices in schools around the world, I'm not sure we're reflecting the true meaning of assessment. For far too long, assessment is what we have done *to* students rather than *with* them. Students need to stop being the people to whom we apply assessment processes, as if they were inanimate objects. Similar to how a lawyer might become a "partner" in the firm, students need to transform from being the employee to being the co-owner in the learning process.

Furthermore, this is not a student issue but a human one. People want to know the standards by which they are being assessed, how they will be evaluated, and whether they will have some input into the reporting of the result. I mean, seriously, how intrigued would *you* be as a student if this were the sales pitch:

> Welcome, class. I'm going to teach for a while, and then sometime next week I'm going to assess you. After enough of those experiences, I will rank and sort you compared with others based on how well you've recalled the things I've told you. Your scores may affect your future in some dramatic way. Good luck.
>
> Oh, and I forgot to mention, there may be some effects on your grades that have nothing to do with your understanding, but rather how you behave, treat others, display effort—those kinds of things.

I probably lost you at "I'm going to teach for a while...."

I'm not sure about the rest of you, but that "sales pitch" would largely sum up my assessment model over the first 10 years of my career. Clearly, it needed to change.

Support for a Student-Centered Approach to Assessment

A more learner-centered model of assessment has ample support. The Organisation for Economic Co-operation and Development (OECD) is an international governmental forum whose purpose is to "promote policies that will improve the economic and social well-being of people around the world" (www.OECD.org). This Paris-based forum, to which Australia, Canada, Italy, the United States, and more than 30 other countries contribute, has taken a decade-long approach to helping governments respond to new developments and concerns around education in an information economy. In *The OECD Handbook for Innovative Learning Environments* (OECD, 2017), this multinational think tank presents seven principles for designing learning environments. Thankfully, the OECD states that it's "unrealistic for a school or district to start working on all seven principles with equal priority" (p. 22). Although all seven are worthy of further study, for our purposes we will summarize three that support the student being the primary agent in assessment:

- The learning environment recognizes the learners as its core participants.
- The learning environment is acutely sensitive to the individual differences among learners.
- The learning environment operates with clarity of expectations and deploys assessment strategies consistent with these expectations. (OECD, 2017)

In his groundbreaking synthesis of research on factors affecting student achievement, *Visible Learning for Teachers*, John Hattie (2012) presents a ranked list of 150 items. The highest-ranked factor is "student self-reported grades." To be clear, by Hattie's own admission, he would rather have phrased this as "student expectations," meaning that students are incredibly accurate in predicting their own level of understanding and achievement. Hattie states it bluntly: "Students are the best people to report on themselves" (personal interview, 2018).

Let's pause for a moment to consider the ramifications. How is it possible that many of our traditional assessment models largely ignore the voice of the student when reporting learning, while research suggests that the student is the most important agent in the conversation?

In *Embedded Formative Assessment*, Wiliam (2018) makes a strong case for teaching to be adaptive to the needs of the student, an approach that is impossible if we're not involving the student in assessment. In establishing five key elements upon which we would base our assessment system, Wiliam includes three that directly and overtly involve the student:

- Clarifying, sharing, and understanding learning intentions and success criteria.
- Activating learners as instructional resources for one another.
- Activating learners as owners of their own thinking. (p. 52)

Involving students in assessment has powerful side effects. In his book *Rigorous PBL by Design*, Michael McDowell (2017) underscores how a student growth mindset is supported by students having the ability to monitor their own progress and take actions to improve their achievement. In a vein similar to the OECD principles and Wiliam's elements, McDowell goes on to encourage the supporting of "assessment-capable learners" who can monitor their own progress by being able to answer these questions:

- Where am I going in my learning?
- Where am I now in my learning?
- What's the next thing I need to improve in my learning?
- How do I improve my learning and that of others?

Inviting students into the realm of assessment is linked to increased motivation, confidence, self-regulation, and performance. Moss and Brookhart (2012) make a compelling argument as to why students must be at the center of the assessment conversation:

> Students who take ownership of their learning attribute what they do well to decisions they make and control. These factors not only increase students' ability to assess and regulate their own learning, but also boost their motivation to learn as they progressively see themselves as more confident and competent learners. (p. 11)

As we dig even deeper into the research, involving the student goes beyond boosting motivation and confidence. Not only should students understand the elements of assessment as McDowell, Wiliam, and Moss and Brookhart propose, but also their understanding of its very *purpose* relates directly to their performance (Brown & Hattie, 2012). There is a positive relationship between assessment and performance when students believe that assessment (1) legitimately helps determine their grades, (2) helps regulate their own learning, and (3) is used by teachers to modify or improve instruction (Brown, Peterson, & Irving, 2009). Conversely, if students perceive that assessment is irrelevant, is given for fun, reflects external factors beyond their control, or is related to overall school quality, they perform worse (Brown, 2011).

Voice and Choice: Key Factors in Student-Centered Assessment

If *assessment* means "to sit beside," we need to stop figuratively placing the learning outcomes on the table *between* us and our students, informing them of what's right and what's wrong, and instead slide our chair around to the same side of the table to facilitate a conversation. Assessment would then become a process by which we collectively strategize and codesign how *we* will best approach, evaluate, and report on the learning objectives. Students would ideally be able to demonstrate understanding over a period of time, drawing on examples and discussing challenges and what's been learned from these experiences. Just imagine the transformational potential if learning were to truly become a *partnership* between the teacher and the learner.

The Power of Voice

In their book *Student Voice: The Instrument of Change*, Russell Quaglia and Michael Corso (2014) argue for such a partnership, one built upon authentic and valued student voice. As educators, we might *think* we are listening to our students, but Quaglia and Corso question our traditional approach, offering a challenge to transform. They write,

> Sure, we have had student protests, student marches, student sit-ins, and student walkouts, but we are talking about student voice not that reactively opposes something, but rather *proactively participates* in the greater good of learning. We are talking about genuine and authentic student voice, where teachers ask for their students' opinions, listen—*really* listen—to what students have to say, and incorporate what they learn and students themselves into leadership of their classrooms and schools. (p. 1)

Student voice can be very powerful. Over the decade from 2009 to 2018, the Quaglia Institute for Student Aspirations polled more than 450,000 students, in 820 schools across 34 states, and found that when students have voice, they are

- Three times more likely to experience *self-worth* in school.
- Five times more likely to be *engaged* in school.
- Five times more likely to have a sense of *purpose* in school. (Quaglia Institute for Student Aspirations, 2018)

Despite student voice being a powerful force in learning, statistics suggest that we are failing to support this teacher-student partnership—especially as our students get older. In 2012–2013, the Pearson Foundation administered the national My Voice survey to just under 60,000 students in grades 6 through 12. The survey found that although 61 percent of students entering middle school felt they had a voice, this number dwindled to 37 percent by grade 12. Just as alarming, only 46 percent felt that they had any say in decision making in their schools, and just over half believed that teachers were willing to learn from students (Quaglia Institute for Student Aspirations, 2013).

If we pause long enough to listen—*really* listen—students will tell us what's going on. What they need is the opportunity and avenues to share their thoughts, opinions, and reflections concerning their own learning. The thing is, you can't really listen to someone else while you are speaking. Perhaps that's why Hattie contends that we need to stop talking once in a while and "create that space to listen with them" (ASCD, 2019).

In this book, we'll look at specific examples of how we can incorporate student voice into all stages of the assessment process. We'll explore how to create a safe climate of sharing and reflection. Throughout the book, I'll share assessment tools and strategies that empower students and welcome student voice. For instance, when I incorporated a "sharing circle" in my classroom, I experienced a revolutionary change in the learning climate—both during our sharing-circle activities and in classroom conversations that followed long after the circle disbanded. (See Chapter 6 for more on sharing circles.)

Many educators have told me how listening to their students is transformational for them and their practices. One of the best examples was from an educator in Minnesota who listened in on a homework conversation between her daughter and a friend. At one point, her daughter stopped at a question and was trying to explain a key math concept. Barely into the explanation, the daughter was interrupted by her friend, who said, "Listen, I don't have time to learn this. I just need to get it done." Is there a better "elevator pitch" for why traditional homework regimens need to change? Again, we just need to stop and listen—*really* listen—to the learning.

More recently, a whole other sector of the population has been challenged to truly listen to students about their learning experience. The COVID-19 era of home-based learning has placed parents on the front lines of their children's education, charging them with delivering curriculum and assessing how well kids have attained learning objectives. Probably for the first time in the modern era of education, legions of parents have heard their children thinking aloud about their learning, witnessed their children's (desirable) learning difficulties, and been forced to move beyond whether it is right or wrong to help children think about a problem. Trust me—I fled the room while my wife Tracey earned a Purple Heart working with my son, Elijah, through his grade 10 math course! Globally, it will be interesting to witness the long-term effects of the COVID-19 crisis as parents everywhere have dived into the language of learning. If my own house is any indication, the way parents speak about learning may evolve from such traditional queries as "Did you complete your homework?" and "What did you do at school today?" These millions of parents, together with their children, may now demand a more sophisticated conversation surrounding *what* their children learn, *how* they learn it, and *why*.

Students are in a unique position to report on their own learning, so it's imperative that we ask them. When I first met Dave Van Bergeyk, a senior math teacher from Salmon Arm, British Columbia, I was astonished to learn that he met with each of his calculus students and negotiated their grades based on a *body of evidence* and a *conversation*. My reaction was swift: "Seriously—you negotiate with the student to determine the final grade?" How could a senior calculus and math teacher be basing his grades on a conversation? (See page 147 for Dave's story.)

Soon after I had met Dave, a few colleagues and I started a system that we informally called *conversation-based grading*. At about the same time that I first offered students in my Leadership class a chance to comment on their progress, Marnie Mennell was asking learners in her Foods class to share their own successes and struggles. Troy Stubbert offered his Auto and Metal students the chance to self-report, and Rachel Stubbert threw the doors open to her math students to track and report their progress on both formative and summative assessments. At times it felt like we were opening up a new frontier. (Templates and resources reflecting these kinds of changes are presented throughout this book.)

I wondered if asking students at Summerland Secondary to report on their own learning was having a positive impact, so we... asked them. Here are some of their responses:

> "Instead of just getting marks back from my teacher telling me what I'm doing, or what they think I'm thinking, they get an idea of what's actually going on." —Xavier

> "I know about me; teachers think they know me." —Morgan

> "No one knows me like I know me!" —Malaina

These students' comments are compelling. *Giving Students a Say* is about engaging and empowering students in all conversations about learning—particularly assessment. The time has come for teachers to provide opportunities for students to articulate their understanding and be given a voice in reporting it. It's time to create space to listen with them.

The Importance of Choice

Voice and choice are arguably inseparable factors when looking at empowerment and engagement—and that goes for all of us. The 20th century saw an explosion of choice in areas ranging from careers and educational opportunities to food products and entertainment. In my lifetime alone, the expansion of choice has been both amazing and numbing. Growing up, I recall "channel surfing" the *three* available TV stations. I bet I watched *The Sound of Music* eight times because there was nothing else on—literally! My kids struggle to understand how I can possibly know the lyrics to "Do-Re-Mi." Limited choice in TV stations has a lot to do with my singing, "Fa, a long, long way to run." For all of you who now have that song in your head for the remainder of the day, you likely had limited choice also. Now I have hundreds of TV channels to choose from, and too many options for streaming.

Our students live in a world filled with contexts where choice is prevalent, but too often school is not one of them. In *The Motivated Brain*, Gayle Gregory and Martha Kaufeldt (2015) note how many of our youngest learners benefit from the exploratory nature of full-day preschool and kindergarten. They cite research, however, that suggests that much of the learning benefits enjoyed by these children, such as increased vocabularies and better social skills, are snuffed out by the time they reach high school due to the "sit and get" nature of grades 1 through 8 (Brownell et al., 2015). It's probably time to learn from our early learning colleagues and invigorate student learning by giving choice a more prominent place in the classroom.

In essence, there is little debate to be had on voice and choice. All you have to do is ask yourself: *What role do voice and choice have on my own feelings of empowerment and engagement?* Few of us would choose to exist in a cookie-cutter environment compared with one that valued our input and offered options.

The Structure of This Book

Our approach to student-centered assessment should follow logical and clear steps from start to finish, with ample room to be creative within those stages. *Giving Students a Say* will present an assessment plan that fundamentally and authentically involves the student. Specific steps covered in the following chapters include

- Sharing and cocreating student-centered learning targets.
- Using rubrics linked to standards to provide success criteria and ongoing performance assessments.
- Involving students in ongoing assessment opportunities.

- Devising grading systems that are reliable, fair, and sensible.
- Designing student self-reporting structures.

In covering each of these topics, we'll address some of the problems with traditional approaches to assessment. With each theme, we'll consider some of the research and concepts that support student-centered systems. We'll also look at examples of educators empowering and engaging students in elementary, middle, and high school and the tools that can transform the nature of student-centered assessment. Last, we'll continually measure tools and ideas by the extent to which they employ and foster student voice and choice, self-assessment, and self-reporting.

Returning to the anecdote that opened this chapter, if you were in John Sculley's shoes, how could you possibly ignore the question posed by Steve Jobs: "Do you want to sell sugar water for the rest of your life? Or do you want to come with me and change the world?" Pardon my extension of this notion, but maybe we should ask ourselves a similar question: "Do we want to continue to shut kids out of testing, grading, and reporting decisions, or do we want to explore ways to truly and authentically involve them in the realm of assessment?"

We can empower students in the assessment process; we just need to establish why it's critical to do so, and then explore how it can be done. On that note, perhaps this book requires an elevator pitch. For now, I'd suggest the following:

> In every aspect of assessment, we will engage and empower the student by offering opportunities for student voice, choice, self-assessment, and self-reporting.

Without further ado, it's time to *give students a say!*

SHARING AND COCREATING STUDENT-CENTERED LEARNING TARGETS

How can we specify what we want students to learn in a way that promotes student involvement and understanding?

If you don't own a copy of Tim Ferriss's book *Tools of the Titans: The Tactics, Routines, and Habits of Billionaires, Icons, and World-Class Performers* (2017), I suggest you buy one. Of the many "titans" Ferriss highlights, few are more intriguing than Joe De Sena. When the stresses of a job on Wall Street were getting to him, De Sena sought to get back to the basics of life—namely, to seek water, food, and shelter. Out of this need was born the "Death Race." Now, let's be clear about one thing: I've never entered the Death Race, and I have no intention of doing so (I would rather chew on chunks of concrete). The "race" is grueling beyond measure. Besides running and swimming ridiculous distances under extremely difficult conditions, activities along the way include chopping piles of wood, excavating old tree stumps, and moving piles of cinder blocks up a mountain (Dupont, 2012). According to Ferriss, when De Sena was faced with a government directive that he remove a one-ton steel beam from the river on his property, rather than pay a contractor thousands of dollars to do the job, he simply included its removal as one of the challenges in his race—the January edition. Essentially, the race participants, through their rather expensive entry fees, paid De Sena for the opportunity to spend eight hours in the icy water removing the beam. What a deal.

De Sena designs each race element with a simple goal: get participants to give up. Although most race organizers might be discouraged if more than half the competitors threw in the towel, that's not the case with De Sena. As he commented on the Tim Ferriss podcast devoted to the Death Race (https://tim.blog/2014/07/01/spartan-race/), "he knew he had a winner" in the race concept when five of the first eight participants quit. Elements that encourage quitting are not that complicated, just bold and a little twisted. For instance, once the race is well under way, De Sena lures desperate people to withdraw from the event by depriving them of water and strategically positioning buses along the way, with signage and announcements such as "You could quit here. This is not for you" (Ferriss, 2017, p. 39). By design, only about 20 percent of entrants are expected to complete the race (Dupont, 2012). De Sena was delighted when a former Olympian was brought to tears as he gave up, arguing he was a world-class athlete, but the race was "f----g crazy." One marathon runner completely broke down and, in his exasperation and tears, struggled to understand why chopping a pile of wood should have anything to do with a running race. (For more details, listen to this clip: www.youtube.com/watch?v=-U3UFtqR-hY.)

In a clever twist, De Sena's competition pitches racers' fatigue and frustration against their own determination—exacting tremendous pressure on their will to continue. His goal is to have them struggle immeasurably on the razor edge between finishing the race and hitting their breaking point. You can't accuse the race's promoters of hiding their intent. As cofounder Andy "the Undertaker" Weinberg states, "Our goal is to break people… emotionally, mentally, physically, that's the goal. But we tell them that from the start" (Dupont, 2012, para. 3).

One of the many ways that De Sena and Weinberg nudge people closer to giving up is by being intentionally vague and misleading around *really* important race details. Competitors are often a little surprised, and frustrated, to find out that the race has started without notice (Ferriss, 2017). Participants should be extremely wary of any offers of assistance. Competition officials once offered racers a choice when moving a pile of cinder blocks up a mountain: use a wheelbarrow or carry by hand, but regardless, the decision is final. Those who selected "wheelbarrow" were understandably disappointed to find it was still in the shipping crate, unassembled, with no tools provided (Dupont, 2012). You know you've made a poor decision when you're dragging cinder blocks—and a complete set of wheelbarrow parts—up some godforsaken hill. Picture the poor sap paying a hefty entrance fee to lug that conglomeration up a mountain. As long as it's not you, the image is pretty funny.

The idea of the unassembled wheelbarrow is as warped as it is clever, and I can't help but smirk at the thought of people *paying* De Sena to clean up his property. Those depraved and malicious strategies aside, the Death Race has an even more frustrating element. De Sena typically doesn't tell the racers where the finish line is located or when the race ends. For all intents and purposes, *they don't have a target.* By design, this missing element helps transform the Death Race from difficult to *desperate.*

Stories like that of the Death Race cause me to wonder about my own teaching practices and beliefs, with questions such as these:

- *How clear are the learning targets for my students?*
- *Do my students get any opportunity whatsoever to determine the course of their learning?*
- *Do I proclaim democracy while acting like an assessment dictator—the person who gets to make all the critical decisions?*

Unlike the murky finish line in the Death Race, the target or goal of learning should not be shrouded in mystery. We need to clarify, share, and, when possible, codesign learning targets *with* our students. This is arguably the most important step in building an assessment plan that both engages and empowers students. The learning targets should help us design our instruction, be the benchmark for determining the extent to which students have met the targets, and form the basis for how student achievement will be reported.

The importance of sharing learning targets *with our students* is well documented. In their book *Learning Targets: Helping Students Aim for Understanding in Today's Lesson,* Connie Moss and Susan Brookhart (2012) write that "without a learning target, it's unlikely that teachers, students, and administrators will make informed, evidence-based decisions about student learning" (p. 21). Anne Davies, in *Making Classroom Assessment Work* (2000), suggests that although "an education system may define the learning in broad terms through its documents, teachers must translate and summarize the hundreds of statements into language that parents and students can understand" (p. 20). In *Grading for Impact,* Tom Hierck and Garth Larson (2018) suggest breaking down our array of standards into student-friendly learning targets. Ken O'Connor (2018), in *How to Grade for Learning,* contends that grades must be "directly related to the learning goals" and that students must "understand clearly what the learning goals are so that they know what they are expected to know, understand and be able to do" (p. 46).

At this point, I can imagine the voices of 1,000 educators exclaiming in unison, "Oh, you're referring to standards-based grading!" And I would answer, "Well, sort of." For the purposes of this book, the terms *learning objectives* and *learning standards* will be used interchangeably, just as they are across many jurisdictions. To be clear, however, a learning standard or objective is not necessarily a usable *learning target* for students.

We will now delve a little into the transformation of learning *standards* into learning *targets*. However, for a more thorough study, I suggest looking at *Making Standards Useful in the Classroom* (Marzano & Haystead, 2008) or *Grading for Impact* (Hierck & Larson, 2018). It's imperative to distinguish between *what* and *how* when discussing transforming learning standards into clear targets for our students. For instance, all Wyoming grade 4 science teachers will have the same learning objectives or standards regardless of where they teach in Wyoming. These mandated objectives are *what* they should teach. Identifying the *what* of learning standards is relatively easy. *How* we communicate, clarify, share, and cocreate learning targets based on these standards is considerably more difficult, but arguably more important.

In the case of De Sena's Death Race, the *what* is getting from point A to point B (even if the precise location of those points is known only to De Sena). The *how* of the Death Race is the steps De Sena takes to craft the deprivation and exhaustion of the experience. *How* De Sena structures his endurance race reveals his purpose and mission. Similarly, *how* a teacher tackles the transformation of learning standards into student-centered targets, and the way these are shared and cocreated, will reveal a number of important elements. The *how* will do the following:

- Clearly communicate to the student the direction and intent of the learning.
- Affirm that the teacher is adhering to the standards established for that jurisdiction (rather than winging it).
- Reflect, in accordance with the standard, the depth of the learning experience.
- Determine the amount of voice and choice students have in the learning process.
- Help determine the extent to which the student can demonstrate learning in a multitude of ways.

Throughout the assessment process, the learning target will shape how we grade, evaluate, and report the learning that has occurred. As well, it will expose the extent to which lifelong competencies are being developed. We'll explore more on that later. Let's start with the *what*.

Learning Standards and Learning Targets: What's the Difference?

Given the plethora of terms embedded in education-related debates, declarations, policies, and statements, it's understandable that many people are confused by some elements of the vocabulary. A case in point is learning *standards* versus learning *targets*. Moss and Brookhart (2012) make the following distinctions:

Learning *standards*
- Are written from the teacher's point of view.
- Serve to unify outcomes across a series of lessons or a unit.
- Are typically broad in nature.

Learning *targets*
- Are written from the learner's point of view.
- Consist of lesson-sized chunks of information.
- Are specific in nature.

To increase our understanding, let's take a closer look at standards and targets.

Learning Standards

In most jurisdictions, the *learning standards* or *objectives* are mandated for teachers by the state, province, international school, or country. Generally speaking, the teacher has a list of learning standards that must be covered at a particular grade in each subject area. An internet search that includes the name of the jurisdiction and the term *learning standards* will usually lead to an organizational structure of the objectives for grades K through 12. In Texas, learning standards are referred to as TEKS, or Texas Essential Knowledge and Skills. Wisconsin simply calls them Wisconsin Academic Standards and indicates they are to "specify what students should know and be able to do in the classroom. They serve as goals for teaching and learning" (Wisconsin Department of Public Instruction, n.d.). If your future includes living in Switzerland, you may be interested to know that the 26 cantons, or states, in that nation each manage the learning standards up to postsecondary school; and similar to the intent of the Common Core State Standards in the United States, they've sought to align the learning standards of each jurisdiction. The Swiss use the term *performance standards*, which "describe subject-related skill levels to be achieved by the pupils. They are measurable and testable" (Swiss Education, n.d.).

Many schools and districts are somewhere between exploring and incorporating *standards-based grading* or *standards-referenced grading*, and one of the seemingly obvious steps would be to list the standards and have teachers assess the extent to which students have met them. If only it were that simple. In their book *Making Standards Useful in the Classroom*, Marzano and Haystead (2008) list two main issues with simply using state or national standards *as they are published*:

- *Too much material.* It's often unrealistic for a teacher to cover the stifling number of items embedded in the standards. By some estimates, teachers would need about 70 percent more time with students to meet all the established learning outcomes.
- *Lack of unidimensionality.* Many standards include a number of dimensions in a single statement, making accurate assessment difficult. How is a teacher to accurately assess and provide feedback on one dimension if it's packaged with another? For instance, imagine a standard that read, "Students should know the locations of the 13 American colonies and the main concerns each had with British rule." Clearly, there are two different outcomes embedded in this standard—geographic locations and colonial issues.

It should be noted that sometimes a state, provincial, or national standard is suited for use as a learning target (Marzano & Haystead, 2008) and makes sense as stated. Consider the following examples:

- Obtain and combine information to describe climates in different regions of the world. (National Science Teaching Association, Next Generation Science Standards, Grade 3)
- Understands key ideals and principles of the United States, including those in the Declaration of Independence, Constitution, and other foundational documents. (Washington State Learning Standards, 2019)

Even these, however, are a bit of stretch to be given to students as is. When reading them, one is reminded that standards are almost always written for their intended audience—teachers. Our objective is to examine how standards can be transformed, written, and used for and by students.

Learning Targets

In *Learning Targets*, Moss and Brookhart (2012) define a learning target in terms of both students and teachers. On one hand, it's "a student-friendly description—via words, pictures, actions, or some combination of the three—of what you intend students to learn or accomplish in a given lesson" (p. 9). On the other hand, learning targets help teachers "plan, monitor, assess, and improve the quality of the learning opportunities" (p. 9). Although I agree that, historically, this second component is largely intended for adults, perhaps we can more broadly consider learning targets as elements that assist "those who are planning the learning experience"—whether that be teachers or students.

From a teacher's point of view, whether using them for instruction, grading, or reporting purposes, I've become so accustomed to clear learning targets that I'd feel lost without them. A few years ago, I was asked to teach a leadership course at our high school. I looked for the learning targets, only to discover they didn't exist. My first step was to establish them in a clear, student-friendly unit plan (see Figure 2.1). Although in the past I may have considered a lack of learning targets quite freeing—the license to do whatever I pleased—over the last decade, things have certainly changed. Clear targets derived from the learning standards are the essential starting point for everything I do. The bottom line is that our evaluation, assessments, and grades should be based on the extent to which the student has mastered the learning targets.

Figure 2.1
Unit Plan with Learning Targets

Name: _____

Student-Friendly Learning Target Statements	

Knowledge Targets
 	
What I need to know
	☐ I can *define* the following:
	    leadership stealth leadership
	☐ I can *list* and *contrast* the qualities of a **leader** and of a **manager.**
	☐ I can *list* and *describe* the <u>three main leadership styles</u>:
	    autocratic democratic/participative laissez-faire
	☐ I can *define* **positional power base** and *describe* it in terms of **coercive, legitimate,** and **reward** elements.
	☐ I can *define* **personal power base** and *describe* it in terms of **connection, expert, information,** and **referent** elements.
	☐ I can *list* and *state* the importance of at least seven **leadership qualities.**
	☐ I can *define* and *describe* what is meant by **ethics,** an **ethical dilemma,** and **cognitive dissonance.**

Reasoning Targets *What I can do with what I know*	☐ I can *evaluate* what **leadership styles** might be best applied to particular situations. ☐ I can *evaluate to what extent* some famous leaders subscribe to certain **leadership styles.** ☐ I can *determine* and/or *argue* the appropriate use of **positional** or **personal power bases.** ☐ I can *explain* the role of **ethical values** when facing an **ethical dilemma.**
Skill Targets *What I can demonstrate*	☐ I can watch, read of, or address a situation and *determine* some of the **leadership <u>elements</u>** involved. ☐ I can watch, read of, or address a situation and *determine* some of the **leadership <u>styles</u>** involved. ☐ I can watch, read of, or address a situation and *determine to what extent* the two **power bases (positional** and **personal)** are involved.

Student-Friendly Learning Target Statements	

Product Targets
 	
What I can make to show my learning
	☐ I can regularly *maintain* a journal in leadership class and *develop* it according to the "journal guide."
	
	☐ I can *produce* a report on **five influential leaders** and identify
	  • The **need** addressed, the **group** affected, and the specific **goals/actions** used to address the need.
	  • Examples of how the person displayed a **leader's** rather than a **manager's** qualities.
	  • Clear examples of how the person demonstrated **leadership qualities and characteristics.**
	  • The person's **leadership style(s)** and supporting evidence.
	
	☐ I can *produce* my personal list of **ethical values.**
	
	☐ I can *compose* a 1–2-page reflection on what my personal view of leadership is. I can incorporate the following topics:
	  • **Leadership styles**
	  • **Power bases (positional or personal)**
	  • **Leadership qualities**
	  • **Ethics**
	
	Major Project—Details to be announced and developed further. Project should be focused on a community/school initiative and/or center on major concepts from the course.
	
	Ideas may include
	  • Working with a local elementary or middle school.
	  • School awareness initiative.
	  • Movie or webpage focused on a leadership issue.

Three Flaws in the Traditional Approach to Learning Targets

Learning targets are by no means a universal component of classroom education, and when they are present, they can be problematic. The "traditional" approach to learning targets—if there is any approach at all—typically has three flaws. Too often, learning targets are (1) teacher-centered; (2) simply copied from the state, provincial, or national standards; or (3) on display but with no apparent plan for relevant learning activity.

Teacher-Centered

Too often, the teacher is the only person who's aware of the learning intentions (be they standards or targets), which results in a top-down approach to learning. This situation is similar to a platoon of soldiers being ordered to take a hill or clear a street, with the only person knowing any of the details or obstacles being the commanding officer. Historically, this has been the approach of many armed forces, but too often it leads to confusion and lack of morale. In their best-selling book *Extreme Ownership* (2015), former Navy SEALs Jocko Willink and Leif Babin describe the necessity of "decentralized command" and the critical importance of "every tactical-level team member [understanding] not just what to do, but *why* they are doing it" (p. 183).

If this principle is true for SEAL team members attempting to secure a military target, it likely applies to other environments also—classrooms included. Similar to the SEAL team's situation, the extent to which students understand the process of learning is inextricably linked to how much they care about and feel empowered in the pursuit of it. Tomlinson and Moon (2013) write that "successful learners understand the learning process, accept it as worthy of time and effort, and accept the centrality of their role in contributing to their success" (p. xii). When teachers are the only ones aware of the learning intentions, it's not only disempowering for the students but also inefficient. Moss and Brookhart (2012) warn that when relying on "teacher-centered instructional objectives," teachers spend "a great deal of energy trying to get students to meet the instructional objective. Meanwhile the students spend the bulk of their energy figuring out how to comply" (p. 18).

Implication for assessment: We should design our assessment plan to include creation and sharing of the learning targets *with* students as partners in the process. We should take on the challenge of cocreating the learning targets when possible. By providing students with a voice in the process, later on they will have a much greater chance of understanding the success criteria and effectively self-assessing and self-reporting on those targets.

Copied from State or National Standards

As mentioned previously, some jurisdictions may have standards that are suitable as learning targets, but this is the exception rather than the rule. It's tempting to acquire a list of already established learning standards, seemingly indicating what we should teach, and systematically hammer through them. However, blindly trusting the standards as written leads to a few problems. First, too often the standards are written in formal language that's difficult for students to access (Dueck, 2014; Hierck & Larson, 2018; Wiliam, 2018), and their complexity may actually "detract from a teacher's ability to teach effectively" (Marzano & Haystead, 2008, p. 7). Second, the standards may define what is to be learned but not be specific enough or lack examples. As Davies (2000) points out, "we may know the standard states 'communicates effectively in writing' but have no idea what it looks like for students at a particular age range" (p. 26). Last, all too often the standards include little or no indication of what it looks like to be successful (Hattie, personal communication, July 11, 2020).

Learning targets are an integral part of a student-centered assessment plan, not an entity unto themselves. Dylan Wiliam (2018) makes the case for education being far more than a list of learning tasks and for why assessment is the critical component. In *Embedded Formative Assessment*, he argues that "assessment is *the* central process in instruction—students do not learn what we teach. If they did, we would not need to keep gradebooks. We could, instead, simply record what we have taught" (p. 54). With this in mind, if assessment is central to instruction, we need to clarify and solidify the targets *as part of* the assessment process. Essentially, we must figure out how to best articulate what that learning looks like, and understanding learning targets is a logical first step.

Implication for assessment: We need to transform state, provincial, or national learning standards into clear, student-centered learning targets that can form the basis for self-assessment and reporting.

Displayed but Not Implemented

I clearly recall the days when I was training to become a teacher and had an advisor who instructed me to write on the board the objective for every lesson. Although the goal of making the learning intention clear was a noble one, this step by itself falls far short of being a comprehensive approach to sharing the learning targets. I have visited many classrooms where the teacher has written out the learning goal on the board or stapled it to a fancy poster. This learning "snapshot" is a form of sharing the learning intentions with our students, but too often the target is disconnected from the overall plan. Students cannot possibly glean from a single objective the contributing ideas, concepts, and procedures. And to be clear, sometimes a lesson or an activity is more effective if the learning target is not posted (Wiliam, 2018). Take the following example.

I wanted to address the global inequities of population distribution and wealth with my grade 6 students, so I concocted an interesting, and rather disturbing, human geography activity. First, we shoved the desks aside, and students worked in groups to create rough outlines of the earth's continents using masking tape. One group marked out North America, another group Asia, and so on. The students had two criteria: (1) as a class, use all our available floor space, and (2) within their groups, accurately mark out the relative size of their assigned continent. It was some organized chaos, that's for sure, but eventually we had a planet on the floor.

Once we had created the map of the earth, each group had to determine the population distribution of its continent. For instance, the Africa group members used a reference book to determine that they represented about 17 percent of the world's population. Next, we discussed as a class how we would distribute the number of students in the class to reflect the proportion of people who live on each continent. We calculated on the board how many students would represent the population of each continent—so, for example, 6 of the 33 students in the class would represent Africa. Next, I assigned the students to the various continents—randomly, to signify the fact that we do not choose where we are born. Once our planet was populated, I introduced the notion of gross domestic product (GDP) and held up a bag of 100 gold chocolate coins I had brought in. Needless to say, once I started distributing the wealth according to each continent's actual GDP, the inequity became clear, and students started either celebrating or protesting. The two kids standing in North America received 27 coins to represent that continent's 27 percent of the world's GDP, whereas the six kids standing in Africa were handed a mere 2 coins in total to reflect their GDP. Gross inequity.

I led this unit-opening activity before sharing the learning target as a way of hooking students' interest and spurring them to launch their own exploration into a related topic. In cases such as this, waiting until *after* the learning moment to establish the learning target can actually make the activity more powerful.

Implication for assessment: Supply students with a comprehensive unit plan and the information necessary to cocreate learning targets. Decide when to refer to the unit plan in accordance with the activities planned.

Giving Students the "Inside Scoop" on Learning Targets

To truly invite students into the realm of assessment—and learning targets specifically—we may want to consider giving them security clearance into the "Office of High Command." I've found that sharing educational theory and terminology with students is a good thing, so long as it's appropriate for the grade level. For example, a number of years ago, I decided to share with my students in grades 9 to 12 the definitions, application, and theory behind the terms *formative* and *summative* when describing assessment. I wanted my students to use these as working terms in their own learning, and an indicator of success was when a grade 9 student asked about our upcoming quiz, "Is it going to be formative, kinda like a check-in for how I'm doing?" These types of responses suggested that students were beginning to understand that the *purpose* of formative assessment is different from that of summative assessment.

Actions (Verbs) and Content (Nouns)

When sharing and codesigning learning targets with students, it will be helpful for them to understand that a target typically consists of two important elements. As Krathwohl (2002) states: "Objectives that describe intended learning outcomes as the result of instruction are usually framed in terms of (a) some subject matter content and (b) a description of what is to be done with or to that content" (p. 213).

Krathwohl's observation alerts us to the fact that when constructing effective learning targets, we need to understand the purpose of *verbs* (actions) and *nouns* (content/object). The verb will largely determine the cognitive level of the learning outcome, whereas the noun (content/object) will determine the knowledge dimension. Consider the following example from Krathwohl: "The student shall remember the law of supply and demand in economics." The verb *remember* establishes the level of cognitive demand, whereas the noun phrase "the law of supply and demand in economics" establishes the knowledge dimension. To be clear, both are crucial to the learning and assessment process, and we should be cautious when we're tempted to say one is more important than the other. That said, with many recent curriculum changes throughout the world, learning standards today are populated with verbs that often require a higher cognitive demand than the word *remember*. Verbs such as *evaluate, analyze, determine, argue,* and *create* are just a few that are used to establish the action in contemporary standards.

The focus on verbs is critical when designing learning targets with our students. If we are going to articulate student-friendly learning targets, and later establish clear performance measures, build effective assessments for self-evaluation, and ultimately design student self-reporting structures, let's keep in mind that verbs should be actionable, achievable, and not shrouded in the "you have it or you don't" world of nouns. Furthermore, teachers are reminded that it's OK to question whether their instruction and assessment match the verb phrase of their target. As grade 9 science teacher Helen Carelse commented,

> My learning standard read, "*Apply scientific knowledge and understanding to solve problems in unfamiliar situations.*" I have realized I needed to carefully examine what I am doing in my classroom to make sure I was providing enough "practice" for the students to improve at this skill. Easier said than done! (personal communication, February 4, 2019)

Categories of Targets

Moss and Brookhart (2012) argue that an objective only becomes a learning target when it's shared with students and, furthermore, that students can only aim for a target once they understand it exists. Clearly, we can achieve both these things through sharing and cocreating learning targets with our students. Let's delve further.

Moss and Brookhart (2012) suggest three key aspects of planning for instruction:

1. What are the essential knowledge (facts, concepts, definitions) and skills (procedures) for the lesson?
2. What are the essential reasoning requirements?
3. How do the knowledge, skills, and reasoning items fit into the larger "learning trajectory" (the big picture)?

Elaborating on the knowledge component, McDowell (2017) presents an interesting and applicable model that separates knowledge into three levels: surface, deep, and transfer. It could be effective to have our students understand that at the *surface* level are the building blocks of learning, whereas the *deeper* level refers to the learner's ability to relate multiple ideas. The *transfer* level of knowledge asks learners to apply their understanding within and between contexts. McDowell argues that "the critical challenge is for teachers to find instructional approaches that balance surface and deep learning and also provide opportunities for students to transfer their understanding to real-world problems" (p. 15).

This position aligns closely with the work of Chappuis, Stiggins, Chappuis, and Arter (2012), who separate learning targets into four categories. In my first book, *Grading Smarter, Not Harder* (Dueck, 2014), I explored a unit plan design for the 1919 Paris Peace Conference based on this structure:

- Knowledge targets (What do I need to *know*?)
- Reasoning targets (What can I *do* with what I know?)
- Skill targets (What can I *demonstrate*?)
- Product targets (What can I *make* to show my learning?)

An updated version of the Paris Peace Conference unit plan appears in Figure 2.2. What's different about this unit plan is that it provides students with the opportunity to create some of the learning targets while still maintaining the unit's structure and adherence to the standards.

Student-Created Targets

I don't know why it didn't dawn on me years ago to give students more voice and agency in creating learning targets. There were indications that students had something to offer in this area; apparently, I was either not listening or not ready to give up the steering wheel. Consider the following experience around retesting, for example—one I cited in *Grading Smarter, Not Harder*.

I had a student, Sam (a pseudonym), who had made one tiny error on our unit test on the Paris Peace Conference and had lightheartedly demanded a retest,

Figure 2.2
Unit Plan for History 12: Paris Peace Conference

Name: _____

Is Peace Achievable?
An Examination of the Paris Peace Conference

Learning Target Category	Learning Target
Knowledge Targets *What I need to know and understand*	☐ I can *define* these terms and *explain* how they were factors affecting the Treaty of Versailles: **capitalism communism imperialism militarism** **nationalism neo-imperialism self-determination**
	☐ I can *identify* the countries on a pre-1919 map of Europe and a post-1919 map of Europe. ☐ I can *identify* major differences between the pre-1919 and post-1919 maps of Europe such as (a) land lost by Germany, Austria-Hungary, and the Ottoman Empire and (b) newly formed countries of Europe.
	☐ I can *define* the following terms and *explain* how they applied to Germany in 1919: **Anschluss Article 231 (War Guilt Clause) "blank check"** **diktat Polish Corridor reparations Rhineland** **Saar Schlieffen Plan self-determination** **"stab in the back" theory Sudetenland**
	☐ I can *define* the following terms and *explain* how they applied to Italy in 1919: **Dalmatian Coast "Italia Irredenta" South Tyrol** **"stab in the back"**
	☐ I can *list* and *describe* **Wilson's Fourteen Points.**
	☐ I can *describe* the main conditions placed on Germany by the Treaty of Versailles: **territorial losses, military conditions, reparations;** and *explain* how each led to German discontent.
	☐ I can *explain* how the **Treaty of Versailles** may have led to increased **nationalism** in a number of different groups/nations.
	My personal knowledge outcome. Include information here you believe should be included in this unit. ☐ I can _____ *(verb)* _____ _____ .

(continued)

Figure 2.2—(continued)

Unit Plan for History 12: Paris Peace Conference

Learning Target Category	Learning Target
Reasoning Targets *What I can do with what I know and understand*	☐ I can *assess* to what extent **Wilson's Fourteen Points** are reflected in the **Treaty of Versailles.** ☐ I can *evaluate* to what extent **France** or **Britain** was satisfied with the **Treaty of Versailles.** ☐ I can *argue* the role that **nationalism** and **imperialism** played in the formation of the **Treaty of Versailles.** ☐ I can *determine* instances where **self-determination** was and was not applied to people after 1919. *Student-created learning target:* ☐ I can _____ (verb) _____ _____ .
Skill Targets *What I can demonstrate*	☐ I can *apply* the interests of Britain, France, or the USA in a Paris Peace Conference negotiation. ☐ I can prepare a short presentation for the Paris Peace Conference that will *justify* or *argue* a minority claim or national position (e.g., Palestinian Arabs, Romanians). ☐ I can prepare a presentation to *justify* and *decide* how Britain, France, or the USA will approach one of these key issues: • **War costs and reparations** • **Map of Europe and colonies** • **Future military strength considerations** • **War guilt and prevention**
Product Targets *What I can make to demonstrate and expand my learning*	☐ I can *create* a reflection on our PPC, to *report* and *discuss* the following: 1. My impression of the experience—frustrations/successes. 2. My understanding of the complexities of national issues. 3. Long-term consequences of national decisions. 4. Addressing the question **Is peace achievable?** **"Time Machine"** ☐ I can *formulate* a comprehensive plan for an alternative decision to one of the contentious issues with the Paris Peace Conference. ☐ I can *modify* a decision to achieve a different result and *predict* how it may have affected subsequent events. *My own product outcome as discussed with my teacher:* ☐ I can _____ (verb) _____ _____ .

cheekily muttering that there was nothing I could ask him that he didn't know about our unit. "Just give me my inevitable 100 percent," he said. In reaction, I made his "retest" an interesting mission. He needed to find out something about our unit that I (1) didn't know and (2) would find intriguing. Furthermore, he needed to tell me when he was ready, and I'd choose the time and place for him to present his findings.

"How am I supposed to know what you'd find intriguing?" he asked with some frustration.

"I guess we'll just have to find out now, won't we?" I responded.

As frustration instantly switched to ardent determination, he stomped out of the room exclaiming, "OK, Dueck, it's on!"

A few days later, Sam came to class early and was excited to tell me what he had discovered. When he was about to launch into his diatribe, I reminded him of the third element of the "retest": *I would choose the time and place.*

"I didn't think you were serious about that!" he said with exasperation.

"Oh, I was serious," I responded. "I want to be sure you really know it."

Several days passed before I came across Sam at a local hardware store and promptly ambushed him.

Setting down a box of nails, he asked, "Hey, Mr. Dueck, why don't you address the topic of Class C Mandates in our unit?"

"Class C Mandates? I haven't heard of them." I answered.

With a wry grin, Sam retorted, "Ah! Intrigued, are you?"

Sam went on to share an in-depth account of groups of people that the leading powers of 1919 thought to be incapable of *ever* ruling themselves—most of which were African colonies that are independent countries today. I was intrigued.

For the longest time, I looked at this story through the lens of retesting, but not cocreating learning targets. Clearly, Sam had developed a personal interest that was aligned with our topic of study, but on a matter that I had not included. In hindsight, I've had students explore personal-interest areas in project work, but for some reason, I've not extended this opportunity in a more formal way to delve into cocreating targets. It's time to change that.

Implication for assessment: Note in Figure 2.2 that it's relatively simple to modify my original unit plan to include student voice and choice. Students can write their own learning targets by completing the "I can" statement. They simply select a verb and then insert the content material that will accompany it. Here are examples of learning targets that reflect actual student interests from my class and that could have been transformed into learning targets aligned to existing standards:

I can *explore* (verb) *the training and tactics of a specific WWII tank ace (Michael Wittmann).* (B.C. Standard: "Examine the role of technology in major conflicts.")

I can *determine* (verb) *the extent to which landmines have had a detrimental impact on elephant populations.* (B.C. Standard: "Assess the short- and long-term causes and expected and unexpected consequences of people's actions, events, phenomena, ideas, or developments [cause and consequence]).")

If you adhere to the Next Generation Science Standards, a student could create the following target:

I can *create* (verb) *a model using plastic parachute figures to indicate the force of Earth's gravitational pull.* (NGSS 5-PS2-1: "Support an argument that the gravitational force exerted by Earth on objects is directed down.")

Allowing students to create their own targets is not a far stretch from offering them choice on inquiry projects. Overtly providing these opportunities simply underscores our elevator pitch.

Collective Student Efficacy and Cocreated Learning Targets

John Hattie's meta-data analysis of the factors that most affect student achievement shows "collective teacher efficacy," or CTE, as the number one factor (Waack, 2013). Donohoo (2017b) defines CTE as "a staff's shared belief that through their collective action, they can positively influence student outcomes, including those who are disengaged and/or disadvantaged" (para. 1). At first, I was surprised that CTE would be number one, but if you think about it further, it makes sense. When teachers believe that they are the most important factor influencing the success of their students, they're more likely to attend professional development sessions, read more books, and spend more time planning effective activities. Conversely, they will spend less time blaming socioeconomic factors, class size, and scheduling issues for their students' lack of success (Donohoo, 2017a).

It's possible that you're reading this book because you believe that you wield considerable power in determining the success of your students and you're looking for more tools to influence this effect. Now imagine assembling a group of teachers of that type and harnessing the synergistic power of that collective. That's how CTE became number one.

Considering the power of collective teacher efficacy, what might *collective student efficacy* look like, and how might we develop it in our learning environments? Consider those epic moments in your classroom, when the right factors collide and you see the power of student-led groups working toward pursuing questions, finding solutions, and learning from one another. Unfortunately, these instances were too rare in my classroom, but when they occurred, the experience was amazing.

If you have found it challenging to organize group-work activities in your classroom, take solace in some research suggesting that the learning potential of the group does not hinge on its being successful initially. In fact, the ability to learn effectively can be triggered when a group struggles and *doesn't* seem to understand the material or process. In a remarkable series of studies done in Singapore, students who worked in groups that explored a possible self-generated solution—and made mistakes along the way—were compared with students who received the "correct" solution through direct instruction. The study concluded that situations involving groups struggling to come up with solutions, even when they are completely incorrect, seemed to better prepare students to learn the "correct" solution once the teacher demonstrated it (Kapur, 2015).

As we pursue a student-centered approach to assessment, we want to imagine not only including the student but also attempting to harness this "power of the group." In designing clear, student-centered learning targets, consider elements that could be determined by the student collective—even if you end up tweaking these after students have struggled with the activity. Ben Arcuri and Russ Reid at Penticton Secondary School in British Columbia did just that.

In a novel approach to cross-curricular learning, Ben (who teaches chemistry) and Russ (who teaches geography) decided to combine their classes for a unit pursuing "geo chemistry." Specifically, their students sought to learn about the causes and effects of acid precipitation. Each group of students approached the topic of acid precipitation and its effects—such as those on soil, water, or infrastructure. The bulk of the learning targets were created by Ben and Russ, as shown in Figure 2.3 (p. 30).

Once the classes had tackled the general targets, students constructed their own learning targets based on interest or curiosity. In most cases, these targets were more specific and sophisticated as students delved deeper into a specific issue around acid precipitation. Their questions included the following:

- What is the effect of acid precipitation on salmon spawning habitats?
- What is the effect of acid precipitation on coral reefs?
- How is the population of small freshwater creatures affected by acid precipitation?
- How are both ancient and modern-day infrastructures affected by acid precipitation? Have building processes changed owing to acid rain?

Figure 2.3
Chemistry and Geography Learning Targets

Chemistry Learning Targets	Geography Learning Targets
Identify and *explain* the causes of acid precipitation based on the chemical equations.	*List* the polluting chemicals that are associated with acid precipitation.
Describe the pH conditions required for normal precipitation to be termed "acid precipitation."	*Identify* and *explain* three different types of acid precipitation.
Investigate and *summarize* the impacts and general environmental problems of acid precipitation.	*Describe* the sources of human activity associated with acid precipitation.
	Outline solutions to minimize the damage of acid precipitation.

Source: Courtesy Ben Arcuri and Russ Reid. Used with permission.

Once students had chosen a focus question, they conducted research to craft their response and designed a classroom display to present their findings. Students then did a gallery walk, examining the various displays, asking questions, and having conversations on what they'd learned.

Grade 12 student Emily commented on the experience of creating her group's question:

> At first, our group didn't really know what to do because we've always been told exactly what to study. Then, after a few minutes of talking in our group, we all agreed on a big topic, then narrowed it down a little. In the end, we were a lot more comfortable sharing out what we researched because we got to pick our own topic.

Ben reflected on the process, particularly on the effects of letting the students determine the focus of their final learning goal:

> I witnessed that students appeared to be more confident when sharing information and understanding they had chosen to investigate. Many students were uncomfortable with the assignment at first but became more self-assured throughout the process. It seemed they were more engaged researching a topic of interest rather than one assigned.

It was during the gallery walk that Russ saw the results of student-directed learning:

> During the gallery walk, students were more prepared and confident to share their research. Typically during these types of assignments, student reread the information directly from their poster. However, this time they were more apt to go off script and [were] capable of answering questions not directly found in their responses.

Ben and Russ's approach to developing learning targets *with* students aligns closely with Dylan Wiliam's concept of *co-construction*. Wiliam (2018) argues for a "mechanism whereby students can discuss and come to own the learning intentions and success criteria, making it more likely that they will be able to apply the learning intentions and success criteria in the context of their own work" (p. 64). To be clear, this is not about unleashing your students to take over the learning targets. Wiliam contends that the process is not wholly democratic, in that teachers are in a "privileged position with respect to the subject being taught" (p. 64) and therefore should have a strong presence when learning targets are being cocreated.

Learning Targets at the Elementary and Secondary Levels

While revising my assessment structures to allow for more student involvement, my environment was grades 9 through 12 social studies and leadership classes at a public high school. As I gained experience and confidence in changing my practice, I saw similar shifts occurring with colleagues teaching math, chemistry, PE, English, and other courses at the middle and high school levels. I've had the opportunity to share this journey with educators all over the world, but some of those visits have included difficult conversations. An experienced elementary teacher recently looked at my Paris Peace Conference unit plan and commented, "Your examples look really 'high school'—you should spend some time with elementary kids." I took up the teacher's suggestion and decided to design a more user-friendly template for younger students.

Helping Elementary Students Understand Learning Targets

Addressing the challenge of involving elementary students in the creation of learning targets, I began by investigating my daughter's experiences at the time (in grade 3) and developed the unit plan template shown in Figure 2.4 (p. 32).

The design was influenced by the idea that students will need to learn or know a variety of things, and these separate elements will coalesce into a combination of demonstrations to further embed understanding and memory. As one elementary teacher told me, "It's critical that our students show their understanding through building, manipulating, and movement. It's not about memorization and studying; it's about doing." Based on this advice, the last section of the template allows the student to demonstrate and blend the separate pieces. It's the elementary-level equivalent to the "Product" section of the secondary unit plan.

Figure 2.4
Elementary Unit Plan Template

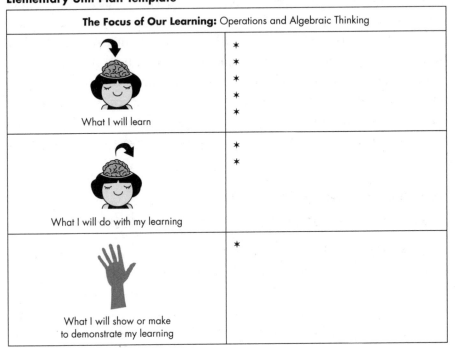

While designing the plan, I found myself stumped at trying to come up with an interesting final product. I decided to seek input from my young daughter, Sloane. Here's my recollection of the conversation, and ample proof of why the teacher told me to spend some time with elementary kids.

"Hey, Sloane, I need an idea for a grade 3 math project."

Sloane approached slowly, likely a little wary of getting involved in another one of Dad's assessment projects. "What's it about?" she asked.

"It's about the idea that a letter can take the place of a number and...."

"Wait! What do you mean, a letter can take the place of a number?" Sloane interjected.

"Like *X* equals 5," I responded.

"I don't like *X*," Sloane said with immediate certainty.

"It's just an example, Sloane!" I replied, slightly frustrated that we had already hit a snag in the process.

"Yeah, but I don't like *X*," she persisted.

I became a little more annoyed. "What's wrong with *X*? Everyone just says '*X* equals 5.' It's an example!"

Sloane remained resolute. "*X* usually means it's wrong, or it's used to cross stuff out. It's not friendly. I don't like it. The only time I like *X* is on a buried-treasure map like you did for my birthday."

Not friendly? Only on treasure maps? I pondered in frustration. I changed to an admittedly insincere conciliatory tone, just hoping to get past this letter issue. "Do you have another letter you prefer, Sloane?"

"*P*," she responded instantly.

"Why *P?*" I inquired.

"*P* stands for *princess*. And she's 5 years old," Sloane stated, suddenly taking a regal stance.

"OK. *P* it is. The princess is 5," I conceded, and, in doing so, I began to consider how this math concept might be addressed in an elementary class environment.

"OK, Sloane. So imagining the princess is 5 years old, how old will she be in four years?"

Sloane thought for a moment and replied, "She'd be... 9."

"OK, so as an equation, we would write it as $P + 4 = 9$."

"Sure," Sloane agreed, but added, "I'd want to draw the princess instead of putting in the letter *P*."

Draw it? That'll take forever! Seizing the opportunity and scheming how this might play out, I agreed. Sloane drew a tiny princess and then included the rest of the equation (see Figure 2.5).

Figure 2.5
Sloane's Equation

After she completed this artwork and math combination, I asked her to do a few more equations, with Sloane insisting each time on drawing the character. Predictably, she began to tire of drawing the intricate little royal and soon sighed with frustration, "This is getting tiring, Dad!"

"So maybe just use P from now on instead of drawing the princess *every* time."

And with that, she looked up with an unmistakable air of understanding and simply commented, "I get it now. P equals 5."

Perhaps this approach could have students use any little drawing to represent a number concept, such as C to represent four tires on a *car*, or S to represent eight legs on a *spider*. Once they've drawn it a few times, students could substitute the letter for the drawing. Thanks to Sloane for inspiring the product in Figure 2.6.

Figure 2.6
Completed Template for a Grade 3 Common Core Math Standard

3.OA.D.8. Solve two-step word problems using the four operations. Represent these problems using equations with a letter standing for the unknown quantity. Assess the reasonableness of answers using mental computation and estimation strategies including rounding. Show details.

The Focus of Our Learning: Operations and Algebraic Thinking	
 What I will learn	✴ Two-step word problems ✴ The four operations ✴ Letters acting as numbers ✴ Three estimation strategies with rounding ✴ How to "show" my work
 What I will do with my learning	✴ Solve two-step word problems with the four operations. ✴ Estimate if a number I am given could take the place of a letter in an equation.
 What I will show or make to demonstrate my learning	✴ I can make my own equations that use the four operations. I will also make a cartoon of number characters that try to take the place of the letter.

Engaging Secondary Students with Learning Targets

Kari Straube, a grade 11 and 12 English teacher, attended one of my professional development sessions and was inspired to involve her students in the sharing and construction of learning targets. Shortly after the session, she sent me her version of a student-centered unit plan for the study of *Beowulf* (Figure 2.7, p. 36). Straube underscores the notion that there is more than one way to structure a unit plan. Key features of her design include

- Essential or "Big Idea" questions.
- Student self-reporting of an academic goal.
- Student voice and opportunity to create their own "Epic Hero" project.

To see other examples of secondary unit plans, visit my website (www.myrondueck. com).

Sydney Jensen, a 9th grade English teacher from Lincoln, Nebraska, contacted me to tell me about the impact of digitally sharing a unit plan on Shakespeare with her students, who logged in daily to view it. On printouts of the plan's learning targets, students highlighted objectives they believed they had become proficient in, using markers of different colors each week to self-assess their progress. They used Google Forms to report to Sydney, and she used the feedback to plan for the next week. She reported that at the end of the unit, students had achieved a proficiency rate of higher than 70 percent on every objective, and every student received a score of 80 percent or higher on the summative assessment of the unit. Summing up the experience, Sydney said, "I would not have believed that this would have such a huge impact if it had not happened to me."

Closing Thoughts

Establishing clear, student-centered learning targets is one of the most important steps in engaging and empowering our learners while creating a student-centered approach to assessment. The targets will act as a rudder in making many of the follow-up decisions around grading, ongoing self-assessment, and reporting. With the standards largely stipulated by educational jurisdictions, it might be predictable that teachers have felt somewhat powerless in this arena, and therefore including students may have seemed impossible. However, as we've seen, we can take definitive steps to ensure our students understand where the learning path leads and, with our guidance, even affect the destination.

Figure 2.7
Unit Plan for *Beowulf*

Name: _____ Block: _____

In this unit, students will understand the following elements:

Knowledge Targets: I can *define* the following terms and use them in my analysis:

☐ **Anglo-Saxon**   ☐ **archetype**   ☐ **epic hero**   ☐ **hero**   ☐ **hero's journey**

Reasoning/Skill Targets *(check the box beside each row once you confirm your understanding):*

	I can *identify* the role of the **epic hero archetype,** including its influence on **character, plot, setting, theme, point of view, tone,** and **style.**
	I can *explain* and *classify* the traits of the **epic hero archetype** and *apply* that knowledge to an **analysis of characters** in literary works across genres and formats.
	I can *identify* and *explain* the **hero's journey** as it appears in literature and film.
	I can *evaluate* the influence of historical context on the **epic hero** and the **hero's journey.**
	I can *compare* and *evaluate* oral, written, or viewed works from various **eras** and **traditions.**
	I can *create* and *defend* an argument for a character's **heroic status.**
	I can *utilize* research skills, word processing, and footnotes to create a product.
	I can *identify* **kennings** and **alliteration** in literary works as well as *create* my own.

Essential Questions:

* **How do heroes reflect the values of a particular culture?**

* **How do archetypes influence how we perceive others?**

A portion of this unit consists of reading various epic hero myths and comparing them to *Beowulf.*

What is my academic goal for this unit?

Formative Assessments: Daily journals, group work, in-class work, discussions, reading quizzes

Summative Assessments: Beowulf résumé, "Create an Epic Hero" project

Source: Courtesy Kari Straube. Used with permission.

It's imperative that we not replicate Joe De Sena's Death Race by obscuring the finish line. Instead, we should follow the SEAL teams' example by letting everyone in on the goals of the mission. Now that we've established that students have a rightful place at the table when learning targets are being built, shared, and used, let's consider *how* we can help students achieve those targets.

3

USING RUBRICS TO ASSESS PERFORMANCE

How can students better understand the path to success?

I've watched many professional athletes with a degree of envy. To be a Formula 1 driver would be exhilarating beyond description. At each race, the driver commands the automotive equivalent of a fighter plane, in front of cheering crowds and millions of TV viewers. Few of us will ever experience the 6g of force generated while an F1 car maneuvers a turn at high speed. The closest experience we might have is the tightest turns on an extreme roller coaster, which are generally designed at a maximum of 3g ("g-Force," n.d.). I'm envious of professional hockey players as well. Just imagine touring major cities with a group of fellow athletes, signing autographs for adoring fans, and perhaps having the rare opportunity of stepping onto the ice for game seven of the Stanley Cup playoffs. I'd love to feel the pressure of the final green at the Masters golf tournament in Augusta, Georgia, and drain the winning putt. Oh, to be serving for the tennis final at Wimbledon. Can you imagine?

My sports envy does not extend to all top athletes, however. I've never envied springboard divers. The height alone would strike this sport off my list. Do I ever wish to perch 10 meters (just under 33 feet) above a pool with the intention of dropping straight into it? Nope. I'd have that nasty surface tension of the water awaiting me should I garner the courage to leave the board. Gravity more or less governs that you will accelerate toward the water at 33 feet per second. Therefore, not even accounting for any upward movement from the board, a diver falling from 10 meters will reach the water in a mere 1.42 seconds (Allain, 2012) and be traveling at about 35 miles per hour (*From the Lab Bench*, 2012). How efficiently the diver pierces the water surface will determine the extent to which it feels like hitting pavement. As in any sport, mistakes happen, but with diving they seem amplified. Unfortunately, YouTube contains no shortage of videos of dives that did not go as planned. Should you desire to see how bad an Olympic dive can be, search "Stephan Feck."

Included in my lack of desire to be a diver is the assessment, or judging, of the sport. In a track and field event, performance in the 100-meter sprint is straight-forward: *the first person across the line wins*. With diving, however, it's a little murky—at least to me. I'm amazed at how judges can determine the quality of a dive that occurs in less than two seconds and has numerous elements. Sometimes I witness a dive thinking, *That's really good*, only to have the television commentators immediately remark on how it went awry. I've some hope of understanding the errors once it is reviewed in slow motion, from a few different angles, but the judges have this uncanny ability to assess it in the moment!

It was during the 2016 Summer Olympics that I was watching diving and wondered, *How exactly do they assess these dives?* So I went looking.

USA Diving, part of the Team USA website (www.teamusa.org), has a portal labeled "Diving 101" that's particularly helpful. Information under the heading "Judging and Scoring" explains how dives are judged and scores calculated. After reviewing the site, however, I reached out to Leslie Hasselbach Adams, USA Diving's High Performance manager, for her personal opinion. Adams works with some of the world's top divers and is a judge certified for Olympic water sports events. I asked her this question: "In under 30 seconds, how would you describe how an Olympic dive is judged?" Adams responded:

> Basically, a dive is judged by the [diver's] approach, flight through the air, dive position, distance from the diving board, the entry into the water and the overall impressions of the dive. (personal communication, August 28, 2019)

Dan Laak, the High Performance director for USA Diving, agreed with Adams's succinct description but added an interesting twist that reflected his role in developing athletes over the long run:

> In High Performance we are definitely looking for these things, as this is what the judges are looking for. However, we also look for divers that may have the ability to

achieve these things over time, meaning when we are evaluating a diver for potential greatness, we look for more than just the scores they receive at a competition. (personal communication, August 28, 2019)

When it comes to designing and using performance assessments, all this talk about diving has left me wondering about a few things:

- *Can I break down projects, assignments, and other complex learning opportunities into clear, manageable pieces?*
- *Can I invite students into the realm of self-assessment and self-reporting of their learning, while focusing less on scores?*
- *Can rubrics be designed to be used by both the student and the teacher?*
- *Could my students understand the elements of good assessments and even play a role in designing them?*
- *Could we discuss and report learning as we look for "more than just the scores"?*

With these questions in mind, let's take another step toward engaging and empowering our students in the assessment process.

Rubrics: Why They Matter for Student-Centered Assessment

I've worked in education for well over 20 years, 12 of which have been specifically in the area of assessment. I'm not sure if it's the same in other professions, but each year leaves me feeling that I still have so much to learn. Through recent work with the Alberta Assessment Consortium (AAC), I discovered elements of a rubric I had not thought of, and tools for building rubrics that I'd never considered. Many elements of this chapter are inspired by the fantastic work of the AAC, and specifically Sherry Bennett and Anne Mulgrew's document *Building Better Rubrics* (2013). As well, Susan Brookhart's book *How to Create and Use Rubrics for Formative Assessment and Grading* (2013) is a clear and useful read for anyone wishing to explore rubrics in detail. Brookhart's work will certainly help inform our discussion.

With so much having been written on rubrics, how to construct them, and their uses, perhaps it's worth asking: do we really need to revisit the topic of rubrics? I'd argue we do, for at least three key reasons:

1. **There is much to learn.** I'll be the first to admit that for much of my teaching career I did not have a confident grasp of the elements of a rubric and some of the finer details of their construction and use. In visiting many

schools and districts, I've concluded that there's a fair degree of confusion surrounding rubrics. Some of the questions I most frequently encounter include

- What's the purpose of a rubric?
- How do I build one?
- When should I use a rubric?

2. **The verbs are changing.** In a world demanding higher-order thinking, we need to adapt our assessment methods. Assessing learning standards driven by verbs such as *create, design,* and *analyze* will require more sophisticated assessment tools than ones starting with *list, define,* or *recite.* There's no question that assessing for student performance related to these kinds of standards is harder than grading traditional content, and good rubrics can help us face this challenge.

3. **Assessment means "to sit beside."** Recall from Chapter 1 that the translation of the Latin root of the word *assessment* is "to sit beside." If we are truly going to embrace the notion of tackling and assessing our learning outcomes *with* our students, then we will need common language and assessment tools that everyone understands. This chapter will examine how our construction and use of rubrics can help invite students to not only understand the elements of more complex learning opportunities, but also provide success criteria, a tool to better self-assess and self-report.

What Is a Rubric?

When I typed the word *rubric* into Google, the search engine took under a second to churn up 75 million results. This is not the 1969 moon landing—people have been here before!

The word *rubric* originates from the Latin for *red.* In medieval times, writers used red ink when listing the rules for conducting liturgical services with the hope that these edicts would easily catch the reader's attention (Brookhart, 2013). If this were a book focused on conducting church services in Latin, that would be the end of our discussion—*pay attention to the rules in red!* Obviously, our needs are different, so we'll need to dig a little deeper.

A rubric is a tool used to score and describe performance. Brookhart (2013) defines a rubric as "a coherent set of criteria for students' work that includes descriptions of levels of performance quality on the criteria" (p. 4). The Eberly Center for Teaching Excellence and Educational Innovation at Carnegie Mellon

University describes a rubric as "a scoring tool that explicitly describes the instructor's performance expectations for an assignment or piece of work" (Eberly, n.d., para. 1).

What Is the Purpose of a Rubric?

As suggested by Brookhart's and Eberly's definitions, the word *performance* will loom large in our conversation. One purpose of the rubric is to provide for the student a "coherent set of criteria." Ideally, this will help the student understand what is needed to be successful on the activity, project, or pursuit. Second, the definition of a rubric is inextricably tied to its purpose of evaluating student performances. Bennett and Mulgrew (2013) define a rubric as "a tool used to evaluate student performance" (p. 2), and Brookhart (2013) writes that "the main purpose of a rubric is to assess performances" (p. 4). This is not to suggest that students must *perform* for a rubric to be appropriate. Brookhart offers a clear distinction of the use of this terminology and the link to learning outcomes:

> State standards, curriculum goals, and instructional goals and objectives are the sources for what types of performances your students should be able to do. When the intended learning outcomes are best indicated by performances—things students would do, make, say, or write—then rubrics are the best way to assess them. Note that the performances themselves are not learning outcomes. They are indicators of learning outcomes. (p. 4)

Just to be clear, performances can be the *act* of a student doing something—such as diving, conducting an oral presentation, or performing a basketball layup. As well, the performance can be the *product* that results from a student endeavor—an essay, a webpage, a sculpture, or a robot. Brookhart provides examples (see Figure 3.1) that are useful in guiding both teachers and students in understanding the dual nature of performances.

When Should I Use a Rubric?

Like many teachers, I've been confused about when and where it's most appropriate to use a rubric. Bennett and Mulgrew (2013) suggest that a rubric should be used in assessment situations when it's possible to

- Give feedback on various aspects of student work.
- Delineate various levels of quality.

Looking back at my interview with USA Diving's Leslie Hasselbach Adams, a dive would clearly fit these two criteria. A dive has five elements, and quality varies from dive to dive and from diver to diver.

Too often, I've thought of a rubric as a tool used to judge student work. By contrast, Brookhart encourages us to view rubrics as a tool for describing performance. Once the purpose of a rubric becomes *description* rather than *judgment*, Brookhart suggests it shifts to a tool "that can be used for feedback and teaching" (p. 5). This notion certainly fits with our quest *to sit beside* while seeking to empower and engage students. Personally, I'd find a conversation around *describing* my construction project, book, or pie crust far more inviting than one focusing on the *judgment* of these things.

Figure 3.1

Types of Performances That Can Be Assessed with Rubrics

Type of Performance	Examples
Processes • Physical skills • Use of equipment • Oral communication • Work habits	• Playing a musical instrument • Doing a forward roll • Preparing a slide for the microscope • Making a speech to the class • Reading aloud • Conversing in a foreign language • Working independently
Products • Constructed objects • Written essays, themes, reports, term papers • Other academic products that demonstrate understanding of concepts	• Wooden bookshelf • Set of welds • Handmade apron • Watercolor painting • Laboratory report • Term paper on theatrical conventions in Shakespeare's day • Written analysis of the effects of the Marshall Plan • Model or diagram of a structure (atom, flower, planetary system, etc.) • Concept map

Source: From S. M. Brookhart, *How to Create and Use Rubrics for Formative Assessment and Grading* (p. 5), 2013, Alexandria, VA: ASCD. © 2013 ASCD.

Rubrics as a Tool for Teacher *and* Student

One of the greatest benefits of rubrics is that they can be incredibly useful to both the teacher and the student. For teachers, a rubric can bring consistency to describing (and scoring) student performances. Numerous studies, some dating back to the early 20th century, have shown that without consistent criteria, the grades for a particular assignment can vary widely from teacher to teacher (Guskey, 2015; Guskey & Brookhart, 2019). I would add that in the absence of clear criteria and descriptions of performance, grades can vary widely from the *same* teacher—me!

During my first teaching assignment, I clearly recall sitting down to grade student work and more or less "winging it." I hereby apologize to my class of grade 5 students in Morris, Manitoba, Canada. First, I'm sorry for assigning a title page at the beginning of each unit and grading it. No aspect of the title page, such as coloring or neatness, was remotely linked to the science or social studies learning standards. And even if for some bizarre reason these things *were* in the standards, we hadn't even begun the unit and I was grading a representation of your understanding. Yikes! Second, I'm sorry for arbitrarily deciding to score each title page based on a top score of 10, with no clear success criteria whatsoever. Why did I choose 10? *I don't know!* Maybe it seemed like an appropriate number (not a good answer). Last, I'm sorry that my grading process may have involved first looking for Taylor's title page, knowing it would be perfect, and using that as a benchmark for the rest of them. Taylor gets a 10 and everyone else gets a score somewhere below that. My only shoddy defense is that I truly didn't know any better. Really.

If you think this approach was a secretive grading system known only to a rookie teacher in Morris, Manitoba, think again. Comedian Gerry Dee plays a rather inept and misguided teacher in the CBC television series *Mr. D.* In an early season of the show, he uses a grading system remarkably similar to the one I described for the title page. His hilarious spoof depicts him and his buddy grading papers at the local pub. Watch it on YouTube when you need a good laugh: www .youtube.com/watch?v=0fn_vAhu_Lw.

Benefits for Teachers

Many university websites serve as a resource for understanding and developing better rubrics. Some of these sources highlight the benefits of a rubric for the *teacher*. Queen's University in Kingston, Ontario, lists the following:

- It can develop a matrix that will be used for assessment.
- It can ensure consistency when assessing students.
- It can provide expectations and assessment requirements prior to assessment.
- It can justify and communicate evaluations of students.
- It can define what quality entails by adding detailed descriptors. (Queen's University, n.d.)

It's worth noting that Queen's has an effective rubric generator online at www .queensu.ca/qloa/rubric-builder-cognitive-skills/creating-rubric.

Learning Tools for Students

Even if an experienced teacher were to ignore the benefits of rubrics, arguing, "I don't need a rubric! I've been teaching this course for 465 years and I'm a consistent grader!" that claim still relates only to the *teacher's* perspective. It does not change the fact that students benefit from being aware of, interacting with, and possibly helping produce the criteria and related performance levels for a rubric.

To make better sense of the dual purpose of rubrics, let's venture outside education. Chris Van Bergeyk, a fantastic principal in my school district, compares the value of placing a good rubric in the hands of the student to the grading of lumber in a wood mill. According to the Canadian Wood Council (CWC), dimensional lumber is graded on a scale of 1 through 3, based on "the presence of wane (bark remnant on the outer edge [of a board]), size and location of knots, the slope of the grain relative to the long axis and the size of shakes, splits and checks" (CWC, n.d.). Although terms such as *checks* and *wane* may not make a lot sense to you, they do to certified wood graders. A lumber grader with 25 years of experience in the mill might quickly identify a plank of spruce as grade 1, 2, or 3 and be very accurate in that assessment. However, Chris argued that for a young worker who just started at the mill, a clear set of criteria that describes the various elements of wood grades would be incredibly useful. The worker would be more empowered to make good decisions, and a beautiful piece of oak would be saved from becoming plywood!

Similarly, in the hands of a student, a good rubric can help clarify what the student is being asked to do and describe the various levels of quality related to these tasks. You could argue that an effective rubric helps the student understand what might be inherent to an experienced teacher.

The Centre for Teaching and Learning at Western University in Ontario is one of many sources listing how *students* benefit from the use of rubrics. According to their website, a rubric

- Clarifies the instructor's expectations.
- Gives them a goal to work towards in producing their work.
- Helps them understand all of the components of the work.
- Gives them greater clarity on how they can improve in [the] future.
- Helps them understand why they achieved a specific grade. (Western University Centre for Teaching and Learning, n.d., para. 4)

Cornell University's Center for Teaching Innovation states that rubrics can help students

- Understand expectations and components of an assignment.
- Become more aware of their learning process and progress.

- Improve work through timely and detailed feedback. (Cornell University Center for Teaching Innovation, n.d., para. 5)

With such a litany of student applications, there's no question that rubrics are critical in inviting students into the world of assessment. With that established, let's delve deeper into their types and construction.

Holistic or Analytic? Deciding Which Type to Use

Over the last two years, I've helped California's Roseville City School District shift its middle schools from a percentage grading system to one based on a four-level performance scale. Brandon Blom, Roseville's director of educational technology, and I have witnessed more than 250 teachers and administrators making bold and significant changes in how they communicate about student learning. I encourage readers to explore some of Roseville's examples and literature at the following link: https://sites.google.com/rcsdk8.org/afg/home.

Among the design considerations we covered with all Roseville educators were the similarities and differences between holistic and analytic rubrics. When looking at the two examples from Roseville addressing a California state standard for grade 7 history and social science (Figures 3.2 and 3.3 [p. 49]), we see that both the holistic and the analytic rubric are

- Designed around three critical elements: criteria, a measurement scale, and descriptors. (In Figure 3.2, the criteria appear in the paragraph above the chart.)
- Written in language friendly to both students and teachers.
- Clearly linked to one or more learning standards.
- Focused on verbs and content specific to the learning standard.
- Designed to offer teachers a nongraded way to report a missing element (insufficient evidence).
- Reflective of our goal to indicate that a standard is either met (*Mastery* or *Proficient*) or not met (*Beginning* or *Approaching*).

We were clear with all Roseville teachers that the choice of which rubric type to use is more about *purpose* than *preference*. When comparing analytic and holistic rubrics, Bennett and Mulgrew (2013) point out that "neither format is superior to the other; they simply serve different purposes. What is most important is that the choice of rubric format matches the assessment purpose" (p. 4).

Figure 3.2

Holistic Rubric for a Scientific Revolution Project

7.10 Students analyze the historical developments of the Scientific Revolution and its lasting effect on religious, political, and cultural institutions

Theory and Invention: How New Ideas Changed My World

I can *create* a model, newspaper, cartoon, or video that focuses on a <u>new scientific theory</u> (from Copernicus, Galileo, Newton, Kepler, etc.) and a <u>significant invention</u> (telescope, microscope, barometer, etc.) that resulted from that theory. I will discuss the <u>origins of the theory</u> (exploration; science from Muslim, Greek, Christian sources; humanism, etc.).

Level	Descriptors
Mastery	• Provides an **in-depth** description of a scientific theory, including an **insightful** understanding of the origins of that theory. • Includes a **comprehensive** illustration or summary of an important invention (related to the theory). • Provides an **extensive** variety of sources used and includes **compelling** comments on credibility.
Proficient	• Provides a **considerable** description of a scientific theory, including a **meaningful** understanding of the origins of that theory. • Includes a **substantial** illustration or summary of an important invention (related to the theory). • Provides a **substantial** variety of sources used and includes **convincing** comments on credibility.
Approaching	• Provides a **basic** description of a scientific theory, including an **appropriate** understanding of the origins of that theory. • Includes a **basic** illustration or summary of an important invention (related to the theory). • Provides a **partial** list of sources used and includes **believable** comments on credibility.
Beginning	• Provides an **emerging** description of a scientific theory, including a **partial** understanding of the origins of that theory. • Includes a **brief** illustration or summary of an important invention (related to the theory). • Provides a **few** sources used and may include **plausible** comments on credibility.
Insufficient/Blank	• No level can be determined at this time due to insufficient evidence of student performance.
Comments:	**Beginning** **Proficient** **Approaching** **Mastery**

Source: © 2018 Myron Dueck. Used with permission.

Consider the holistic rubric we designed for Roseville (Figure 3.2). Holistic rubrics have advantages in certain situations:

- They are faster to design and build.
- They are efficient to use.
- They provide interrater reliability—particularly when evaluation teams are asked to assess state, provincial, district, or school exams/essays.
- They provide overall justification of a grade or score.

The benefits of holistic rubrics are the very reasons we will not be spending a lot of time on them. Formative feedback and active student assessment experiences are not the domain of holistic rubrics, and therefore render them fairly useless for our discussion. As Brookhart (2013) states, "For most classroom purposes, analytic rubrics are best" (p. 6). With that advice in mind, let's explore analytic rubrics in more detail.

Analytic Rubrics: A Closer Look

Brookhart (2013) states the key feature that supports the use of analytic rubrics with students: "Analytic rubrics describe work on each criterion separately" (p. 6). Let's use the analytic example from Roseville (Figure 3.3) to further our understanding, looking more closely at the three elements—criteria, fixed measurement scale, and descriptors of student performance.

Criteria

A major assignment, project, or performance will typically involve criteria that are designed to address one or more learning standards—in this case, California History and Social Science 7.10. As many districts shift to a standards-based grading model, teachers will need to become accustomed to designing instruction and assessment tools that correspond to specific standards. Furthermore, I don't think this is a teacher-only conversation. It's important for students and parents to understand the notion of standards and know that the criteria embedded in our assessment tools are clearly linked to them. The Roseville example has four criteria that address standard 7.10.

Notice in the example that each criterion starts with a verb (*discuss, illustrate* or *summarize, assess*). I garnered this idea from Bennett and Mulgrew's work, and it's a game changer. When I looked at my rubrics, I saw that nearly all my criteria were nouns. Examples included "important invention," "list of sources," and other *things*. To be clear, knowing a lot of things matters, but it's the verb that determines the action and, hopefully, drives the thinking.

Figure 3.3

Analytic Rubric for a Scientific Revolution Project

7.10 Students analyze the historical developments of the Scientific Revolution and its lasting effect on religious, political, and cultural institutions

Theory and Invention: How New Ideas Changed My World

I can *create* a model, newspaper, cartoon, or video that focuses on a *new scientific theory* (from Copernicus, Galileo, Newton, Kepler, etc.) and a *significant invention* (telescope, microscope, barometer, etc.) that resulted from that theory. I will discuss the *origins of the theory* (exploration; science from Muslim, Greek, Christian sources; humanism, etc.).

Criteria	Beginning	Approaching	Proficient	Mastery
	Standard Not Met		Standard Met	
Discuss a new scientific theory that emerged in the 1550–1700 era. No Evidence: ☐	Provides an **emerging** description of the scientific theory.	Provides a **basic** description of the scientific theory.	Provides a **considerable** description of the scientific theory.	Provides an **in-depth** description of the scientific theory.
Discuss the origins of the theory (exploration, science, humanism). No Evidence: ☐	Provides a **partial** description of the origins of the chosen theory.	Provides an **appropriate** description of the origins of the chosen theory.	Provides a **meaningful** description of the origins of the chosen theory.	Provides an **insightful** description of the origins of the chosen theory.
Illustrate or summarize significance of an important invention (related to chosen theory). No Evidence: ☐	Provides a **brief** illustration or summary of an important invention.	Provides a **basic** illustration or summary of an important invention.	Provides a **substantial** illustration or summary of an important invention.	Provides a **comprehensive** illustration or summary of an important invention.
Assess the credibility of list of sources that are varied and appropriate. (Analysis Skills) No Evidence: ☐	Provides a **few** sources used and **plausible** comments on credibility.	Provides a **partial** list of sources used and **believable** comments on credibility.	Provides a **substantial** list of sources used and includes **convincing** comments on credibility.	Provides an **extensive** variety of sources used and includes **compelling** comments on credibility.
Comments:			**Proficient** **Mastery**	
			Beginning **Approaching**	

Source: © 2019 Myron Dueck. Used with permission.

If a criteria item is listed as a noun, such as "topic sentence," it raises the question "What about it?" Should I analyze, discuss, or identify a topic sentence? Should I *write* one and *send* it to my mom? People are unclear on what to do if they are supplied with only a noun. Put this book down right now and try a fun little noun/verb activity. Walk up to the person nearest to you and adamantly state, "Bicycle!"

(I'll wait for your return.)

So, how'd it go? I'll bet the person looked at you with a rather puzzled expression, perhaps asking, "What about a bicycle?" Just as with our noun criterion "topic sentence," a verb would offer much-needed direction. If you instead stated something such as, "I think you should *buy* a bicycle, *ride* a bicycle, or *design* a bicycle," at least the conversation would have an objective. In any case, the verb offers students immediate direction on what they should *do*.

Assessment implication: I've challenged recent attendees of my workshops to critique their own rubrics—namely to see if criteria are listed as noun or verb statements. Tim Van Ness, a 7th grade teacher I met at an international school, EIS Honduras, came to me during this activity, showed me his rubrics, and declared, "Sure enough—all nouns! That's something I can change right away." I could see pen scratches showing that he'd already performed a rough edit of shifting the criteria to verb phrases. Find one of your favorite rubrics and check to see if one or more of the criteria are listed as nouns. Don't be surprised if your experience is similar to mine and Tim's.

Fixed Measurement Scale

The second element of a rubric is the fixed measurement scale. Typically, rubrics will have between three and six descriptor levels. It's not that four is better than five or six (or vice versa), but rather that the scale

- Is appropriate for the task.
- Allows for clear differences between descriptors.
- Is easily understood by the student.

Remember that less is more, and this certainly holds true for the number of descriptor levels. Guskey and Brookhart (2019) argue that using more grade categories means an increased number of borderline cases, ultimately resulting in a greater chance of misclassification—instances when you are torn between describing student performance as being at one level or another. Building on this notion, let's call these tough spots the *zone of potential misclassification*.

To illustrate this point, say schoolteacher Bob had a two-level scale to describe his day: *good* day or *bad* day. Imagine a shaded zone of potential misclassification covering the lower end of *good* and the upper end of *bad*. Now imagine Bob heard that his district would be giving all teachers a raise in pay next year. However, while considering this nugget of good news on his drive home, he ignored the speed limit in a construction zone and incurred a $500 fine. As he walked through the front door of his home, a family member greeted him with "Welcome home, Bob. Did you have a *good* day or a *bad* day?" Because of his conflicting experiences, he is unsure. He might answer, "Bad," still feeling the sting of the traffic ticket. A little later, however, as he calms down, his focus might shift to next year's increase in pay, and he might revise his report: "Upon further reflection, I actually had a *good* day." Or perhaps he'll remain torn, falling asleep that night never able to decide what kind of day he had. In any event, while he ponders, Bob finds himself in the *zone of potential misclassification*.

A performance scale with four levels of descriptors will have three potential zones of misclassification, whereas a six-level rubric will have five. Thankfully, in deciding between a three-, four-, five-, or six-level fixed performance scale, none are as drastic or daunting as the 100 zones of potential misclassification present in a percentage-based system (see Figure 3.4, p. 52). We'll delve further into this topic later in the book when we look at grading and reporting. The most important consideration is that, whichever scale is chosen, the student recognizes that the descriptors are distinct from one another. The more levels, the greater the chance the student is confused over the differences between one level and another that's adjacent to it. Considering Bob, if he had to describe his day with one of 100 levels, he'd likely struggle all the more to come up with an answer.

For many teachers, the educational authority of their school, district, state, province, or country will likely determine the number of levels in their performance scale. In my province, British Columbia, a recent pilot suggests that students in grades kindergarten through 9 will have their learning reported on one of the four levels seen in Figure 3.4. Given this significant, challenging, and exciting change, we've been incorporating some four-level language into our rubric design. Examples appear throughout this chapter.

Descriptors of Student Performance

Once the criteria and a fixed measurement scale are established, it's time to describe the varying levels of performance. I've found it useful to start at the level describing how a student would meet the basic requirements—often termed as *Proficient* or *Meeting*. With one descriptor established, I will cut and paste that descriptor into the other cells in that row and then change the adjective and perhaps a few other words to have it reflect a different level of demonstrating understanding or competency. Let's look at the first row in Figure 3.3 to see how this is done with the first criterion of the Roseville rubric.

Figure 3.4
Zone of Potential Misclassification

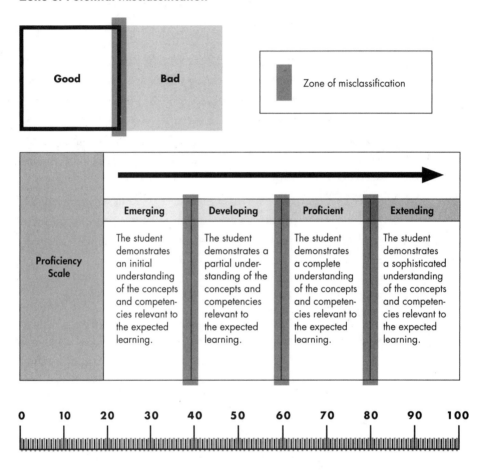

Recognize how changing only one word provides the student a degree of distinction between the levels. Unfortunately, distinction may not equal clarity. There's no question that the language in our example leaves plenty of room for judgment and subjectivity. For instance, what's the difference between a *considerable* description and one that's *in-depth*? Experiencing this challenge in our district, we've found that four steps can help bring more clarity:

1. Spend time discussing and defining terms such as *emerging, basic, considerable,* and *in-depth* relative to the students' age and the subject area.
2. When possible, consider showing students examples of what you would describe as *considerable* and *in-depth*. (When I graded provincial exams with teams of teachers, we spent time looking at exemplars before grading actual student papers.)

3. Consider adding success criteria with more details and specifics.
4. Work through the rubric with your students. Give them voice and agency in the process.

When Scott McIntosh and I were designing a rubric for his grade 3 students to use in designing a planner cover, we initially followed our traditional approach: *adults create rubrics that they then administer to students, never asking if they make sense.* We had limited buy-in from most students.

Thankfully, we had started a practice of sitting down with students at their level (yes, seated in the little chairs or on the carpet) and observing how they used the assessment tools in the classroom. To our surprise, what we had considered to be clear, student-friendly language turned out to be rife with confusion and ambiguity.

Only when we *sat beside* the students, observed the process, and *truly listened* did we hear comments such as "I don't know what this means," "This makes no sense to me," and "What's the difference between *often* and *sometimes*?" We realized immediately that one way to clarify our descriptors was to build them *with* our students. Figure 3.5 (p. 54) shows the resulting rubric. The check-box items in each cell use language that the students consider to be clear and understandable. Don't be discouraged if your first draft is met by criticism. Getting this right involves mistakes and experimentation. For the record, Figure 3.5 is version seven of our rubric!

Some educators go beyond "sit beside" when developing descriptors. Nicola Korvin is an elementary educator who took an innovative approach with her grade 2 students when she was developing more outdoor education opportunities. In an interview, she discussed her attempts to clarify what acceptable and productive behavior would look like when her students were engaged in exploratory learning in the community. She noted that one of the challenges with leaving the classroom is that not all students know how to self-regulate, and some of these negative behaviors can distract students from the learning experience. She was struggling to describe positive behavior in student-friendly terms when she had an epiphany—*get the students to write the descriptors!* Nicola builds an initial structure, starting with simple criteria outcomes and a three-level fixed measurement scale, but she leaves the description boxes blank. As she describes it,

Once we've spent time learning what appropriate behavior would look like, and then we go outside and experience it, we then come together to build the rubric descriptors. We talk about what "approaching" would look like, what "meeting" would look like, and so on. (personal communication, June 25, 2019)

Figure 3.5
Rubric for Designing a Planner Cover

Name(s): _____

Emerging	Developing	Proficient	Extending
Designs a logo that's... ☐ basic. ☐ beginning to show parts of our school.	*Designs* a logo that's... ☐ quite interesting. ☐ beginning to show specific parts of our school.	*Designs* a logo that... ☐ is creative. ☐ is interesting. ☐ completely represents our school.	*Designs* a logo that... ☐ is creative. ☐ is very interesting. ☐ represents the school in a unique way.
Includes text that's... ☐ basic. ☐ spelled correctly in some places or close to correct.	*Includes* text that... ☐ makes sense. ☐ is mostly spelled correctly.	*Includes* text that... ☐ clearly relates to the planner. ☐ is almost always spelled correctly. ☐ is easily read and understood.	*Includes* text that... ☐ clearly and thoughtfully relates to the planner. ☐ enhances the cover. ☐ is spelled correctly. ☐ is easily read and understood.
Designs and *uses* artwork that... ☐ looks like a draft copy. ☐ is starting to be shaded/colored.	*Designs* and *uses* artwork that... ☐ is interesting. ☐ has a little bit of shading/color.	*Designs* and *uses* artwork that... ☐ is interesting. ☐ fits the planner theme. ☐ uses quite a bit of shading/color.	*Designs* and *uses* artwork that... ☐ is creative and really pops out. ☐ clearly fits the theme. ☐ is fully shaded/colored.
Designs and *uses* a border that... ☐ is at the very beginning steps of a design. ☐ partly surrounds the cover.	*Designs* and *uses* a border that... ☐ is basic and simple. ☐ mostly surrounds the cover.	*Designs* and *uses* a border that... ☐ is creative. ☐ completely surrounds the cover.	*Designs* and *uses* a border that... ☐ is creative and original. ☐ helps the cover look unique and complete.

Other thoughts or comments about my learning

Student comments:
Teacher comments:

Source: © 2019 Myron Dueck. Used with permission.

She shifts to inviting student voice and choice by getting the students, working in groups of three, to develop the criteria descriptors. She sees an increased level of engagement in this process compared to when she spent time and energy trying to explain what *her* descriptors meant. As well, once the students have a stake in stating the outcomes, they're better able to self-assess. Speaking of the importance of amplifying student voice and empowerment, Nicola said,

> We're demonstrating that we value [the students'] own experiences.... The fact that I'm recording their descriptions makes them feel special—it shows that they have a voice. I give the rubric some structure, but after that, I don't want to hear me, I want to hear them. (personal communication, June 25, 2019)

Three of Nicola's students filled in the descriptors in Figure 3.6.

Figure 3.6
Rubric with Student-Provided Descriptors

Criteria	Approaching	Meeting	Mastering
I observe the world around me. *I walk the land/ practice silence.*	"It's kind of going to the same places, playing games, not looking."	"It's like when we go hiking and see flowers and go to new places."	"It's like going on new walks to see more places, walking really slowly, really looking and touching."
I explain my thoughts reasonably. *I create stories.*	"You have something to say, but it's hard to explain and you forget your idea."	"It's like telling our stories after our hikes. When something happens, you need to explain it later."	"In our community circle we share thoughts and feelings. When we use art and explain in different ways."
I make connections. *I create stories, learn names of people and places, relate it to my life.*	"My story uses a few details, but could use more. It's also similar to other stories I heard."	"I see animals, trees, and other things and connect them to my projects at school."	"It's like memories of the things you do with parents." "Connects to my life like families and emotions, like collecting sticks when camping."

Source: Courtesy of Nicola Korvin. Used with permission.

Whatever the level of student involvement, there's no question that selecting and changing one or more key words in the descriptor to correspond to different performance levels can be difficult and time consuming. In response to this challenge, I developed a Rubric Support Document for teachers in our district (to view this document, visit www.myrondueck.com). Drawing on work done by Sherry Bennett and Anne Mulgrew of the Alberta Assessment Consortium, as well as other districts such as Nanaimo, British Columbia, this type of tool can be incredibly useful for educators who want to build effective rubric descriptors. I encourage leaders of departments, schools, or districts to look for ways to support teachers in developing banks of common language. Doing so not only assists teachers but also helps students begin to see consistency across different learning environments.

Developing language for each descriptor level is not the end of the line but, rather, one more step toward effectively inviting students to communicate their learning. I encourage educators and students to look at rubrics as "living documents," open to change and revision.

It's also important to note that language is only as valuable as the sense it makes to those using it. Once students see examples of what it means to "provide an in-depth description of the scientific theory," they will be in a better position to do this in their own way and in different situations. I'd encourage individual teachers, departments, schools, or districts to consider a central location—for example, a portal of their website—as a place for storing and sharing anonymous student examples and corresponding rubric assessments.

Seven Design Considerations

We've already discussed a few elements of a good rubric, such as the value of using verbs in our criteria, but there are more ideas to address. The following considerations are a result of rubric work I've done with teachers in many jurisdictions and are strongly influenced by the work of Bennett and Mulgrew (2013), who've identified "common flaws in rubric design and construction" (p. 6). Although these can be viewed as errors, I prefer calling them "design considerations." This moderate terminology reflects the many different situations and scenarios that exist in our diverse classrooms and communities. An effective rubric in one classroom may not work as well in another.

These design considerations are intended to help build capacity and understanding. Perhaps they might serve as interesting discussion prompts in a staff or department meeting. They could be used to reexamine the rubrics already employed in your classroom or school. Personally, I've used them to help answer this enduring question: *When designing and using rubrics with our students, how can we continue to make them more accessible, usable, and effective in both encouraging and communicating learning?*

#1: Ensure That the Highest Level Can Be Modeled and Is Attainable

It's been my experience, in working with many educators, that we often struggle to design instruction, activities, and assessments that match the highest level of a proficiency scale. For a student's performance to match the description of mastery or sophistication, I've heard teachers describe the performance by stating, "I tell my students I need to be wowed." Really? That's the extent of the direction for students? I know the feeling of being pleasantly surprised by the quality and depth of a student's performance, but we'll need a little more structure than "I was wowed" or any similarly ambiguous statement.

In British Columbia's draft of a four-level performance scale, the upper level is labeled *Extending* and is described as "the student demonstrates a *sophisticated* understanding of the concepts and competencies relevant to the expected learning." Similarly, the American School Foundation of Monterrey, Mexico, focuses the highest level on students' ability to "*transfer*" their learning to a new scenario or situation. Whether the term used is *sophisticated, transfer, mastery,* or *advanced,* it's important that we teach and model what student performance *could* look like at the upper end of the scale. Once modeled, students should be able to practice and explore the skill or process for themselves. Once it's the students' turn to formulate an answer, to design a response, or to create a project, they can more confidently chart their own path.

While on the topic of the highest level, I'd suggest we avoid the word *exceeding.* This term is commonly used in proficiency-scale rubrics, and I find it confusing and ineffective. First, I'm unsure exactly how a student—or anyone else, for that matter—might *exceed* a standard. Perhaps the origins of *exceed* come from the hospitality industry, in comments such as "the service at that restaurant exceeded my expectations." Maybe you were expecting mediocre service at the local diner, but Agnes seemed surprisingly cheerful as she poured your coffee. Restaurants aside, many industries and professions have standards, and once they are established and made clear, it can be hard to imagine how they would be exceeded. How would an air-traffic controller *exceed* in guiding numerous aircraft at a busy airport? Would she need to do it blindfolded? Manage a few UFOs?

I've frequently heard educators say, "Exceeding means tackling next-grade-level material." This too is problematic. I'm not sure we want to be framing the highest level of grade 7 math in terms of grade 8 curriculum. Grade 8 math teachers may find it frustrating that entire grade levels of students have already encountered the topics and standards they are planning to cover. To be clear, I have no issues with teachers using extension activities that involve higher grade-level concepts to challenge students at the borderline of their competencies—whatever that might entail—but "next year's material" should not form the basis of "mastery" for all students at any given level. Remember, in most jurisdictions, the existing number of standards at a particular grade level is already more than what can be accomplished in a given year (Marzano, 2010).

#2: Use Strength-Based Language at the Emerging Level

Increasingly some districts are attempting to frame the lowest-level descriptors using *strength-based* terminology. I'll admit, at first I was somewhat skeptical when British Columbia stated the following in its Draft K–9 Reporting Policy:

> Strength-based feedback: A strength-based approach recognizes that student learning is dynamic and holistic, and that students demonstrate their learning in different ways and rates. Feedback is focused on what the student can do and what they are working toward. (British Columbia Ministry of Education, 2019, p. 3)

While reading this, remnants of my traditional mindset rose to the surface. I wondered, *Is this just another version of "Everyone gets a prize"?* and *Don't some students need a dose of reality?* But when I thought of my own experiences in dealing with adults, students, and even my own kids, I began to see the merit in developing this idea for all students.

I currently coach my son's competitive high school volleyball team. He mainly plays the setter position—volleyball's equivalent to a quarterback. He's getting better at orchestrating our offense, but he's young, and as a developing athlete he has much to learn. As the coach, I often give him instruction, discuss strategy, or challenge his game-time decisions. As his parent, I'm tempted to use the drive home from the game to express frustration, ask questions, or offer advice—especially after a loss. After more than a decade of being a sports parent, I'm realizing that I've yet to succeed when I start a conversation with what I believe went wrong. As an administrator, the same has been true when there's been a problem to discuss with a staff member and I begin with what the person did wrong. As a husband, the same has been true when talking with my spouse about a family issue and I start the conversation with what I think she did wrong. Do we detect a pattern here?

Seriously, I don't think we appreciate someone else starting a conversation that's focused on our deficiencies. And on another note, if I'm willing to discuss my challenges and shortcomings, I feel better if I'm granted the opportunity to help identify them on my terms. The key is to develop constructive and respectful conversations that help students to detect errors, to remediate, to see failure as an opportunity to learn. I'm reminded of Michael Jordan, arguably the greatest basketball player of all time, regularly citing failure as a key to his success. As he put it, "I've failed over and over and over again in my life. And that is why I succeed" (Hardy, 2016).

If Jordan is right, we have the challenge before us in education to reframe the importance of failure. However, if the emerging level is built on negative language, this challenge will be all the more difficult. Consider some of our most fragile learners, who often come from homes steeped in negativity and eroded relationships. Do you honestly believe they'll sooner embrace your suggestions and opinions if they are centered entirely around their errors? I doubt it.

Although it may surprise many educators, we can use strength-based language to describe the accomplishments of our most struggling learners—or, stated differently, *students at the first steps of learning.* When challenged by teachers on this point, I often tell the story of an acquaintance who, in his 40s and having never skated in his life, decided to pick up ice hockey. Invariably someone would ask, "Hey, how's the hockey going?" Although he couldn't skate backward, take a slapshot, or come to a stop when he wanted to, he didn't frame his progress around his deficits. Rather, with a wry grin, he'd offer a five-word report: "I can tie my skates." What a perfect example of strength-based reporting!

(Note: The "Comments" section of the rubric can always be used to indicate to the student [and sometimes the parent] what needs changing or adjustment. This language need not be strength-based but instead can describe what is detrimental to that student's learning path and how it needs to change.)

Recall that Brookhart (2013) suggests our rubrics should describe, rather than judge, student performance. If judgment is not the goal, then perhaps we should develop descriptive language that helps build confidence and positive learner identity. During a recent visit to the South Kitsap School District in Washington state, an educator asked, "Should we encourage all students to achieve the highest level of a rubric?" A special education teacher spoke up immediately. She challenged the group to think critically concerning our tendency to level and rank students. She suggested that rather than arguing that everyone strive for the upper level, we should look at learning as a personal and individual pursuit *for each student.* For some students, achieving the descriptors at the *Initial* or *Emerging* levels is an incredible accomplishment. She reminded us that some students (and their parents) would be ecstatic if they moved from *Emerging* to *Developing* and would not see this as failing to achieve *Proficient* or *Mastery* levels. She argued that we should look at our scales not as a hierarchy but, rather, through the lens of individual student learning, and recognize that everyone is at a different place on that continuum. While she offered this invaluable perspective, I was reminded of my friend's self-report: "I can tie my skates."

Students and parents need to see the value of progress *and* achievement; we do not need to choose between the two. As John Hattie phrases it, "It's through progress that we achieve" (personal communication, July 23, 2020). With this in mind, we should exercise caution when focusing mostly on achievement—which is something I've certainly been guilty of. Too often, I've lauded the high-achieving student who has made barely any progress while giving little merit to the student who started very low and progressed significantly.

#3: Include Only Criteria That Are Linked to the Established Standards

In many instances, we want to encourage students to produce work that conforms to expectations not specifically mentioned in the standards. For instance, we might want to see that a paper, script, or paragraph has been proofread to ensure proper spelling, grammar, and punctuation. Perhaps students were instructed to include a list of at least five sources, to completely fill in a poster, or to cite a source using APA style. Whatever the expectations, teachers might feel they need to include these requirements in the levels of the rubric. This assumption can be problematic for at least three reasons. First, typically these types of requirements are not reflective of the learning standards. Second, the language around these types of descriptors is typically focused on compliance rather than learning. Third, it can be challenging to develop levels of proficiency for a static requirement— typically it's either done or not done.

A solution to consider is developing a checklist of "must haves" for elements that are defined by their existence rather than their quality (Brookhart, 2013). Brookhart suggests that "a checklist be used to make sure directions have been followed and that all required elements are present" (p. 78). This checklist could be separate from, or incorporated into, the rubric. Notice how the following requirements are well suited to a checklist:

- _____ I have proofread my paper.
- _____ I have included at least five sources.
- _____ My paper is typed, and all formatting and citations are in APA style.
- _____ I have read the rubric used to assess this paper and completed one as a self-report.

The importance of separating compliance from learning targets when establishing a standards-based grading and reporting structure cannot be overstated (Dueck, 2014; Guskey, 2015; Hierck & Larson, 2018; O'Connor, 2007, 2018).

#4: Avoid Quantitative Language

While looking over some of my rubrics, I found examples in which the amount or number of items is what distinguished one level from the next. For example, if the criteria asked a student to "*compile* a list of appropriate and varied sources," the *Emerging, Developing, Proficient,* and *Extending* levels required one, three, five, and seven sources, respectively. From the student's perspective, numbers like these can detract from the true purpose of the learning or activity. In *Building Better Rubrics,* Bennett and Mulgrew (2013) argue that quantitative language can shift the student's focus away from quality to "How many should I do?" My experience in the classroom certainly reflects this. I've seen students immediately look at the numbers (usually the minimum requirement to achieve their academic goal) and use this figure to decide how much effort to exert or how deeply to engage.

From the teacher's perspective, it's tempting to use quantitative language. Doing so provides a clear parameter for students and seems to add a measurable variable that reduces subjectivity when determining a grade or score. Perceived benefits aside, I now acknowledge that typically quality and learning are far more important than how many items are present. If you had to choose, wouldn't you want a student to research and discover *one* insightful journal-article source rather than list three from Wikipedia? If so, let's be sure to build descriptors that reflect what we most value.

Some teachers will undoubtedly be thinking, *But the number of items gives my students a clear goal, and some students need specific direction!* Returning to design consideration number three, if a student is required to have numerous sources, then perhaps make this a "must have" or incorporate it into a checklist. Bennett and Mulgrew (2013) suggest the following:

> A teacher may determine that a minimum of four sources are needed in order to gather evidence of student ability to demonstrate this skill. Students who submit work without the minimum number of sources may need support in locating additional sources before completing their assignment; they would not, however, be penalized by lower grades. (p. 7)

#5: Avoid Using Absolutes Such as *All, None, Every,* or *Never*

Rob Reinalda has spent nearly 30 years in the print industry and regularly contributes writing and language articles to *HuffPost.* In his ironically titled article "Why You Should Never Use Absolutes," he writes, "Face it, 999,999 times out of a million is a lot, but it's not *always.* Adverbs such as *almost, nearly,* or even *seemingly* can alloy these terms, which can otherwise be perceived as bellicose or accusatory" (2014, para. 5). His argument is *always* worth considering when designing rubrics.

Perhaps the biggest issue with absolutes is that the teacher is painted into the proverbial corner when grading or assessing student performance. The moment the descriptor includes a word such as *every*, much of the judgment and discretion afforded the teacher flies out the window. Adding to the case against absolutes, Bennett and Mulgrew (2013) argue that "one significant error in an otherwise carefully constructed piece of work automatically relegates the assignment to the next lower level" (p. 8). More important, from the student's perspective, when faced with absolute language, entirely reasonable and strategic decisions could be made that run counter to learning, exploration, and risk taking. For instance, if a descriptor says that *all* examples are to be in-depth and a student is quite confident in the five examples she's collected, then she'd be discouraged from including a sixth that might involve a hunch, is new to the field of study, or is underdeveloped because only a few sources are available.

#6: Avoid Combining Multiple Variables in a Criterion Row

Read the criterion in Figure 3.7 (borrowed and revised from the earlier Roseville example) and the descriptors for the four levels. Do you recognize the challenge in trying to determine a particular level of proficiency?

Figure 3.7
Rubric Combining Multiple Variables

Criterion	Levels and Descriptors			
	Beginning	**Approaching**	**Proficient**	**Mastery**
***Illustrate* or *summarize* the significance of an important invention that relates to your chosen theory and include images.**	Provides a **brief** illustration or summary of an important invention and **an** image.	Provides a **basic** illustration or summary of an important invention and **few** images.	Provides a **substantial** illustration or summary of an important invention and **some** images.	Provides a **comprehensive** illustration or summary of an important invention and **many** images.

When one criterion row includes two very different variables, students may be confused and frustrated when self-assessing their performance. Although their summary of an important invention might be comprehensive, what descriptor should they use if they included only a single image? Furthermore, even the natures of these two elements are quite different—one involves writing or drawing and the other involves gathering or compiling. For the example in Figure 3.7, ways to avoid this issue include

- Adding a separate criterion row for the inclusion of images.
- Including the use of images in a checklist or set of "must haves."
- Omitting one of the two assessment elements and considering it for part of a future assignment.

#7: Ensure That Descriptors in the Same Row Describe the Same Characteristic

Examine the criterion and descriptors in Figure 3.8 and try to explain the problem in a way that grade 7 students might understand. This example again uses the Roseville rubric, although the idea is adapted from the work of Bennett and Mulgrew (2013).

Figure 3.8
Rubric with Ambiguous Descriptors

| Criterion | Levels and Descriptors | | | |
	Beginning	**Approaching**	**Proficient**	**Mastery**
Illustrate or summarize significance of an important invention (related to chosen theory).	Provides a **surface** illustration or summary of an important invention (related to chosen theory).	Provides a **partially correct** illustration or summary of an important invention (related to chosen theory).	Provides a **substantial** illustration or summary of an important invention (related to chosen theory).	Provides a **precise** illustration or summary of an important invention (related to chosen theory).

Did you struggle to define the problem? When I've challenged a group of educators to explain what the issue is, some have simply reported, "It doesn't sound or feel right." I agree, but why? Educators have described the issue as follows:

The descriptors are not describing the same thing.

Surface refers to depth, whereas *partially correct* refers to accuracy.

You can have a summary that's *partially correct* and *substantial*.

To avoid this type of issue, it's important to identify the quality you want to describe and then determine the sequenced family of words that refer to it. For the example in Figure 3.8, consider the following:

- *Beginning:* Provides an **emerging** illustration or summary…
- *Approaching:* Provides a **basic** illustration or summary…
- *Proficient:* Provides a **considerable** illustration or summary…
- *Mastery:* Provides an **in-depth** illustration or summary…

Once you have determined an appropriate family of words, remember that showing student examples, having a class conversation, and adding specific success criteria will lessen ambiguity and subjectivity.

Figure 3.9 provides a checklist that will help you create rubrics that address the seven design considerations.

Figure 3.9
Checklist for the Seven Design Considerations

#1: Ensure that the highest level can be modeled and is attainable.
- ☐ Language describes characteristics that are attainable and quantifiable.
- ☐ All items are *within* the standards of the grade level.
- ☐ Potential avenues to success at this level have been defined/modeled.

#2: Use strength-based language at the emerging level.
- ☐ Language at every level reflects what students *can* do.
- ☐ Descriptors for struggling learners reflect growth and ability.

#3: Include only criteria that are linked to the established standards.
- ☐ Criteria are reflective of established learning standards/targets.
- ☐ Descriptor language reflects different levels of quality.
- ☐ A checklist is used for compliance elements such as spelling or format.

#4: Avoid quantitative language.
- ☐ Leveled language avoids amounts or numbers as the determining variable.
- ☐ Required or compliance elements are reflected in a checklist format.

#5: Avoid using absolutes such as *all, none, every,* or *never.*
- ☐ Leveled language leaves room for small errors or risk taking.
- ☐ Descriptors empower the teacher and student to use discretion.
- ☐ Learning and exploration are valued over compliance.

#6: Avoid combining multiple variables in a criterion row.
- ☐ Criteria reflect one variable or closely related variables.

#7: Ensure that descriptors in the same row describe the same characteristic.
- ☐ The language in each descriptor refers to the same characteristic.

Providing Examples

To effectively build and use rubrics, students and teachers need a combination of tools and practice in using them. For instance, students will benefit from seeing examples that show the difference between an *in-depth* summary and a *considerable* one. A common concern is that showing students examples of others' work will lead to copying. Although I've had the same concerns, recent experience in schools and the "real world" has made me think differently. When I am about to embark on a building project or renovation, I typically look for what else is out there. I encounter others' ideas, and my thinking is influenced for the better. I think our students can safely look at examples of other students' work so they can learn more and better understand the assessment process.

Students will benefit from seeing working examples that illustrate all levels of proficiency, and teachers will be in a better position to demonstrate the differences once they are equipped with examples. Through our recent work in building rubrics in School District 67 in British Columbia, we've identified a goal for the next few years: compile examples of student work that we can use to illustrate differences in our descriptor language.

Walkabouts—An Innovative Assessment Tool in Need of a Rubric

Earlier I mentioned my friend Russ Reid, a thoughtful educator who currently teaches social studies at Penticton Secondary School in British Columbia. Russ has taken a lead in his department around constructing rubrics that make sense for students. Russ was compelled to get his colleagues on board shortly after he decided to design a unique assessment opportunity called a "walkabout" for his Human Geography class. His notion of a walkabout entails students encountering something in the environment *outside* the classroom that relates to a concept or theme previously covered *inside* the classroom. Once students make the connection, they *capture* the phenomenon (say, with a digital image), *connect* it to a concept, and then *support* that connection.

A Secondary-Level Example

For his Human Geography class's year-end assessment, Russ decided to extend the one-day exam into a multiday experience. His objectives were to

- Clearly determine how effectively his students could *apply* their understanding of the course within their own community.

- Allow students to use personal technology devices, such as cell phones.
- Provide students with voice and empowerment in their own final exam.
- Assess spur-of-the-moment application and long-term understanding, rather than regurgitated information typically crammed, memorized, and soon forgotten.

Although he used a relatively traditional final-exam format for day one of the year-end assessment, for the second phase, Russ decided to venture well off the beaten path—literally. On day two, students arrived in class having been told to be prepared to take a walk into the surrounding community. Little did they know that over the next two days, they'd be immersed in an engaging and personal assessment experience. Russ guided them through the following steps:

1. *Introduction:* Russ provided each student with eight quotes that reflected central themes from the course. These included "Pollution knows no borders" and "Urbanization and industrialization have had extremely degrading impacts on the environment."

2. *Activity:* Students were informed that they'd be embarking on a 35- to 40-minute supervised walk through the community. Russ displayed a map of their intended route.

3. *Purpose:* Students were to look for examples, symbols, or structures in the community that embodied or exemplified the course themes. Working individually, when students saw an example of the theme, they were to capture an image of it using their own phone or one of the tablets provided.

4. *Task:* Each student was to take a total of two photos—each relating to a different quote.

5. *Demonstration of Learning:* Once the class returned to the school, students would write a three- to five-paragraph response explaining how the image related to the quote, using supporting information and examples from one or more of their units of study. Students could access supporting data and other sources via the same device they had used to capture the images.

6. *Timeline:* Completing the activity required two class periods. Students would spend the first day walking, taking photos, and beginning some preliminary research to support their choices, and write their responses on the second day.

In each of the written responses the student was to explain the relationship among three elements: unit of study, quote, and image. Here's an example:

- **Unit:** Urbanization
- **Quote:** "The future will either be green or not at all."
- **Image:** Street-side recycling bins

Russ's foray into a new and innovative assessment process—*with* his students—is an impressive example of incorporating our key themes: voice and empowerment, engagement, and self-assessment.

Voice and empowerment. Students could make their own decisions about three different components. They could start by choosing a theme and looking for a photo opportunity to match it. Alternatively, they could wait for an image opportunity to arise and select a corresponding quote. Finally, they were given the latitude to explain how their choices related to the course and to choose their own supporting data and information.

Engagement. By giving students choice, by being outside the walls of the school, and by looking for real examples in their own community, students seemed much more engaged. Russ knew things had changed when he heard students say things he had never imagined, such as "Hey, Mr. Reid, I've got my images. Let's get back and get this exam started" or "I can't wait to get back! I've got things to say!" As Russ noted, "I've never had students excited to begin an exam!"

Self-assessment. To assess the results of this innovative approach to demonstrating learning, Russ and I collaborated to build a rubric that had clear criteria and corresponded to the curricular standards (Figure 3.10, p. 68). Students could use the rubric when deciding how to construct their responses and later use it to self-assess their work before submitting it.

Russ was amazed at the student responses he received. Students had selected a wide array of images while on the walk and related them to the course in personal and innovative ways. One student took a picture of a discarded fast-food container lying beside the road, related it to the theme of urbanization, and supported her response with research on the effects of drive-through restaurants and associated emissions. Another student took an image of a stop sign and went on to discuss how we might "stop" the negative effects of urban sprawl.

As an aside, Russ has been pursuing a personal inquiry as to whether assessments could incorporate student electronic devices rather than forbid them. As Russ commented, "There seems to be something artificial, or unnatural, in the way that students have constant access to their devices, every day, everywhere, except while we assess their understanding of that world. I wonder how we could design assessment tools that incorporate these devices rather than ban them."

Figure 3.10
Analytic Rubric for a Secondary-Level Walkabout

Task: After capturing two images from our community, *create* a 200–250-word document for each image, and *relate* the image to one of the nine statements provided.

Product: Generate your document on a tablet or personal device, and ensure that you (1) *discuss* a clear connection between the quote and the image, (2) *demonstrate an understanding* for how topics/concepts from Human Geo 12 enhance your connections, and (3) *support* your argument or position with data, research, or facts.

** Be sure that your document includes (a) your name, (b) the quote, (c) the supporting image, and (d) your response. **

Criteria	Emerging	Developing	Proficient	Extending
***Discuss* a clear connection between the quote and the image.** **No Evidence:** ☐	Attempts a **basic** connection between the quote and the image.	Provides an **appropriate** connection between the quote and the image.	Provides a **meaningful** connection between the quote and the image.	Provides an **insightful** connection between the quote and the image.
***Demonstrate* an understanding for how concepts from Human Geo 12 enhance connection.** **No Evidence:** ☐	Begins to demonstrate an **initial** understanding by **attempting** to use ideas from course to enhance connection between quote and image.	Demonstrates a **basic** understanding by **somewhat** using ideas from course to enhance connection between quote and image.	Demonstrates a **practical** understanding by **meaningfully** using ideas from course to enhance connection between quote and image.	Demonstrates a **comprehensive** understanding by **skillfully** using ideas from course to enhance connection between quote and image.
***Support* argument or position with relevant, accurate information (data/research/facts).** **No Evidence:** ☐	**Attempts to support** the chosen position with evidence.	Provides **partial** support of chosen position by including **some** evidence.	Provides **considerable** support of chosen position by including **substantial** evidence.	Provides **in-depth** support of chosen position by including **comprehensive** evidence.
Checklist (I have…)	☐ Included 2 images	☐ Cited 3 sources	☐ Self-reported w/this rubric	☐ Proofread my response
Comments: (Student or Teacher)				
Overall evaluation of walkabout (check one)	**Emerging** ☐	**Developing** ☐	**Proficient** ☐	**Extending** ☐

BC Learning Outcome: Assess a variety of interpretations of geographic evidence after investigating different perspectives, reliability of sources, and adequacy of evidence (evidence and interpretation).

Source: Courtesy Russ Reid and Myron Dueck. Used with permission.

An Elementary-Level Example

In his book *Essentialism: The Disciplined Pursuit of Less*, author Greg McKeown (2014) asks, "What if schools eliminated busy work and replaced it with something that made a difference to the whole community?" (p. 25). Scott McIntosh, the elementary teacher we discussed earlier, has done exactly what McKeown suggests.

Inspired by Russ Reid's work at the high school, Scott decided to embark on his own elementary school version of the walkabout. He recognized that his colleague Nicola Korvin was routinely incorporating outdoor education into her students' learning experience, and he wanted to take advantage of her expertise. Preferring collaboration over isolation, Scott asked if she and her grade 2 class would join in the activity.

The purpose for Scott and Nicola's walkabout was to get their students to think more deeply about kindness and community. The medium used to achieve this purpose was similar to Russ's Human Geography model. Students were to capture an original image that reflected a quote and then combine the two into a poster. Through this project, students would develop a multitude of useful skills, including

- Use of a camera, editing, and other design technology skills.
- Effective use of words and imagery to communicate an idea.
- Purposeful and inviting poster layout and design.
- Group work and cooperation.
- Responsible behavior in an outdoor educational setting.

Ultimately, the posters would be used to spread the message of kindness and community throughout their school. The steps for the project were as follows:

1. As a class group, they discussed the importance of kindness and community in making their school a better, more welcoming place.
2. Working in groups of two or three, students cocreated quotes about kindness and community. Here are some examples:

   Nature can make people happy!
   Everyone is different in their own ways.
   Do the right thing even when no one is watching.
   Be kind to others and they will be kind to you.

3. Next, they discussed how messages are conveyed through the use of images. Scott and Nicola presented various posters to the group, providing the opportunity to discuss image, layout, type font, and other design elements.

4. Students were then given the opportunity to find examples of effective poster design—both through secure online portals and around the school—to reinforce the concepts discussed in class.

5. Scott and Nicola then challenged each group to take a photo that reflected their quote. The students were allowed to roam a supervised area of the school grounds and use a tablet to capture a few images.

6. Once students had a photo that reflected their quote, they worked in their groups to design a poster that would be displayed in the school to promote kindness and community.

For the assessment portion of this activity, Scott and I designed the rubric shown in Figure 3.11. By incorporating empty spaces in the section for the first criterion, Scott provided a way to get students to better understand the rubric and reflect on the extent to which their quote and images matched the descriptors. As well, he found a way to greatly increase student voice, engagement, and self-assessment—accomplishing all this with a very simple use of technology.

In an interview, Scott provided some details:

> I put the rubric up on the whiteboard using the digital projector. The students then placed their quotes in the empty space on the rubric to show where their thinking landed.... The powerful part was the conversations to be had as kids brought them up and placed them on the board. I wish I had videotaped the whole thing. (personal communication, July 12, 2019)

Scott used the projection of the rubric onto his whiteboard as the medium for student interaction and discussion of their quotes. Students wrote their ideas on sticky notes and then attached them to one of the empty spaces on the projected rubric.

How a Simple Rubric Transformed a Journaling Assignment

While teaching at Princess Margaret Secondary School in Penticton, British Columbia, I was fortunate to work with principal Don MacIntyre. From my perspective as a young teacher, Don's office was a welcoming place where I could share frustrations, challenges, and questions. Without the open-minded support of leaders like Don, there's no way I would've found the courage to question, and act upon, so many of my traditionally held beliefs about grading and assessment. A few years later, he was working at the board office while I cut my teeth as a high school vice principal. As a rookie administrator, I'd experienced many tough

Figure 3.11
Analytic Rubric for an Elementary-Level Walkabout

Student task: While on our walk, <u>take a picture</u> that **connects** to your group's quote around <u>positive living and mindsets</u>.

Product: Using your picture and quote, design and create a poster with a frame, with the quote attached.

Parents: The curricular competencies used in this assessment are taken from the BC Career Education K–3 curriculum. In the section for the first criterion, there is room for student self-assessment.

Criteria	Emerging	Developing	Proficient	Extending
Discuss a clear connection between the quote and the image. No Evidence: ☐	Attempts a basic connection between the quote and the image.	Provides an appropriate connection between the quote and the image.	Provides a meaningful connection between the quote and the image.	Student creates own quote and provides an insightful connection between the quote and the image.
Student voice! ***I can explain why my quote and picture are connected.***				
Recognize the importance of positive relationships in their daily lives. No Evidence: ☐	Is beginning to recognize positive relationships in their life.	Can sometimes recognize and describe positive relationships in their life.	Can regularly recognize positive and negative relationships, and how they can influence others.	Uses detail to recognize and explain positive and negative relationships in their life. Can use examples to explain how healthy communities rely on positive people.
Share ideas, information, personal feelings, and knowledge with others. No Evidence: ☐	Is trying to share ideas and feelings with others. Is beginning to listen to others.	Sometimes shares ideas, feelings, and knowledge with others. Attempts to listen to other people's perspectives.	Regularly shares ideas, feelings, and knowledge with others. Often listens to other people's perspectives.	In different situations can share complex ideas, feelings, and knowledge. Builds upon the ideas of others to contribute to the whole group.
Work respectfully and constructively with others to achieve common goals. No Evidence: ☐	With lots of support is beginning to work with others.	With support can sometimes work with others respectfully toward a goal.	Can independently work with others respectfully toward a goal.	Consistently works with others respectfully; solves problems in creative ways to help others.
Student or teacher comments:				

Source: Courtesy Scott McIntosh, Nicola Korvin, and Myron Dueck. Used with permission.

situations, and Don offered valuable behind-the-scenes advice. When I encountered a few particularly difficult and complicated parent meetings, he would offer to attend the meeting to provide measured support. Don prioritized learning and relationships for both his students and his staff. He offered guidance and support that were free of judgment—arguably the greatest gift educational leaders can give young teachers and administrators.

Don had a seemingly endless bank of time-tested truths that applied to many situations. Here's one example: "Kids over curriculum. Establish your class as a safe, caring, and equitable learning environment before you start working through the curriculum." This was sage advice!

It must have been five years since I had worked with Don when I was developing a grade 10 Leadership course at a different high school. You might recall from Chapter 2 that I inherited this course without any standards or learning outcomes. I had decided that regular personal journal entries would be a part of the student learning experience and hoped that students would use them to express their thoughts and reflect upon key themes. The routine went something like this:

1. I would introduce a concept or an idea to the class. An example was "*stealth leadership*—the act of service or assistance, typically quietly or behind the scenes, without wanting, or expecting, any recognition or accolades."

2. I might show a short video to support the idea and initiate class discussion. (As an aside, when visiting schools and conferences, if I mention "leadership class," I invariably get approached by some poor soul who's also been assigned a course with little or no structure. For all of you on the deserted Leadership Class Island, feel free to steal this activity and make it your own. For an example of the video I use to support the topic of stealth leadership, check out the TED Talk by Drew Dudley titled "Everyday Leadership," in which he tells the story of his "Lollipop Moment." Here's the link: www.ted.com/talks/drew_dudley_everyday_leadership. You are also welcome to visit www.myrondueck.com for resources specific to running a leadership course.)

3. We would then discuss the video in small groups or as a class.

4. Within a day or two, I might show another example—this time a video of two runners about to conclude a long-distance race (www.youtube.com/watch?v=Dy_LxkRZEbI). About 30 seconds into the clip, we see two runners approaching a finish line area. The lead runner begins to slow down and check his watch for his time, believing that he has completed the race. Unfortunately for him, the actual finish line lies a few steps ahead. We viewers can tell that the runner in second place, Ivan Fernandez Anaya, realizes the "winner" has made an error. That's when I stop the video, make

sure everyone understands what's transpired, and ask the class, "What would you do if you were the second runner?" The class typically erupts in a bit of chaos. Students immediately exclaim, "What happens?!" or "Press play! I gotta see this!" I resist all pressure to resume the video, and instead we discuss the question in pairs and then as a class. The responses in class vary incredibly, though there's an unmistakable split between two camps:

- Tough Luck Camp: The first-place runner made a mistake, and this is a competition. As the second runner I would pass him and win.
- Fair Play Camp: The first runner is the rightful winner who made a simple error. I would inform him of the real finish line and let him win.

5. After our impassioned class discussion, I would then ask students to write a short journal entry to explain their personal thoughts and how these tie to the concept of "stealth leadership" or other related themes. I encourage them to think of an example or a scenario from their own lives that might relate to the topic.

6. I would then play the rest of the video to reveal the decision made by Anaya, the second runner. (If you want to see the outcome of the race, access the link provided earlier.) We then have further opportunity for discussion or journaling.

Although I thought the journals would be a great idea, they turned out to be a bit of a disaster. Despite lively class discussions and debate, upon reading the journals I found the entries lacked depth, care, and detail. To be clear, many of them were terrible. I was alone in my class, staring at yet another shallow submission, when I wondered aloud, "Have these students ever learned to write a decent journal entry?"

At that moment, I could have been Luke Skywalker in *The Empire Strikes Back*. Fans of *Star Wars* will be familiar with a scene in which Luke, injured and alone, is seemingly going to die on the frozen, windswept wasteland of Planet Hoth. At the moment he seems to collapse and expire, his mentor, Obi-Wan Kenobi, holographically appears in the blizzard and offers him advice on seeking out Yoda. As Obi-Wan fades, Han Solo shows up to save Luke.

Back to Don MacIntyre. As I was about to collapse and fade as a result of my journal frustration, Don may as well have appeared in the fluorescent shimmer of my whiteboard. His message was simple: "Young Myron, remember this truth: never assume your students know something unless you teach it."

Although I cannot recall exactly what issue originally spawned Don's advice, I'm sure it involved slowing down my pace of instruction and taking time to teach something I'd assumed my students already knew. In any event, I was reminded in that moment that my students were likely unaware of what made an effective journal entry. If so, how could I help them? How could they help themselves? Much of the answer came through student self-assessment with a codesigned rubric.

Guided by Obi-Don's advice, I started the next class by asking my students a few questions: "Have you guys ever done journaling before?" It turns out most students either hadn't or couldn't remember. "Could we brainstorm what makes a good journal entry?" A few ideas came forward, and we discussed these as a class.

Following this conversation, I provided a number of anonymous examples for us to critique. In the end, we designed the rubric in Figure 3.12. I was using a six-point scale at that time (a topic we will cover in more detail in subsequent

Figure 3.12
Rubric for a Leadership Journal

Criteria	Expert 5/6	Apprentice 3/4	Novice 1/2
Incorporate and *synthesize* topics (example: marathon runner making decision, organizing school event)	Creates a **comprehensive** summary of the topic or event.	Creates a **thorough** summary of the topic or event.	Creates a **surface or simple** summary of the topic or event.
Communicate information (use sentences, diagrams, mind maps, cartoons)	Communicates information in a **compelling** manner to **engage** the reader.	Communicates information in an **effective** manner to **interest** the reader.	Communicates information in a **simple** manner to **generally hold** reader's attention.
Develop and *support* position using leadership concepts (marathon runner using "stealth leadership"; Power Base used to lead school event planning)	Synthesizes concepts discussed in class to develop a **perceptive** position supported by **significant** evidence.	Synthesizes concepts discussed in class to develop a **convincing** position supported by **relevant** evidence.	Synthesizes concepts discussed in class to develop a **reasonable** position supported by **basic** evidence.
Comments:			

☐ There is no level determined at this time due to insufficient evidence of student performance.

Source: © 2020 Myron Dueck. Used with permission.

chapters). I encourage you to note how we attempted to incorporate the seven design considerations discussed earlier in this chapter. As well, I've experimented with placing the "expert" level on the left side of the rubric, knowing that likely students will read that first. I'm not sure who decided that rubrics generally read from left to right, but this tradition is worth revisiting.

Don was right: never assume your students understand something unless you address it. The implementation of this codesigned rubric immediately transformed the quality of the journal entries. Students were provided with a clear path to success without compromising voice or creativity. There were other benefits and observations:

- Students self-assessed their journals using the rubric *before* submitting them for periodic review and grading.
- Often students would identify a problem, or an opportunity to elaborate, *through* the process of self-assessment.
- Students had three clear, verb-driven criteria to follow, which still provided ample room for personalization and creativity.
- Students came up with different ways to use the rubric to support their learning. For instance, one student glued a rubric template into her journal as a helpful reminder when composing an entry.

Closing Thoughts

Old habits and traditions do not change easily. In every situation, I need to remind myself that we're all evolving to increasingly make assessment useful for the *learner*. Although this perspective might sound great, it's not typically our first priority, and once in a while we need a reality check. For instance, when the leadership team in Roseville was fundamentally shifting its grading and reporting structure, it first focused on educating parents. The team produced videos, designed informational webpages, e-mailed people, and held meetings. Once the dust settled, however, perhaps most interesting was Brandon Blom's epiphany on who mattered most in the communication cycle: "My big learning from last year is that we need to first educate our students about these changes, and then the parents" (personal communication, August 13, 2019). I found this observation intriguing and asked Blom to elaborate. Here's his response:

> By educating the students first, the students were able to hear directly from their teacher before their parents heard the information. They could ask questions and have a discussion with their teacher and classmates about the changes. The questions from students also gave teachers the opportunity to clarify any

misunderstandings and hear student excitement or concerns. It also showed the students we value their voice and that they must understand the changes since they are the learners. After the school day was over, parents did receive an e-mail with information, and when they asked their children about it, the students were better able to talk to their parents than if we had informed parents first and then educated the students. (personal communication, August 13, 2019)

Whether assessing an Olympic dive, a walkabout reflection, or a grade 10 Leadership class journal entry about some runner's decision, it's critical that we provide our students with actionable criteria and clear descriptors. Countless forms of rubrics are available, from a single column to quite complex configurations. Perhaps this discussion has provided some elements and ideas on how you can use them with students—for learning, teaching, and assessment. Above all, I think the examples in this chapter provide evidence that we can truly invite students into the realm of performance assessments in our mission *to sit beside.*

INVOLVING STUDENTS IN ONGOING ASSESSMENT

How can we give students opportunities to strive for and demonstrate mastery?

A number of years ago, when I was coaching my son's ice hockey team, an initiative issued by the sport's governing body required that all minor-level hockey players be put through a series of baseline tests. The *purpose* of these assessments was to measure six key skills for each player. These data, related to skating speed, shooting accuracy, agility, and a few other skills, were to be entered into a national database to establish a baseline measure for all players. This baseline would help coaches monitor each player's ongoing development from year to year.

As a coach, an educator, and a writer on topics related to assessment, I was certainly intrigued by these tests. In preparing to put our 11-year-old players through six different testing stations, the other coaches and I discussed how many chances each player should have at each station. We decided to establish a rule that each player would get a maximum of three opportunities to demonstrate each skill.

I was put in charge of timing and recording players skating forward and backward over a distance of 100 feet. Three players were assigned to my station, and the first skater to go through the course was David (a pseudonym)—one of our team's fastest skaters. David was a very good hockey player. He was one of our top scorers, and despite his age, even I found it difficult at times to wrestle the puck from his possession in scrimmages.

When it came time to test his skating speed, he crouched eagerly in the starting position. He may have imagined he was being tested for an NHL team, as the moment I finished saying "On your mark, get set, *go!*" he exploded off the line. As he reached the halfway point of the forward-skating portion of the test, his feet became tangled and he fell, sliding off course. He got back to his feet and completed the route, but his time was compromised greatly by his fall.

After the two other skaters took their turns, successfully remaining on their skates, David stepped up to the line to try again. It was not lost on either of us that he was typically the fastest skater on our team, but his fall relegated him to last place at my station. I attempted to both encourage his enthusiasm and remind him of the rules: "OK, David, stay on your skates. You get three chances to record your fastest time."

"Got it, coach. I'm ready!" David replied as he got set into his starting position.

Once again, he bolted off the line, successfully completed his 100 feet of forward skating, and was generating speed on the backward portion of the test. Suddenly he "blew a tire" (in hockey lingo) and fell backward. Clearly frustrated, David once again completed the course, but with a time slower than those of the other two skaters. In kid-friendly terms, I reminded David that it was imperative that fast skaters also maintain control throughout the two legs of the test. Trying not to ratchet up the pressure he was clearly putting on himself, I pointed out that he only had one chance left *according to the rules.*

Despite employing my best coaching strategies—most notably incorporating well-intentioned but amateur sports psychology—David's third and final attempt did not go much better than the first two. He again lost his footing and concluded the session in last place. I stared at the single box on the stats sheet where I was supposed to record his skating time. *One* number in *one* square would establish his baseline speed for all future tests! I wondered what to do—especially considering my strong belief, based on years of observation, that he was arguably the fastest skater in the group, if not on the entire team! Struggling with the thought of recording his "best" time in his three tries, I looked for room in the margin or end notes to let someone know that David had wiped out in every one of his attempts. I wanted to note something like "David's speed would likely be much higher if he had not fallen every time," or "Player's enthusiasm appears to be compromising his results." I also would have noted, "He's arguably the fastest player on the team!" Unfortunately, there was no box or field for writing a comment. In that moment,

I contemplated a philosophical collision at the icy intersection of the rules, our purpose, and my beliefs!

This example raises a few questions about coaching, classrooms, and all other testing arenas:

- *What should I do if my ongoing observations and experiences are not consistent with the testing data?*
- *What concessions should I make for one or more variables possibly corrupting my assessment data?*
- *Do I abide by the rules, even if seemingly arbitrary, and override my beliefs and long-term observations?*
- *When is it time to say, "Tough luck, kid. You crashed every time!"? Was this an appropriate time to exercise that kind of life lesson?*

When I think back over my 20-plus years in the classroom, I often felt there was a disconnect between what I knew to be true of my students and the testing results some of them achieved. I believe I was handcuffed for much of my career as I followed the old unwritten rule: "There are no retests." As I explain in more detail in *Grading Smarter, Not Harder* (Dueck, 2014), I came to question this mantra as I encountered students who

- Clearly understood more than they cared, or were able, to demonstrate.
- Became easily frustrated or defeated in the testing process.
- Struggled with English as a second language and therefore could not effectively convey their level of understanding.
- Did not have the same resources, time, or safe study spaces afforded to some of their peers and therefore were less prepared on the test day I chose.
- Responded much better to some testing structures and methods than others.
- Had become disengaged and lost motivation through their schooling (and particularly assessment) experiences.

Countless times in my classroom I encountered my on-ice coaching dilemma: *What should I do when the testing data contradict my professional judgment?*

In the end, *purpose* should act as the rudder for all of my assessment decisions. Oh, right—that elevator pitch! Rather than paging back to find it, here it is:

In every aspect of assessment, we will engage and empower the student by offering opportunities for student voice, choice, self-assessment, and self-reporting.

The purpose of this chapter is to look for ways to deliver on our elevator pitch through the testing we do in our schools and classrooms. Owing to the pressure and stigma so often associated with testing, I would argue there is no more important arena in which we need to slide our chair around to the student's side of the table and truly "sit beside."

When I first changed my assessment routines in 2006 and offered students more than one opportunity to demonstrate their learning, I had many reservations and concerns—not to mention plenty of challenging conversations with colleagues. Friends on my own school staff argued, "We should not give retests" or "We're eroding student responsibility by offering reassessments." One well-intentioned colleague even argued that I was "unraveling the moral fabric of our school." Make no mistake—while enacting significant changes to my students' testing routines, I had some of the same concerns.

We'll now cover some concepts that are undoubtedly inspired by thought leaders such as Dylan Wiliam and John Hattie. We'll examine some research on memory and testing, as well as explore a few studies that specifically underscore the importance of student-centered, ongoing assessment. Some of these topics will have undeniable links to the importance of ongoing assessment, whereas others are indirectly related to it. After addressing some of the research, we will look at a variety of examples of how teachers are incorporating student voice and choice in ongoing assessment routines.

Storage Strength Versus Retrieval Strength

Memory has two elements that I wish every teacher, parent, and student better understood: storage strength and retrieval strength. And it turns out that our memory works very differently than that of computers (Wiliam, 2018). According to Bjork and Bjork (1992), we have *storage strength,* which is a measure of how well we have placed something into long-term memory. Storage strength refers to what we have truly learned, and seemingly it only grows as we pack more things into it. The size of our long-term memory has been estimated to be a mind-boggling 2.5 petabytes—or the equivalent of about 300 million hours of television programming (Daspin, 2018)!

We also have *retrieval strength*—the extent to which we can access or recall what we have stored (Bjork & Bjork, 1992). Over time, our retrieval strength can grow weaker as the interval between learning something and retrieving it grows longer. You've likely found yourself trying to recall someone's name while picturing his face or the place you met, all the while saying something like "Hang on... I know his name... wait, I know it!" At that moment, you are confirming Bjork and Bjork's contention that you have stored the name *and* you know it's in storage, but you just can't retrieve it. Storage strength and retrieval strength are indeed two different things.

The relationship between storage strength and retrieval strength is both astounding and paradoxical. A widespread belief contends that we continually increase storage strength whenever we study something, but we also increase storage strength when something is retrieved. The paradox arises from the fact that we embed something deeper and more profoundly in storage when our retrieval strength is low compared to when it's high (Bjork & Bjork, 1992; Wiliam, 2018). Put bluntly, when we retrieve something after struggling to do so, we entrench it deeper into memory. This benefit to long-term learning, developed by our very struggle to retrieve, is what Bjork and Bjork (2014) have called "desirable difficulties."

Desirable Difficulties

Bjork and Bjork (2014) describe desirable difficulties as follows:

> Desirable difficulties, versus the array of undesirable difficulties, are desirable because they trigger encoding and retrieval processes that support learning, comprehension, and remembering. If, however, the learner does not have the background knowledge or skills to respond to them successfully, they become undesirable difficulties. (p. 58)

I found this concept particularly interesting when I recalled my own frustrating experience as a math student. I always considered myself a fairly weak math student because I seemed to take much longer to grasp a concept compared with many of my peers. Especially in algebra and physics, exasperated and with my forehead planted squarely on my desk, I might have found some solace in hearing that difficulty could be "desirable." (Incidentally, Ericsson and Pool [2016] suggest in *Peak* that some influential person likely had a massive, and unfortunate, influence on my contention that I was not a "math person," but we'll get into that matter later.)

Bjork and Bjork have four concrete suggestions for how we can build "desirable difficulty" environments. For each suggestion, we will consider the implications it might hold for our assessment conversation.

1. Vary the conditions of practice. Avoid having the learning always take place in the same location, under the same conditions. If the learning space is predictable, we as humans tend to contextualize the learning so it's most effective only if we replicate the same conditions (Smith, Glenberg, & Bjork, 1978). I recall some of my own students voicing concern that final school exams would take place in the gym rather than the classroom, where the vast majority of instruction had occurred. Now I know why.

Assessment implication:

- Learning, practicing, and testing with our students, in a variety of ways, and in different locations, is better than in one way, in one room.

2. Space study or practice sessions. The reality that humans learn better when we spread out learning sessions over a longer period of time is one of the most robust conclusions of memory research (Bjork & Bjork, 1992). Therefore, cramming all evening for a test may seem effective the morning after, but the learner will be able to retrieve very little of that information in the long term.

In a related study, Cepeda, Vul, Rohrer, Wixted, and Pashler (2008) discovered that we transfer learning more effectively into long-term memory when we encounter longer periods of time between learning sessions. The longer the span between learning something new and then revisiting it, the longer the retention interval we can sustain once we are tested. One conclusion of the study is that the typical unit structure of many schools—namely, one or two weeks spent on a topic—may be highly ineffective, and that "current results indicate that this compression of learning into a too-short period is likely to produce misleadingly high levels of immediate mastery that will not survive the passage of substantial periods of time" (p. 1101). The bottom line: we don't retain much from cramming sessions, and our typical one- or two-week unit structures may be far from optimal for learning.

Assessment implications:

- Spacing out instruction, study, and testing situations encourages long-term retention of learning.
- Testing a concept multiple times over a period of time may increase long-term learning of that concept.

3. Interleave instruction rather than delivering it in blocks. Whether examining the learning of motor skills related to typing (Simon & Bjork, 2001), the math skills involved in calculating volume (Rohrer & Taylor, 2007), or the styles of 12 different artists (Kornell & Bjork, 2008), interleaving the topics of instruction can prove far more effective than blocking topics. (Blocking involves addressing topics in this fashion: A, A, A; B, B, B; C, C, C; whereas interleaving uses this approach: A, B, C, A, C, B, C, A.) An interesting point is that this conclusion was typically revealed through test results rather than asking people what instruction format they preferred. Although people tend to favor learning by blocking, the test data overwhelmingly suggest that we retain more when instruction is interleaved versus blocked.

Assessment implications:

- Consider revisiting topics previously covered while presenting new ones.
- Interleave topics during instruction, review, and testing to create deeper connections.
- Consider cross-curricular initiatives in schools.

4. Consider the "generation effect" and use tests (rather than presentations) as learning events. The "generation effect" refers to "the long-term benefit of generating an answer, solution, or procedure versus being presented that answer, solution, or procedure" (Bjork & Bjork, 2014, p. 61). We discussed the findings of Manu Kapur (2015) in Chapter 2 while discussing the benefits of group struggle. Now let's dig a little deeper. In his research around what he calls "productive failure," Kapur concluded that students who spent two out of four periods coming up with their own solutions—even if those solutions were misguided or incorrect—demonstrated better retention of the canonical solution once it was presented by the teacher. It's particularly interesting how much better these students did when compared with students who experienced four periods of direct instruction and group work. Kapur (2015) refers to this as the "solution generation effect." He concludes, "The more solutions students generated, the better they performed on the procedural fluency, conceptual understanding, and transfer items on the posttest" (p. 55).

Some of the same principles found in the work of Kapur as well as Bjork and Bjork have surfaced in what Ericsson and Pool call "the largest effect ever seen in education" (2016, p. 243). In a remarkable study conducted at the University of British Columbia (UBC), researchers Louis Deslauiers, Ellen Schelew, and Carl Wieman (the latter the winner of the 2001 Nobel Prize in physics) pitted two groups of first-year physics students with similar levels of understanding against each other in an epic battle of instructional styles.

While one group of 270 students continued week 12 of their studies in the typical fashion—three 50-minute lectures, homework assignments, and tutorials—the other group took a different path. Led by two "instructors" who had never taught a physics class before, the second group would be assigned a short reading on a physics concept. Arriving to class somewhat familiar with a chosen concept, students were put in small groups and given calculus and intensive math problems. Using electronic responders, the students would generate an answer to the problem, and the instructor could make various decisions depending on the data received. For instance, the instructor might ask groups to discuss the range of responses, give a minilecture for clarity, or provide a little more detail and ask students to respond again. A key feature is that students were afforded the opportunity to discuss, debate, and ponder the problem within the group before responding (Deslauiers, Schelew, & Wieman, 2011).

The results of the study were nothing short of astounding. Although the two groups' level of engagement with the material was identical before the change in instruction, it nearly doubled for the electronic-responder group after the change (Ericsson & Pool, 2016). In an even more amazing twist, after 12 weeks of different instructional styles, both groups were tested for their understanding of the material. The results? The electronic-responder group got two-and-a-half times more responses correct than the traditional lecture group (Deslauriers et al., 2011). You read that correctly—two-and-a-half times! In his aptly titled article "Transformation Is Possible If a University Really Cares," Mervis (2013) documents that many of the changes highlighted in this study have been adopted across nearly 100 science and math classes at UBC.

Similar to the conclusions related to "desirable difficulties" and "productive failure," Ericsson and Pool (2016) suggest that we should "keep students out of their comfort zone but not so far out that they cannot master that step. Then give plenty of repetition and feedback; the regular cycle of try, fail, get feedback, try again and so on…" (p. 253). I'm not sure I've read of a study that better represents the power of our elevator pitch.

The further we investigate the topic of ongoing assessment, the more evidence we uncover in favor of it. For instance, students learn more by experiencing a test situation than if they read that same material over and over (Pyc & Rawson, 2010). Dunlosky, Rawson, Marsh, Nathan, and Willingham (2013) conclude that students learn more from an hour of testing than they do from an hour of studying the same material. We might want to reconsider the timing of testing in the learning journey. Studies indicate that students may benefit more in long-term retention when they start working on a new topic by taking a test on it—before any instruction has even taken place (Little & Bjork, 2011)!

Assessment implications:

- Ongoing assessment is a critical element of long-term learning.
- An approach that involves students working together, or as individuals, to explore a solution (especially testing it and failing) can have a greater positive impact on learning than direct instruction.
- Students seem to learn things more deeply through the process of making mistakes, and testing can be a suitable avenue to achieve this result so long as the test can be revisited after learning has occurred.

Performance or Learning: What Are You After?

Have you ever crammed for a test or an exam? Do you remember the introduction of high-caffeine Jolt Cola and the legions of students who made it a staple of all-night study sessions? I've engaged countless times in some sort of cramming, and I'm pretty sure every reader of this book has also. A more important question is, *why* did you cram for a test or an exam? Likely you wanted a good score, grade, or final course standing. Perhaps you consciously or unconsciously knew that your homework scores—perhaps derived from copying the work of your friends—needed to match your test scores or uncomfortable questions might arise. Maybe you wanted to avoid being grounded by your parents and missing the weekend party. Perhaps you would be embarrassed if you had to try *again* to get your driver's license.

Most important, was your goal to (1) learn the material or (2) achieve short-term performance? If you were cramming, I'd suggest it was the latter. I realize we might occasionally need to stuff information into our heads in order to spit it out shortly after, but unfortunately, the results of this process too often get recorded as "learning" in a gradebook, in a software program, or on the driving instructor's clipboard. Once I passed that driver's test, for example, everyone seemed to accept that I *knew* and *understood* the material—and would for the rest of my life. Seriously, isn't it a little odd that I'm entrusted to drive my F-150 pickup truck, pulling a heavy trailer down a busy highway, based in large part on the results of cramming for a test 30 years ago? This potential misrepresentation—namely, the labeling of performance as *learning*—has the potential to keep us awake at night.

I recently read Bjork and Bjork's chapter, "Making Things Hard on Yourself, but in a Good Way," in *Psychology and the Real World* (Gernsbacher & Pomerantz, 2014). What I read leaves me quite concerned. Apparently, we've long been misrepresenting much of the data from our assessments. We label results as evidence of "learning," when really it's performance. They define the difference between *performance* and *learning* as follows:

> Performance is what we can observe and measure during instruction or training. Learning—that is, the more or less permanent change in knowledge or understanding that is the target of instruction—is something we must try to infer, and current performance can be a highly unreliable index of whether learning has occurred. (p. 57)

Yikes! I'm considering plunging my head in the sand.

The notion that performance is not a good indicator of learning has massive implications for our assessment strategies. Just as we can all agree that the testing results from a cramming session are not likely a reflection of long-term learning, the same could be true for other things that boost performance, such as direct instruction and even immediate feedback. Bjork and Bjork (2014) suggest that some of our assistance may be detrimental, whereas struggle can be a good thing:

> We can also be misled by our current performance. Conditions of learning that make performance improve rapidly often fail to support long-term retention and transfer, whereas conditions that create challenges and slow the rate of apparent learning often optimize long-term retention and transfer. (p. 57)

If Bjork and Bjork are onto something here, the implications for how we interpret evidence of student learning are enormous. If performance is inversely related to learning, in that we may well be learning *more* when it appears that we are learning *less*, I wonder how many assessments, done every day, in classrooms around the world, are completely misrepresentative. It's entirely possible that students who are performing well may not be learning much at all, whereas others performing poorly are learning more. Seriously, I could use a sandbox right now.

While you ponder this juxtaposition, staring at the ceiling at 2 a.m., consider this as well: we may want to stop putting an inherent value on how fast or efficiently something is learned. If you listen carefully, our schools still reverberate with the industrial-era notion that *faster is better*. Bjork and Bjork, by contrast, have concluded that we need to slow down the learning process and realize that people who take longer to grasp a concept may indeed learn it more deeply than those who appeared to understand it immediately. In *Thinking, Fast and Slow*, Daniel Kahneman (2011) reminds us that slowing down is a powerful factor in learning and memory, suggesting that our memory holds the "vast repertory of skills we have acquired in a lifetime of practice" (p. 416). Throughout this span of time, when our brain fails to conjure a spontaneous solution, it switches to "a slower, more deliberate and effortful form of thinking" (p. 13).

While we're questioning our routines, let's kick in the door on *immediate feedback*. Long heralded as a key component to effective teaching, the immediacy of feedback is being questioned in light of Bjork and Bjork's work. Wiliam (2018) argues that immediate feedback may boost performance, but the amount of learning may actually decrease, as the student is not the one doing the heavy lifting. He summarizes the idea by suggesting that "supporting students as they work through *desirable difficulties* in their work is likely to have a greater impact on long-term learning than feedback that just tells students what to do" (p. 139).

Of course, the teacher needs to monitor the situation to decide on the timeliness of feedback; but if grappling with a problem and experiencing "desirable difficulty" is proving effective for true learning, we may want to delay the feedback.

When making this determination, Wiliam's advice has proven to be valuable: "We need to ensure that feedback causes a cognitive rather than an emotional reaction" (p. 153).

In light of this research, we should question some of our traditional assessment procedures, grading decisions, and reporting methods. When asked to share what students have learned, teachers may cite their gradebooks, unaware that much of the data may be strictly performance indicators. Bjork and Bjork (2014) contend that when "people interpret current performance as a valid measure of learning, they become susceptible to misassessing whether learning has or has not occurred" (p. 57). Perhaps all of this underscores the reason why we need to involve students directly in their own ongoing assessment routines.

Assessment implications:

- Ongoing assessment procedures, involving challenges and struggle for the student, increase learning. Therefore, students should be given the opportunity to revisit assessments *because learning may have changed during the assessment process.*
- If testing is a way to increase learning, students should be engaged in ongoing assessment—demonstrating understanding on more than one occasion and in different ways.
- Immediate feedback may not be as effective as we once thought. In some circumstances, students can benefit from grappling with a problem (over a reasonable amount of time) rather than receiving immediate correction or help.

A final comment on "performance versus learning" involves implications for how we assess, and later report, the "learning" of students moving from one level to another—be that grade to grade or our high school grads moving on to university or college. I was recently interviewed for a news story on the topic of grade inflation and university preparedness. A particular Nevada community was concerned that recent high school graduates were not as prepared for higher education as their grades might suggest. A strong and predictable reaction by some educators and parents was to blame retesting and grading changes (such as reducing the use of zeros for missing assignments). Rather than casting blame on retesting, which research suggests increases learning, perhaps we need to ask ourselves whether our students have really learned what our data suggest, or whether we may have misassessed their performance as "learning." If a freshman is struggling in their Nevada State College physics class, it might be because they crammed or performed to get a 99 percent in high school, learning little along the way.

Self-Testing Versus
Traditional Study Methods

In *Embedded Formative Assessment*, Wiliam (2018) cites the work of five U.S. education psychologists who looked specifically at techniques that students could use on their own, with little support or guidance from teachers, to increase their level of understanding. Two of the ten techniques, practice testing and distributed practice, received very high ratings. Common study techniques, such as rereading material, pale in comparison to testing—even when this testing is done without teacher correction! As Bjork and Bjork (2014) contend, we've been making some pretty dangerous assumptions about how we remember things:

> Much laboratory research (for example, Landauer & Bjork, 1978; Carrier & Pashler, 1992) has demonstrated the power of tests as learning events, and, in fact, a test or retrieval attempt, even when no corrective feedback is given, can be considerably more effective in the long term than reading material over and over. The reason why rereading is such a typical mode of studying derives, we believe, from a faulty model of how we learn and remember: We tend to think of our memories as working much like an audio/video recorder, so if we read and reread or take verbatim notes, the information will eventually write itself on our memories. Nothing, however, could be further from the way we actually learn and remember. (p. 62)

In his insightful and practical article "Strengthening the Student Toolbox: Study Strategies to Boost Learning," Dunlosky (2013) offers a plethora of research-based suggestions on how students can do well on exams *and* retain the information for longer periods. Practice testing emerges as one of the most powerful tools students can use, especially when the tests require the student to recall something from memory (as opposed to recognizing the correct answer from a list). Dunlosky argues that when students work hard to remember something, it pays off in the long run. Furthermore, when students are in the driver's seat of the testing process, they can see for themselves what they got right and what they did not—and then make important decisions around what to revisit and learn.

I think we need to redefine what it means to study *for* learning, and the way we use tests can play a big part in this reframing. As students test themselves, they are more deeply embedding learning by the very retrieval of it.

Assessment implications:

- Ongoing assessment is powerful, even in the absence of the teacher.
- Student self-assessment can be used simultaneously as a study, learning, and metacognitive activity.

The Hypercorrection Effect

Although the underlying causational factors for it are unclear, the "hypercorrection effect" is a powerful element of ongoing assessment. Imagine someone asks you a question and you respond with an answer you are confident is correct. If it turns out that you are incorrect and subsequently are provided with the correct response, weeks later you will likely test better on this correction than you would on a question you answered incorrectly and with *less* confidence (Metcalfe, Butterfield, Habeck, & Stern, 2012). Hence the name of this perplexing phenomenon: the "hypercorrection effect."

We might think that people confident in an incorrect answer would be hard to sway, but it turns out that doing so is relatively easy. Furthermore, it seems that the discomfort, or perhaps surprise, of being wrong embeds the correction deeper into our memory. The connection among student involvement in the testing process, the hypercorrection effect, and our grading structures is unavoidable. As Wiliam (2018) concludes, "The best person to mark a test is the person who just took it. We need more testing but less grading" (p. 174). I'm reminded of my own students' feedback. When asked if we should involve students in reporting their own learning, recall Malaina's response in Chapter 1: "Of course! No one knows me like I know me!"

Assessment implications:

- When going over an assessment, students who were confident in an incorrect response are highly likely to learn from the correction process.
- All students can learn through ongoing assessment.
- When learning changes through a testing procedure, it's imperative that this new learning moment be reflected in another assessment opportunity.

New Systems for New Ideas

I've come to believe that success can be compromised when new ideas collide with old systems. As we encounter research like that cited so far, it's pretty hard—and possibly unethical—to blend it with some of our traditional testing methods and rules. I find it hard to stomach hearing educators state, "I don't offer retests" when the research is so compelling that we all learn throughout the testing process.

In addition, it's important to consider the role of standards. Around the world, schools, districts, and individual educators are looking for ways to tackle standards-based grading. In my opinion, a massive step in achieving this goal is to organize assessments *by the standards* or the targets derived from those standards. In Chapter 2, we considered how to break down standards into clear, student-friendly, and codesigned learning targets. Now it's time to assess according to that same framework. This step is a critical and natural progression in helping students and teachers assess according to the essential learning goals. The next sections provide examples and tools for how we can harness the power of ongoing assessment while embedding student voice, choice, self-assessment, and self-reporting.

An Updated Retesting Structure

In *Grading Smarter, Not Harder* (Dueck, 2014), I explained how I'd separated my end-of-unit tests into sections based on the topics we'd covered. This approach was a radical departure from the traditional structure I'd followed of separating the sections by the assessment method—true/false, short answer, diagram, and so on—with the topics interspersed throughout these sections. Separating by topics had immediate benefits for me:

- I could quickly determine which topics students did or did not understand and use the data to make instructional adjustments for the class or individual students.
- My grading load was manageable, as each student could decide to revisit one or multiple sections. Revisiting the entire test was *not* required.
- It was far easier for me to determine and document changes in student learning from one test to another.

Benefits for the *learner* were also achieved:

- When taking the test for the first time, students could make strategic decisions about which sections to cover first and the order of the subsequent ones. We observed that students often started with a topic about which they felt most confident.
- Students reported feeling less anxiety as they knew they could revisit sections if things did not go as planned.
- The topics and questions were clearly aligned, avoiding potential ambiguity for everyone and assisting struggling students and English as a second language (ESL) learners in particular.
- Struggling or disengaged learners were far more likely to engage in the retesting process if they could do one or two sections compared with having to redo the entire assessment.

When I returned tests, I included a tracking sheet, which proved to be an effective tool for engaging students in their own learning. This process, and the tools that accompanied it, were monumental in involving my students in the assessment arena for the following reasons:

- Students had the opportunity to go over their test after it was graded and track their results.
- Students could use their own data to decide whether or not to revisit a particular topic.
- Students could report on their study methods and decisions.
- Students could strategize on changes they intended to make concerning their study routines and preparation for future assessments.
- Struggling learners in particular could take pride in small victories—strong scores on certain sections.

This retesting system became the cornerstone of my end-of-unit assessment routine, and I was increasing student agency in the assessment process as never before. Little did I realize at the time, however, that there was another important step to take in achieving a more robust, standards-based assessment structure. Although I had separated my tests by topic, I was still reporting student learning as a testing *event*. I was entering the total score on the test into my gradebook as a single data item, say 39 out of 48, under a heading such as "Paris Peace Conference Test." I saw the need to further design the structure so that the assessment data corresponded to the standards. Simply stated, my quest was to shift from an *event*-based gradebook to a *standards*-based one.

I decided to again look closely at our standards-based unit plan and design the test under three or four broader categories that would align the assessment to those standards. In each of these categories, or strands, I would have a few subsections or subcategories that would help inform both the learner and me on how well the student understood that broader category, or standard. (See the unit test cover sheet in Figure 4.1 [p. 92], where, for example, one of the standards is "I understand the geopolitical issues leading to and affecting the PPC," and one of the subcategories is "General 'ism' definitions." While grading each student's test, I would fill in the cover sheet to reflect the scores for individual sections.) The test tracking sheet that students filled out was reconfigured to align with these standards-based structural changes (see Figure 4.2, p. 93). Overall, this reconfiguration was relatively subtle, but in my quest for a standards-based gradebook, the move was monumental.

While I was considering shifting to a true standards-based gradebook, a few colleagues and I were reexamining our use of percentages. We'll address this change in more detail in the next chapter, but for now, a brief explanation will help make sense of the test structure. We wanted to adopt a more appropriate language than percentage terminology when talking to our students about their learning. We had been looking at the performance scales used at our neighboring middle school, and we decided that reducing our number of grading categories from 100 to 4, 5, or 6 would likely result in language that was more accessible, would be better understood by students, and would increase our grading reliability.

Both my test cover and the corresponding tracking sheet (Figures 4.1 and 4.2) reflect our shift to a six-point proficiency scale. I was pleasantly surprised by how much my students and I liked this shift in language. We were able to calibrate our conversations about learning, grading, and reporting to one scale, based on either words such as *apprentice* or a corresponding number, 3 or 4. I was surprised by how much easier it was to grade when every scoring decision was based on one six-point scale rather than assessing one question based on 3 points, another on 5, and another on 10. (I'll have much more to say on this in Chapters 5 and 6.)

Figure 4.1
Cover Sheet for History 12 Unit Test

"Is Peace Achievable?" A Study of the Paris Peace Conference 1919

Unit Test—History 12

I understand the geopolitical issues leading to and affecting the PPC.

General "ism" definitions	___ / 6
Map section	___ / 6
Underlying problems	___ / 6

I can evaluate how national expectations varied during and after the PPC.

The PPC "losers"	___ / 6
The PPC "winners"	___ / 6
The PPC "hopeful"	___ / 6

I can use and evaluate different historical sources.
I can identify, determine, and analyze point of view and bias.

Point of view	___ / 6
Document/evidence	___ / 6

I can apply my understanding of the issues to different situations.

Comprehensive paragraph/diagram A	___ / 6
Comprehensive paragraph/diagram B	___ / 6

Name: _____   Date: _____

Source: Courtesy Myron Dueck. Used with permission.

Figure 4.2
Unit Test Tracking Sheet for History 12

"Is Peace Achievable?" A Study of the Paris Peace Conference 1919

Name: _____   Date: _____

Topic	Value	Score	Expert/Apprentice/Novice	Retest?
I understand the geopolitical issues leading to and affecting the PPC.				
General "ism" definitions	6			
Map section	6			
Underlying problems	6			
I can evaluate how national expectations varied during and after the PPC.				
The PPC "losers"	6			
The PPC "winners"	6			
The PPC "hopeful"	6			
I can use and evaluate different historical sources. *I can identify, determine, and analyze point of view and bias.*				
Point of view	6			
Document/evidence	6			
I can apply my understanding of the issues to different situations.				
Comprehensive paragraph/diagram Topic A: _____	6			
Comprehensive paragraph/diagram Topic B: _____	6			

Planning, Responsibility, and Preparation:

I (check one) ☐ DID ☐ DID NOT complete all of the term cards and suggested **homework** for this unit.
If **not**, the reason is . . .

I spent about _____ (check one) ☐ minutes ☐ hours preparing for this test.

I can make the following adjustments to improve my understanding:

• _____

• _____

I think I'll be a(n) (circle one)   EXPERT   APPRENTICE   NOVICE   in this course.

Source: © 2020 Myron Dueck. Used with permission.

Once a test was graded, I used the three subcategories to help determine the score the student would receive for the broader category. I could either average them or look for a trend to achieve a score for the standard (category). Once each category had a score out of 6, I needed to adapt my gradebook to reflect this new testing system. Instead of having one column in my gradebook for that assessment, such as "PPC Unit Test," out of an aggregate score, I would have as many columns as I had broader categories or standards. Referring to Figure 4.1, I would have four gradebook headings:

- *Understand* geopolitical issues.
- *Evaluate* national expectations.
- *Use, evaluate,* and *analyze* historical sources, point of view, and bias.
- *Apply* my understanding [the comprehensive questions in this category might combine elements from two or more of the above sections].

Once I recorded the assessment under each of these headings, I had transformed my gradebook from being an event-based percentage system to being (1) standards-based and (2) conforming to a proficiency scale. I didn't fully understand how easy this was to do until I had done it. For this reason, I question those who claim that shifting to a standards-based grading system would be too much work. More important, having data organized into these categories allowed me to have far more effective conversations with my students. We could easily determine their strengths and weaknesses and make decisions accordingly. Last, these data served as valuable feedback, enabling me to determine much more effectively which learning standards I needed to improve upon in my instruction.

An Exemplary Self-Tracking and Pre-Test System

Rachel Stubbert was teaching Math 9 at Summerland Secondary School when she devised a simple and effective student self-tracking and pre-test system. She has designed a template that combines the sharing of learning goals with a way to track evidence of understanding on these goals. Students use this document throughout a unit to track achievement and make decisions on whether assessments will be formative or summative. Rachel's system offers students the opportunity to incorporate ongoing assessment and can help tip the scales to *learning* over *performing*.

Rachel separates the domains of her math course into subsections or strands. As you can see in Figure 4.3 (p. 96), the broader topic of "Rational Numbers" is broken down into five components, such as "Comparing and ordering rational numbers." Although the topic heading is a noun, it's important to point out Rachel's use of verb forms to direct each subsection. Students are immediately aware that they will need to *compare* and *order*, and further down they see they will need to *solve*.

Rachel's system is remarkably simple, while embracing a number of sound grading and assessment themes. Once a learning goal, such as "Comparing and ordering rational numbers," has been covered in class, she encourages students to practice the math procedure on their own. She gives them time in class to practice math problems, and they can continue later at home, on the bus, or in the common area before volleyball or theater practice.

Regardless of where and when the practice is done, Rachel will not grade the homework, for a few reasons:

- It's virtually impossible to determine who did the learning when it's achieved in out-of-class environments.
- Homework is intended as a practice opportunity and therefore should not count for summative data. (I'm pretty sure that no sports league on the planet includes a team's practice results in the official standings.)
- Students are encouraged to take risks and explore different methods without the pressure of a permanent score.

Related to the homework conversation is the fact that some students need more practice than others, and Rachel's system takes this into account. When students return to class the day after a topic has been covered, they are given an opportunity to demonstrate their learning on a short quiz focused on one of the topics—say, "comparing and ordering rational numbers." It's important to point out that during the quiz the students get the opportunity to grapple, consider options, and make decisions on how to tackle and solve the math problems. Rachel is not providing immediate corrective language to students but, rather, leaving them to do the cognitive lifting. Once the students complete the short quiz, Rachel collects the assessments and places them in a folder on her desk.

With the quizzes tucked aside, Rachel and her students revisit the solutions to the problems, and during this stage students can

- Ask questions to clarify understanding.
- Track their understanding on the "Math 9 Learning Goals" self-tracking sheet.
- Make decisions on next steps (extra practice questions, extension activity, etc.).

Both Rachel and her students can use this structure, and the data it provides, to make subsequent decisions. If it's clear that many students struggled with a particular concept, Rachel may choose to consider the quiz formative for everyone

Figure 4.3
Self-Tracking Sheet for Math 9 Learning Goals

Name: _____

It is your responsibility to keep track of your learning goal assessments for this *entire course*. Track your results after each quiz and unit test. You will use this as evidence of your learning. Consider using a different color or symbol to separate quiz and test data in each row (e.g., quizzes in blue checkmarks, tests in black checkmarks).

Learning Goals	Novice		Apprentice		Expert	
	1	2	3	4	5	6
Rational Numbers						
1. Comparing and ordering rational numbers						
2. Adding and subtracting rational numbers						
3. Multiplying and dividing rational numbers						
4. Solving problems that involve multiple operations						
5. Solving word problems that involve rational numbers						
Exponents						
6. Finding the area and side length of perfect and nonperfect squares						
7. Identifying and writing powers and using the zero exponent						
8. Solving problems that involve multiple operations						
9. Solving problems that involve the exponent laws						
10. Converting to and from scientific notation						
Polynomials						
11. Identifying parts of a polynomial (term, degree, variable, etc.)						
12. Adding and subtracting like terms						
13. Multiplying polynomials						
14. Dividing polynomials						
Factoring						
15. Prime factorization						
16. Factoring out a GCF						
17. Factoring a trinomial						
18. Factoring a difference of squares						
19. Factoring using multiple methods						

Learning Goals	Novice		Apprentice		Expert	
	1	2	3	4	5	6
Solving Equations						
20. Solving simple algebraic equations						
21. Solving algebraic equations requiring multiple steps						
22. Solving algebraic equations involving rational numbers						
23. Solving problems with equations						
Linear Relations						
24. Developing and solving an equation from a word problem, picture, or table of values						
25. Creating a graph from an equation or table of values						
26. Demonstrating an understanding of dependent versus independent variables and oblique, vertical, and horizontal lines on a graph						
27. Matching graphs and equations						
28. Interpolating and extrapolating information from a graph						
Financial Services						
29. Identifying the difference between types of income and types of expenses						
30. Identifying the best bank account based on the knowledge given and individual situation						
31. Calculating simple and compound interest						
32. Balancing a budget						

Source: Courtesy Rachel Stubbert. Used with permission.

and subsequently try an alternative instructional approach to the topic with the entire class. Through this informed reaction, Rachel is deciding *with* her students to make that assessment *formative* by *what is done with the data.*

On the other hand, it may become evident that only a handful of students struggled with the concept, and therefore it's left to individual students to make the decision on whether the quiz is formative or summative. If a student asks to revisit that concept, then the first assessment is rendered formative. Considering that each quiz is short, it's relatively easy to have the student revisit the concept in a later class, at lunch, or after school. In this manner, Rachel's system supports student voice and choice in the assessment conversation.

Rachel's end-of-unit assessment structure builds seamlessly from her quiz process. Once all five subsections have been covered and the class is heading toward the comprehensive unit assessment, things take a further turn from the traditional. Rachel intentionally decided to not use the term *retest* as the label for the second unit assessment. Based on conversations with students and colleagues, it became clear to her that the term *retest* carried negative connotations and unnecessary baggage. Some teachers struggled with the idea that if a test could simply be done over again, it ceased to be a test in the true essence of the term. Based on this feedback, as well as her own teaching philosophy, Rachel chose to use the term *pre-test* or *practice test* for the first unit assessment, and she kept the term *test* for the second one.

As the day for the *practice* test approaches, Rachel's students use their self-assessment tracking sheets to strategize and inform the study process. They can quickly reference their level of understanding of the subsections of the unit and make study decisions accordingly.

Rachel schedules the testing events very deliberately. For example, on Wednesday, students complete the pre-test in the exact circumstances that they would find for any regular test—a quiet classroom, working individually, and so on. Rachel grades the tests that evening, records the results, and returns the practice tests to the students the next day. Based on the data of this pre-diagnosis, students can then take various actions and make a number of decisions:

- They can document changes to their learning on the tracking sheet by using a different color or pattern than that used for previous quizzes. This allows them to separate learning goal results on the most recent assessment from those achieved on earlier quizzes.
- They may ask Rachel for help on sections they did not understand.
- They may seek assistance from peers who did well on a particular section.
- They may attend a study session offered by Rachel in class, at lunch, or after school to cover one or more of the goals.
- They may complete some further problems or questions in class or at home to revisit a topic.
- They may do other coursework, engage in extension activities, or read a book if their practice test results were what they desired.

Whatever decisions each student makes as a result of the data from the pre-test, everyone knows that the "real" test, consisting of the same goals but different questions, will typically follow two days later. Everyone has the opportunity to demonstrate understanding on the "real" test. That said, students who did just fine on the pre-test may opt out, as they have already demonstrated a solid understanding of the concepts in the safety, predictability, and authenticity provided by Rachel's classroom environment.

During the filming of *Smarter Assessment in the Secondary Classroom* (ASCD, n.d.), the producer realized that Rachel and I taught some of the same students at Summerland Secondary School. Seizing this opportunity, someone had the brilliant idea to ask students to compare Mr. Dueck's *retest* system to Ms. Stubbert's *pre-test* system. I found some of the comments annoying:

> Ms. Stubbert's pre-test system is waaaay better. I mean, the term *pre-test* just sounds better—like you were just trying out your learning and realized you needed a bit more study time.

> I like Ms. Stubbert's system better. When you say you need to *retest*, it sounds like you didn't understand when everyone else did, like you weren't as smart. If you find out that you need to take the real test, well, that's just a normal thing to do.

> *Retest* sounds like you had to return when you really didn't want to, but *pre-test* just sounds like you tried out your learning and decided on your own to try again. I like that a lot better than Mr. Dueck's retest system; it sounds more inviting.

Student Self-Assessment and Self-Reporting in an IB High School

Josh Eastwood is an International Baccalaureate (IB) teacher at Saint John High School in New Brunswick, Canada. Following a professional development day I helped provide for Josh's district, he revised his assessment system to make it similar to Rachel's. It's interesting to note how his assessment changes affected his approach to homework. After trying out these changes with his students, he sent me an e-mail. Note how his account highlights his use of self-assessment and student voice:

> I've been applying the concept of quizzes in class, in lieu of homework assignments outside of class, and had a really interesting thing happen in my IB 12 class. I had these students last year, in grade 11, and at the end of the year I stopped giving take-home assignments to them in preparation for the test. Instead, I began to give a series of quizzes throughout the unit. In the final survey I had a number of them express that they liked the assignments because they helped them prepare for the test. So, this year, I have been giving the quizzes in class for marks while offering take-home assignments for practice and simply posting the answer key on my Google classroom. The students then have the option of doing the assignment at home, or not, but it is purely for them to prep for the test and they love it. It's interesting what ideas you get from the students when you ask them. (personal communication, October 25, 2018)

As Josh indicated, students like the use of in-class quizzes and *optional* home-work assignments. Here are two of their comments:

> [Homework] assignments are, to me, a take-home test. And to others, free marks to get just by copying. To me, a short 15-minute quiz at the beginning of class is the better option—it gives students more options to improve their marks by working harder in class or on the upcoming quizzes.

> I loved the retest option. I thought it was fair to let everyone retest even if they had a higher mark as well. Not only does it give you the option to get a higher mark, but it also helps you identify exactly what you had trouble with. It allows you to get more help.

Closing Thoughts

So what did I do with David, the young hockey player struggling to balance his will to compete with his ability to remain on his skates? After he had exhausted his three attempts, each time falling to the ice, I stared at the single box demand-ing a time. I wrestled with the fact that not one of his three tests, nor the mean, reflected his ability. At the same time, we had established rules and procedures for these tests, and it was my duty to report David's results in a timely manner. *What should I do, what should I do…?*

In that moment, I returned to the question of *purpose*. The intent of these tests was to gather accurate data to inform future decisions and track David's development. As well, I was David's *coach,* and perhaps this was a learning oppor-tunity for David. Finally, I wondered, *Why am I shouldering this entire decision?* I should meaningfully include the most important player in the conversation—David himself.

I figured I'd note David's fastest time, with an asterisk beside the score and a short comment at the bottom of the sheet explaining the situation. I let David know my plan, but before submitting the sheet I asked if he had any ideas. He sug-gested that if there was time at the next practice, perhaps he could try once more to focus on skating fast and remaining on his feet.

It turned out we were not alone. At other stations, similar situations arose in which coaches felt that the testing data did not accurately reflect a player's true ability. We decided to revisit a few of the stations at the next practice, working with players to overcome pressure so they could perform at their best. David returned to skate a fantastic trial and post a score that we believed accurately reflected his ability. I suppose hockey and diving coaches have something in com-mon after all, remembering Dan Laak's thoughts from USA Diving (as recounted in Chapter 3): "[W]hen we are evaluating a diver for potential greatness we look for more than just the scores they receive at a competition."

Whether on the ice or in a classroom, assessment is an integral part of the learning process. As I examine the research and reflect on my own experiences with students, I've become more convinced that learning is a process that changes over time and through different situations. My goal is to have the assessment of this learning malleable enough to account for the dynamic nature of learning. We all learn through making mistakes, and we all are affected by the personal nature of assessment; and so I believe our greatest challenge is to build testing systems that engage our students through voice, choice, and empowerment.

CREATING FAIR AND SENSIBLE GRADING SYSTEMS

How can we develop systems that reflect actual learning and value student input?

In an airport terminal a few years ago, I was walking toward my boarding gate when I passed a bookstore. Out of all the covers placed strategically to catch my eye, one popped out more than any other: *The End of Average,* by Todd Rose (2016). Picking up the book, I found the descriptor and chapter headings more than intriguing. The biggest hook for me was in noticing that Rose's work explored the futility of using averages to make decisions about the individual. During my 20-plus years in the classroom and my recent work on grading, assessment, and reporting, I must've uttered the word *average* a million times. The term was a fixture of my personal and educational vocabulary! I couldn't leave the store without this book. Two flights later, I had finished reading it. Upon returning home, I read it again. It's been on my bookshelf ever since.

Rose starts the book with a fascinating account of the U.S. Air Force (USAF). In the late 1940s, the USAF was experiencing an inordinate number of "accidents and incidents" (p. 1). From nosedives to botched takeoffs and landings, there was no ignoring the fact that a lot of pilots and planes were going down. Predictably, when the engineers found little wrong with the planes, they pointed the finger at the pilots. Convinced their flying skills were as good as ever, the pilots deflected blame back onto the engineers and mechanics.

Perplexed by the number of crashes, and with inquiries not providing answers, someone suggested they look at the design of the cockpit. It turned out that the dimensions of the cockpit and its myriad design considerations were based on the average size of hundreds of pilots—circa 1926! Some wondered if pilots, *on average,* had gotten taller since those measurements were taken. In fact, they probably had. We now understand that as nutrition and diet improved in the late 1800s, the next 150 years would see the average heights of people living in industrialized nations increase by around four inches (Dougherty, 1998).

Undertaking the task with the scope and complexity of a true military endeavor, in 1950 the USAF set out to obtain an updated average body shape of an American combat aviator. Researchers at Wright-Patterson Air Force Base decided to measure more than 4,000 pilots, taking 140 separate measurements of each one. Seriously. They measured everything from thumb length to the distance from the pilot's eye to his ear (Rose, 2016). Fortunately, a newly hired 23-year-old would arrive at Wright-Patterson with an understanding of some of the challenges of measuring individual humans in hopes of obtaining a group average. As an undergraduate at Harvard, Gilbert S. Daniels had attempted to obtain an average hand size of 250 male Harvard students, only to discover that no one in his sample cohort actually had an average hand. That's right—not one person used to obtain the average actually *had* the average.

Rose goes on to chronicle how Daniels, using only 10 of the USAF's most important measurements, such as height and arm length, arrived at the same vexing conclusion about pilots that he had at Harvard. Once the average size of a pilot was determined, that "pilot" was nowhere to be found among the 4,063 servicemen who made up the average! In case you are tempted to think that this anomaly is reserved only for males at established military institutions, think again. Rose references the 1945 "Norma Look-Alike" contest, which attempted to determine the ideal body shape of more than 15,000 women, and a UC Santa Barbara neuroscientist's attempt to average the results of 16 brain scans. Remarkably, in each case, once an average was determined for each data set, it was impossible to find *one person* in the set that matched the group average! Let that resonate for a second. Not one person in any of these groups was anywhere close to the average obtained from that group!

We use the word *average* a lot in our modern society, and perhaps no more so than in schools. Rose argues that the moment you need to make a decision about an individual—such as how to teach that person, whom to hire, or whom to draft, "the average is useless" (p. 11). Far too long and complex for our discussion here, the history of averages and how we use them is both fascinating and troubling. We seem almost fixated on how much the individual deviates from the average, and we use this deviation to determine student rank, college admissions, school awards, and many other comparison measures. We design and deliver grade 5 math curriculum to suit the needs of the "average" grade 5 student—who may not actually exist.

Averages are not reserved for groups. We like to assign them to the individual as well. Early in my career, I had a teacher planning book and dutifully filled in dozens of boxes for a student, culminating in hundreds of little boxes with numbers for all my classes. Later on, I started using a computer spreadsheet, and finally a digital grading program. Regardless of whether my data were on paper or digital, I'd take an array of measures for a single student, toss them in a virtual blender, and churn out a single number or letter—the average! This single score would be what I referred to in parent-teacher interviews, what I used on the report card, and, disturbingly, what I might use to actually describe the learner: "Grace is a 92 percent student." Yikes! At the end of the year I again resorted to averaging all of the data from terms or semesters and compiling a not-so-valuable score and comment: "Sally earned an average score of 82 percent. Have a nice summer."

According to Rose, we seem drawn to one-dimensional thinking when trying to describe the individual. Maybe we're prone to using the blender approach because it's easier than truly describing a complex situation. Imagine, however, if we considered describing the complexity, or jaggedness, of our students' abilities rather than seeking a one-dimensional average. Rose refers to the first principle of individuality as the "jaggedness principle." He explains it in these terms:

> This principle holds that we cannot apply one-dimensional thinking to understand something that is complex and "jagged." What, precisely, is jaggedness? A quality is jagged if it meets two criteria. First, it must consist of multiple dimensions. Second, these dimensions must be weakly related to one another.... Almost every human characteristic that we care about—including talent, intelligence, character, creativity, and so on—is jagged. (p. 82)

Our students certainly fit Rose's two criteria for jaggedness. Whether considering a student's abilities within a single curricular area or across disciplines, our students exhibit qualities as different as their fingerprints.

The jaggedness principle is not new to educational thought. Gardner (2006) notes in *Multiple Intelligences* that educators have long observed firsthand the jagged intelligence profiles of their students. In his book *On Intelligence*, Stephen Ceci (1996) argues that we have evidence in front of us every day that students have jagged cognitive profiles, "much like... [the child] who may have trouble reading but may be able to do arithmetic satisfactorily" (p. 209).

Just as there's no average USAF pilot, Norma Look-Alike contestant, or brain scan, there's likely no such thing as an *average student*. This leaves me wondering:

- *Should we question the utility and accuracy of using a single numerical average or letter to describe the learning of an individual student?*
- *If we are truly inviting our array of students into the realm of assessment, how can our tools and systems reflect the jaggedness principle?*
- *Can we merge the complexity of student abilities with the goal of reporting by standards, all the while balancing detail and utility in our reporting?*

Standards and Grades: Different but Related

I could buy a really rare Beatles album if I had a quarter for every e-mail, phone call, or conversation that's involved someone from a school district uttering, "We are considering moving to a standards-based grading model." This statement immediately conjures up a few questions. If you're not fundamentally basing your reporting of student grades on the established standards, what are they based on? The alignment of the stars? Lucky 8-Ball? What your next-door neighbor Gus figures they ought to be?

We really should stop proclaiming that we are "moving toward" or "considering" standards-based grading, as the statement implies that up until now we've not been doing it. That's both damning and embarrassing. As the public starts to figure out how this whole education thing is supposed to work, you should prepare for parents to ask, "So if you're *considering* moving toward standards-based grading, what the #@$% kind of benchmarks have you been using until now?" Remember, those people living in that strange place known as "the real world" are surrounded by standards. Whether building a house, operating a restaurant, taking a blood sample, making a commercial box of cookies, or tiling a floor, they typically abide by standards. Once these people figure out that education should have standards also, look out!

(As I'm writing this, the COVID-19 pandemic has resulted in schools being closed around the world, and parents suddenly have been relegated to being stay-at-home educators of their kids. I suspect this situation may have a profound impact on parents taking a giant step toward understanding the need, nature, and existence of learning standards.)

Trust me, I'm all too aware that grading issues are one of the biggest hurdles in moving toward a standards-based structure. Once clear learning targets become the basis for grades, assessment, and reporting student learning, other long-held beliefs turn into questions. Here are a few:

- Should we include homework completion in our grades?
- If something is handed in late, should that lower the student's grade on that assignment?
- Should we include behaviors such as effort or attitude in the student's grade?
- Does the timeliness of an assignment have any effect whatsoever on the measure of how much a student has learned? If so, couldn't it be argued that a late assignment might result in more learning rather than less?

As I described in *Grading Smarter, Not Harder* (Dueck, 2014), I don't believe that any of these elements should be factored into a student's final grade, and I'm not alone in that opinion (Chappuis et al., 2012; Guskey, 2015; O'Connor, 2007, 2018; Reeves, 2010). That said, in any move toward standards-based grading, we ought to address the terms exactly in the order they appear: (1) standards, (2) grading. Therefore, our first step is to establish clear learning targets derived from the standards; later, the extent to which students demonstrate capacity in relation to these standards will form the basis for our grades. Former math teacher, author, and current principal of Penticton Secondary School Chris Van Bergeyk effectively argues that "grading based on established standards is about the only way to clearly record how students are doing on the targets they are supposed to learn" (personal communication, September 20, 2019). Taking the argument one step further, if we're going to include students in the assessment conversation, perhaps we need to choose a sensible grading *language*.

A Pivotal Teacher-Student Conversation

When changing the grading routines of a classroom, school, district, or country, there are bound to be many growing pains. Long-held traditions and beliefs will undoubtedly conflict with new ideas and directions. That's exactly what happened when a number of teachers at Summerland Secondary School shifted away from percentage grading to a proficiency scale. One particularly enlightening interaction took place when a student expressed her dissatisfaction with our new direction. What follows is my recollection of the conversation.

I had just finished a brief presentation to one of our math classes on the topic of desirable difficulties (as described in Chapter 4), and the students, their teacher, and I explored the idea of journaling about their struggles in math. Following the presentation, I was approached by Rayman—a very capable and engaged grade 11 student. She started the conversation.

"That was an interesting presentation, Mr. Dueck; thanks for sharing with us. Is this going to be another big change here at Summerland Secondary? I don't mind the idea of journaling about desirable difficulties or whatever, but I'm not a big fan of another change here recently."

I asked her to elaborate on her concern, and she continued.

"Aren't you one of the people responsible for us shifting from percentages to this… this… six-point scale thing that quite a few teachers are using?"

I affirmed her suspicion with a nod, as some staff had made a significant change to their grading methods. Although all teachers were required by law to report a final course percentage, recently, a number of staff had adopted a six-point scale for the day-to-day academic activities. This six-point proficiency scale could be broken down into three broader categories: *Novice* (1–2), *Apprentice* (3–4), and *Expert* (5–6). The use of this scale was purely voluntary, and about a quarter of the staff used it to some degree. Therefore, it was predictable that some of Rayman's teachers would be using the scale while others continued to employ some version of a percentage system.

She continued, "I wish we'd go back to percentages in all classes."

I reacted with a quizzical look, and she went on. "Percentages make sense—everyone understands them. It's like if I got 97, I know what that is. If I got 95, I know what that is. Now I get a score of 6, and it can include anything between 95 and 100. It's confusing, and I don't like it. Can we please go back to how things used to be?"

By this time, most students had left the class, and Rayman stood waiting for a response, flanked by her good friend Ruth. I knew Ruth was a strong student also, so I asked, "Do you and Ruth share any other classes that still use a percentage scoring system?"

"Yes," she answered.

"Pardon my question, but on your most recent unit test in that other class, how did each of you do?"

They looked at each other a little uneasily, and Rayman responded, "You want to know our results?"

"If you don't mind, I would, yes. Seeing as we're talking about grading scales, I'm just curious how you'd communicate how you did."

"I got, um, a 98 percent." Rayman commented. I looked over at Ruth, and she added, "I think I got a 96."

Addressing Rayman, I remarked, "Oh, so you must be a stronger student on that topic."

She was quick to disagree. "No, I'm not stronger. That was just one test. Sometimes Ruth has a better score, but we're always within a few percentage points."

I countered, "But on *that* test, reflecting *that* unit of study, you were stronger. A percentage score of 98 certainly beats 96, does it not? Is that not what you meant earlier when you said that 'everyone understands the percentage system'?"

Rayman again disagreed. "I don't think it's right to say I'm better than her. One little mistake by me, or one little correction by her, and we could've had the same score, or she'd be a percentage or two ahead of me. It might be more accurate to say we're both strong."

Her comment seemed to hang in the air for a few moments.

"Wait a second," she said. "What did I just say?"

I repeated her last statement. "You commented that it might be more accurate to say you're both strong." And I added, "Like maybe a 6 on the scale, or what we refer to as *Expert*?"

Rayman stood there quietly, appearing to be reconsidering her position.

I took the moment to throw her a bit of a lifeline. "You know, Rayman, what we're talking about here are symbols and language. I think we could agree that whether we choose 98 percent, level 6 on the scale, the term *Expert*, a gold medal, or a gold star out of a sticker collection, all of these are symbols, or language, that are used to represent your learning. And I agree with your initial position that if we're going to talk about learning, the symbols we choose and the language we adopt should make sense to everyone. I'm not saying the six-point scale is perfect by any means, but I'm not sure I want to separate you and Ruth by a percentage point or two when we can all agree that you're both strong students in a particular academic area."

"Hmmm. I'm going to have to think about this a little more, Mr. Dueck. To be continued," she said, as she smiled and left for her next class.

It's taken me a few years to come to a realization around *how* we include students in the grading conversation. In 2006, when I began changing the way I graded and assessed my students, I took very deliberate steps to keep them informed about the process. As mentioned in Chapter 2, I introduced terms such as *formative* and *summative*, and we began weaving this terminology into our everyday conversations. I explained why I was changing our routines concerning learning targets, retests, and homework, and I tried to show students how these changes benefited them, even if it meant more work for me initially. As documented by the many stories in *Grading Smarter, Not Harder* (Dueck, 2014),

I listened to student accounts concerning these changes, and this commentary helped affirm my decisions.

Fast-forward to today, and my thinking has evolved beyond *informing* students of changes to *including* them in the design and implementation of them. I believe interactions such as the one with Rayman clearly demonstrate that we can create an environment in which students take the lead when talking about their learning, assessment, grades, and even policy.

Therefore, whatever grading system we employ, it must make sense to all stakeholders—students arguably being the most important. If our desire is to communicate student learning with clarity, accuracy, and consistency, I think the language of percentages is a poor choice. Unfortunately, percentage-based grading systems still abound—less so at elementary levels, pervasively at secondary, and somewhere in between for middle schools. The tide, however, is turning, with many districts well along the way to changing to fewer categories, such as California's Roseville School District, which we featured earlier.

Summerland Secondary and the Origins of the Six-Point Scale

Rayman was correct—I was one of the staff members at Summerland Secondary School working on shifting from a percentage system to a six-point scale. I swear on my grandmother's grave, however, that we stumbled on this notion by accident rather than intention.

I think it all started when Shona Becker, a senior sciences teacher at Summerland Secondary, organized a voluntary book study for teachers. Offered a choice between *Grading Smarter, Not Harder*, by Myron Dueck (2014), or *Visible Learning for Teachers*, by John Hattie (2012), the 10 teachers who signed up chose Hattie over Dueck in a landslide. (I'm still a little bitter, John.)

Once a month, we met at lunch to discuss a chapter in Hattie's book. In one of our meetings, we covered Hattie's explanation of *effect size* and his argument that a hinge point existed at around 0.4—this being the impact that a regular year of schooling might have on the achievement of an individual student. Hattie (2012) provided a barometer (see Figure 5.1, p. 110) showing that anything above a 0.4 effect size was in the *zone of desired effects*, whereas the area below 0.4 ranged downward from *teacher effects* to *developmental effects* and finally *reverse effects*—things that actually ran counter to achievement, such as summer vacation (−0.12) or television (−0.18).

At one of our last meetings, a pivotal moment occurred. One of the group members directed people's attention to Appendix C, page 266. Not everyone had reached Hattie's list of 150 "influences on achievement," but once discovered, it would spark a spirited conversation. At first, the group quietly scanned the list, considering the rankings compiled from nearly 1,000 meta-data analyses and many thousands of research articles. Then people began to make comments such as the following:

> "Formative evaluation" is number 4. Hey, we do that!

> Good ole "classroom discussion" is in the top 10!

> "Homework" is down at number 94, with an effect size of 0.29! Can you believe that?

Figure 5.1

The Barometer for the Influence of Homework

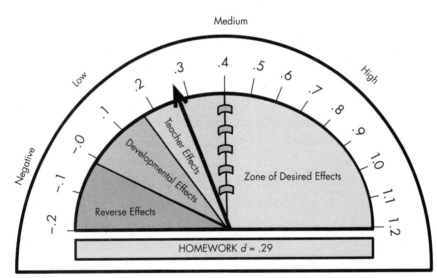

Source: From *Visible Learning for Teachers,* by John Hattie, 2012, New York: Routledge. © 2012 by John Hattie. Reprinted with permission.

It wasn't long, however, before Shona brought our attention to number 1—"self-reported grades/student expectations," with an effect size of 1.44. We pondered what was meant by *self-reported grades,* and people wondered aloud how something that sounded so simple could pack so much power.

This question started a movement that would ripple throughout many curricular areas in our school. It's no wonder that *collective teacher efficacy* has moved ahead of self-reported grades in more recent studies (Donohoo, 2017b). Once our group members began to believe that we could change a system to benefit our students, we were a force of nature! Soon students were self-reporting in classes such as drafting, foods, math, biology, theater, and leadership. We'll address these self-reporting structures in much more detail in the next chapter, but first we have other matters to discuss. As our group would quickly discover, before developing classroom self-reporting systems, we had to choose a language. As it turned out, our traditional percentage language was not 100 percent appropriate.

Problems with Percentages

If we want to include students in reporting their learning, and if selecting the appropriate grading language is an important step, let's explore why we might consider shifting away from percentages. When discussing this shift, students, teachers, and parents often ask me, "What's wrong with percentages?" I typically respond that there's nothing *wrong* with them; it's more a matter of *how* they are used. Let's explore a few ideas that may help frame this conversation.

The "Real World" Argument

Do we really discern between, and make valuable use of, 100 different categories?

The topic of percentages is one of many where we can expect to encounter the "real world" argument. Personally, I've been avoiding the "real world" for quite some time, and I'd argue I'm not alone. I marvel at how often teachers declare with authority, "I'm preparing students for the real world"—as though they've spent a lifetime there. I'd like to pull them aside—and at times, I do—and in a hushed tone ask, "How well do you know that place?"

When looking back at my own educational journey, it went something like this:

Elementary School → Junior High → High School → University… and then → Junior High

Seriously, as my university days were drawing to a close and I stood on the precipice gazing at that mysterious kingdom called the "real world," I just couldn't go there. I had worked at the same summer job at a feed mill from grade 8 through university. I mixed feed ingredients, swept warehouse floors, and carried out countless tasks in hot, dusty conditions. Occasionally I'd tangle with a rat that believed it had first rights to a pile of wet grains that I'd been asked to clean up. This often uncomfortable "real world" environment, where workers started with two weeks of holidays per year, was all the encouragement I needed to remain in the safe, familiar, and air-conditioned confines of a school. To be fair, I learned many valuable life lessons at that job and admire the people there, many of whom did not envy that I was heading off to be a schoolteacher. Anyway, as I neared the end of my undergraduate years and it looked like I might need to actually *leave school*, I sought a permanent solution. Immediately upon graduating from university, I took on a grade 4 and 5 teaching job in Morris, Manitoba, Canada, and I've hung out in the "school world" ever since. Honestly, I consider the "real world" to be a bit like Narnia in the fantasy novels by C. S. Lewis. When asked to hang up my coat in a wardrobe, I prefer to safely fling it over a chair.

I, like many other teachers, have made all kinds of grandiose statements about the "real world." I've said things like, "You better not show up late to class. In the real world, you'll get fired!" Or "I use zeros for things not handed in. In the real world, if I don't complete my assignment, I get fired." In recent years, I've stopped saying these things, as I realize they may not be accurate.

To explore the actual "real world," I recently embarked on a mission to engage in as many conversations as possible with restaurant owners, interior designers, manufacturers, and a host of other "bosses" and "employees." Particularly at airports or on flights, I've had many interactions with people who have access to the "termination button," and according to my unofficial results, the "real world" doesn't seem to be nearly as nasty as some teachers report. Might you be fired for being late for work? Absolutely, but there's a better chance that you won't. Believe it or not, there are rules, or *standards*, around these things—at least in parts of North America. According to the Canadian legal firm Shields O'Donnell MacKillop LLP and the U.S. firm Hudson & Luros, LLP, an employer should exercise caution when moving to terminate an employee struggling with tardiness. Generally speaking, only if tardiness is chronic and the employer has made repeated, documented interventions *might* the employer have grounds for dismissal (Luros, 2015; MacKillop & Nieuwland, 2012).

Furthermore, in my many enlightening dialogues, two critical factors seem to loom large over whether a struggling employee is terminated or not: (1) the job market and (2) a worker's competency. I recently asked a restaurant owner if he would fire any worker who arrived late to work, and he looked at me like I was from another planet. Speaking of his top chef, he commented that she could disappear for two days, and rather than firing her when she returned, he'd simply rejoice that she was back. He commented, "Lots of people are dealing with issues in their lives, so I have to be understanding. But if you want to know, my biggest reasons for retaining her would be personal and selfish. I can spend the weekend with my family if I know she's taking care of the restaurant kitchen."

People who advocate for a percentage system often cite the "real world" as a place that supports it. At a glance, it would appear they're correct. It's common to find percentages scrawled across the news or when watching documentaries. Conversations around health issues and life expectancy are rife with percentages. We discuss sports, the economy, farming, global rain forests, climate change, and countless other things in percentage terms. It would appear that the 100 scale is embedded in our vernacular. To be clear, there's nothing inherently wrong with sprinkling percentages into our daily conversations, but I would question the *utility* of these precise data points.

Let's take the weather forecast, for example. If I'm listening to the radio and hear that there's an 85 percent chance of rain, I may argue that we postpone the family trip to the beach. The thing is, I would likely make the same decision if I heard that the percentage chance of rain was 71, 74, 80, 84, or any other number above, say, 60. Furthermore, it might depend on other factors. If we're already on vacation and paying for a room at a beach resort, we might go to the beach regardless of the rain forecast. Heck, we'd be down at the sandy shore if there was a skiff of ice to contend with! On the other hand, if the trip involves getting ready at home and traveling an hour or more, we might wait for a day when the likelihood of precipitation is *somewhere* below 40 percent. It would seem that I base our likelihood of going to the beach on a *variety of factors* and in a *range of percentages*.

Come to think of it, maybe we don't actually use percentages as we think we do. Just in case you've been convinced by some well-intentioned teacher that you should speak "percentage language" in the "real world," be aware of the potential problems, as in the following examples.

Ski resorts. If you've been saying things like "I've been working on my skiing lately, and I think I'm now a 72 percent skier," that's why you have no friends. Everyone else places the difficulty ratings into simple categories with shapes a 4-year-old can easily recognize: green circle, blue square, and black diamond. Once you start saying things like, "I did OK on the black diamond slope today," people will resume inviting you for drinks after the last run of the day.

Air traffic control school. Before you spend the rest of your life lamenting that "air traffic control training just didn't go my way," stop saying, "I have a 98.5 percent success rate!" My friend Nick, who actually is an air traffic control officer, cites two levels of reporting in the control tower. When lives hang in the balance, they're generally looking for (a) people who can bring planes in safely over (b) people who can't.

Be aware of other precision pitfalls that could be compromising your social and professional acceptance. Temperature is a close cousin to percentages and might better be reported in a range rather than a specific number. Consider the following example.

Appliances. In case you're wondering why no one is showing up to fix your freezer, it's because you sound creepy. Stop saying your freezer is functioning at 34.6 percent, or 71.6 degrees. The tools at your disposal may be contributing to your confusion. Freezer thermometers do incorporate degrees in Fahrenheit or Celsius, but even this scale may be overly precise. Perhaps more useful are three *ranges* that appear on many thermometers: safe freezer zone (-20 to 31 degrees Fahrenheit), referral zone (32 to 40 degrees Fahrenheit), and danger zone (40 degrees Fahrenheit and higher).

The bottom line is that we often speak "percentage language," but we may actually make decisions based on ranges of these numbers, along with other extenuating circumstances.

The Verbs They Are A-Changin': Why Percentages May Not Work with Current Learning Targets

We explored the importance of verbs in Chapter 2 in our discussion of learning targets, and I encourage you to keep that discussion in mind now. When questioning the utility of a percentage-based grading and reporting model, we need to recognize how the verbs used in past learning targets—and our own school experiences with those targets—may shape our beliefs. For instance, I was visiting one of our district high schools recently when I encountered a parent dropping off her son. I knew the parent well, and probably because of our familiarity, she initiated a conversation.

"Hey, Myron, I heard about BC's shift to some kind of four-level language, with no percentages. What's the deal? I mean, when I was a student, we used percentages all the time, and I turned out OK. As a parent, I disagree with getting rid of percentages. They make sense!"

This parent's position is completely understandable and predictable. In chatting with Brandon Blom about his district making a similar shift in Roseville, California, I found he's had the same conversations. We develop our expectations of any environment based on our past experiences (Kidd, Palmeri, & Aslin, 2013). Knowing this, I asked this parent to describe a little more about her schooling experience. In particular, I asked her to recall things she was asked to do in school for which she would receive a percentage score.

"We had to memorize the 50 states in the USA, and, um, I remember doing a lot of spelling tests. I remember having to memorize a poem and recite it."

"This is the point," I responded, "Notice the verbs you're using."

"What?"

I highlighted the verbs she had used to describe her educational experience: *memorize, remember, recite.* I then went on to discuss the global shift we are experiencing, and the types of learning standards being adopted. As discussed earlier, the verb driving the learning standard will determine what students are asked to do concerning the content knowledge, and how deeply they may need to think about that content. Verbs such as *define, memorize, repeat, list,* and *duplicate* are largely associated with acquiring background knowledge, and percentage scores are generally effective for these types of surface knowledge tasks. Verbs associated with higher-order thinking, such as *evaluate, justify, design, generate,* and *create,* are more likely to require student demonstrations of understanding that are more complex and have different elements; descriptors, rather than percentages, may be better suited to these kinds of learning activities.

To be clear, learning standards may include verbs of both types in some iteration, or by necessity. Recall that for a student to perform well on a complex learning standard, background knowledge is essential. Like so many other educators, I've had to understand the importance of both worlds. There are still many examples of learning standards that require students to define, memorize, and list, and for some students, gaining surface knowledge is the first stepping-stone to deeper thinking. I would argue, however, that higher-order verbs are gaining prominence. Just like our society, the tools needed to function effectively in school are changing. The last time I *needed* to remember all 50 states was about the same time I was looking for a phone book.

Thankfully, our contemporary standards are beginning to better reflect that our students need to *solve, predict, argue, design,* and *explore.* Consider the array of standards listed here, noting that I have italicized the verbs for emphasis:

> Next Generation Science Standards, HS-ESS2-3: *Develop* a model based on evidence of Earth's interior to *describe* the cycling of matter by thermal convection. (NSTA, n.d.)

> Texas TEKS Grade 3 Social Studies: The student is expected to... *create* and *interpret* maps of places and regions that contain map elements, including a title, compass rose, legend, scale, and grid system. (TEKS Resource System, n.d.)

> Alaska Arts Standards—Grade 8: *Collaborate* to *select* and *apply* a variety of choreographic devices and dance structures to *choreograph* an original dance. *Articulate* the group process for making movement and structural choices. (Alaska Arts Standards, n.d.)

These are complex and challenging standards. Assessing student work according to these standards can be more difficult and certainly requires a paradigm shift for both students and teachers accustomed to simpler verbs. From my personal classroom experience, when faced with higher-order standards, descriptors of learning turned out to be a better tool for the job than percentages. Educators are constantly faced with trying to differentiate between two different students' work that is similar in quality and detail, but possibly different in approach or process. What teacher out there, who uses percentages every day, has not dealt with questions such as "Why did I get a 95 and not a 96?" or "My daughter says she got an 85. Can you explain why this is not an 86? She needs an A."

In choosing whether to insert grains of sand between my molars or have these types of conversations, it's a close call. When it comes to quibbling over a percentage point or having a more valuable learning dialogue based on a few broader categories, I'd much rather do the latter and *describe* the quality of a student's work using a performance scale. Combined with other tools, such as a good rubric, a performance scale enables students to better see the representation of their learning instead of focusing on a number.

The Illusion of Precision

As my conversation with the concerned parent continued, I could sense that she was not convinced that a shift in verbs should result in the discontinuation of percentage grades. Her next statement made this clear: "I'm fine with moving our students away from memorization and regurgitation. I'm in favor of critical thinking and stuff like that, but I still think percentages should be used. Seriously, Myron, we all know that 90 percent is really good!"

At this moment I had a flashback to a Thomas Guskey presentation I'd witnessed years earlier, and I incorporated it into the conversation.

"So 90 percent is really good?" I asked in confirmation.

"Of course it is," she retorted. "I think everyone would agree on that."

"Do you watch professional baseball?" I asked.

"Like Major League Baseball?"

"Yes."

"Some of it, sure; especially when Toronto is doing well."

"OK. So how would you classify a 90 percent batting average?"

"Well, from my understanding, that would be amazing!"

"Like 'really good'?"

"No, like out of this world. I don't think anyone has ever successfully hit the ball more than 50 percent of the time." (For the record, according to Baseball-Reference.com [n.d.], Ty Cobb came the closest, at .3662 lifetime.)

"So 90 percent can be better than really good?"

"OK, fine. Ninety percent is somewhere between really good and absolutely amazing."

"All right. So I challenge you to hold your favorite glass of wine at your next dinner party and casually pace about the room bragging that you have a 90 percent success rate in picking up your glass of wine and that you're very proud that only 10 percent of the time you spill the wine across the carpet."

She laughed.

I continued, "No, seriously. Successfully picking up a glass of wine 9 times out of 10 is somewhere between really good and absolutely amazing!"

"No, it's not," she laughed. "I'd get to know the carpet cleaner really well."

Continuing in a light mood, we discussed the reasons why we might adopt grading systems in which our students self-report on fewer categories. In conversations such as this one, I'd argue that shifting away from percentages can help bring meaning and context to the student's grade.

I have encouraged many educators and parents to read Guskey's interesting and informative article "The Case Against Percentage Grades" (2013). Guskey uses the history of percentage grading and research spanning more than a century to present a few simple arguments: (1) student grades for the same assignment can vary widely from teacher to teacher—even when these teachers are trained in specific assessment procedures or methods, and (2) given this variation, fewer categories, or classification levels, will result in greater reliability. He summarizes the argument as follows:

> Many educators assume that because the percentage grading scale has 100 classification levels or categories, it is more precise than a scale with just a few levels (such as Excellent, Average, and Poor). But in the absence of a truly accurate measuring device, adding more gradations to the measurement scale offers only the illusion of precision. When assigning students to grade categories, statistical error relates to the number of misclassifications. Setting more cutoff boundaries (levels or categories) in a distribution of scores means that more cases will be vulnerable to fluctuations across those boundaries and, hence, to more statistical error (Dwyer, 1996). A student is statistically much more likely to be misclassified as performing at the 85-percent level when his true achievement is at the 90-percent level (a difference of five percentage categories) than he is of being misclassified as scoring at an Average level when his true achievement is at an Excellent level. In other words, with more levels, more students are likely to be misclassified in terms of their performance on a particular assessment. (p. 3)

Let's return to the argument around baseball and wine glasses. A number only means something once the context is established. Whether a student is reporting a 6 or a 95 percent on the extent to which she has achieved the learning goal is not actually the issue; both could mean the same thing. The most important step is describing *what those symbols mean,* and I think I'd prefer six descriptions rather than a hundred.

The Power of Zero

I worked with Chris Van Bergeyk at Summerland Secondary School for many years, and one of his favorite sayings was "policies just avoid difficult conversations." I'm often reminded of this adage when I'm working in other school districts and hear someone say, "We've adopted a no-zeros policy!" Although I may applaud the *intent* of such a policy, too often the real issue has not been addressed—the percentage system. Across North America, and indeed the world, many schools try to solve the problems associated with zeros while remaining tethered to percentage grading. In his book *On Your Mark*, Guskey (2015) summarizes the underlying issue:

> In a percentage grading system, a zero is the most extreme score a teacher can assign. To move from a B to an A in most schools that use percentage grades requires improvement of only 10 percent at most, say from 80 to 90 percent. But to move from a zero to a passing grade requires six or seven times that improvement, usually from 0 to 60 or 65 percent. (pp. 31–32)

This unhealthy marriage between zeros and a percentage grading system can lead to a host of issues.

"Digging Out." Many teachers use the practice of averaging student scores to achieve an overall percentage score. In such a system, a student sustaining just one zero may have to achieve nine perfect scores to "recover" (Guskey, 2015). In such a grading environment, students who struggle in school or fail to complete graded homework or assignments due to factors beyond their control—dysfunctional home situations, for example—may find that one or two zeros act like torpedoes to the hull of their grading ship—they simply cannot recover. Given this situation, they actually make what research suggests is a predictable, healthy, and rational decision based on their expectations of the environment: they give up (ASCD, 2019).

Many teachers counter with arguments such as these:

- "If there is no work handed in, what choice do I have? A zero is the only appropriate number."
- "I use zeros to teach students a lesson, to teach accountability."

(Just for the record, I've never seen "accountability" in a standard, and therefore it should not be part of the grade.)

Although I understand the intent behind each of these arguments, I respectfully maintain that the consequences of such classroom rules would be far more just and equitable if a scale of 0 through 4 replaced the 101 categories (0 through 100) found in the percentage system. In a four-point scale ($A = 4, B = 3, C = 2, D = 1$, and $F = 0$), all the categories are separated by one point, and the power of zero is equal to all the others. By contrast, on a typical 100-point scale ($A = 90{-}100, B = 80{-}89,$

C = 70–79, D = 60–69, F = 0–59), four of the categories are separated by 10 points, but *60 points* separate failure from a grade of D. The power of zero is incredible!

To illustrate the power of a zero—and the time and effort it takes to "dig out" from one of them—consider the hypothetical student experience depicted in Figure 5.2. After achieving an average of 64.8 from five assignments, the student receives a zero on the sixth, as a result of failing to submit an assignment. (For the record, rarely does a student complete a major assignment or test and demonstrate not a shred of understanding, so a zero is likely far from accurate as a measure of understanding.) With the zero added to the calculation, his average score plummets to 54. Now imagine that the teacher achieved her goal of instilling accountability and the student has an epiphany, declaring, "I need to be a responsible student and better citizen!" Immediately, he bears down on his studies, and on the next assignment matches his top score of 70 percent. Looking at his resulting average score of 56.3, he's understandably disappointed to see that he is nowhere near his original average before receiving the zero. Determined to succeed in light of lessons learned, he again puts in his best-ever effort and receives another 70. Again, this has only a slight impact on his average. To his dismay, incredible improvements as shown by scores of 80 percent followed by 90 percent are still not enough to recover from the zero. Alas, only after his second 90, on his eleventh assignment, does he rise above the effects of the zero received on his sixth assignment.

Figure 5.2
The Power of Zero

Assignments	Scores	Calculation of Average Score
1–5	61, 63, 62, 70, 68	61 + 63 + 62 + 70 + 68 = 324 324 ÷ 5 = **64.8**
6	0	324 + 0 = 324 324 ÷ 6 = **54.0**
7	70	324 + 70 = 394 394 ÷ 7 = **56.3**
8	70	394 + 70 = 464 464 ÷ 8 = **58.0**
9	80	464 + 80 = 544 544 ÷ 9 = **60.4**
10	90	544 + 90 = 634 634 ÷ 10 = **63.4**
11	90	634 + 90 = 724 724 ÷ 11 = **65.8**

Source: © 2019 Myron Dueck. Used with permission.

To call this a "recovery" is absurd. Anyone with the slightest understanding of statistics could see that the zero on the sixth assignment nullified the incredible improvements shown in the last three scores. In most other fields, this zero would be considered an outlier and likely be ignored entirely.

Based on my work with many schools, I've observed that teachers who use zeros in a percentage-based grading system *and* who practice averaging are typically well aware of the devastating effects of zeros. To this point, they hope that the zero acts as a deterrent or threat, encouraging students to make good decisions. Although this may have the intended effect for some students, particularly those who are motivated by grades or who care about their schooling, it's less effective for disengaged, unmotivated, bored, or at-risk students who get zeros by choice or circumstance. I fear this system does nothing to encourage them to "stay in the game." I'm reminded of comments that suggested my own students have melded failing grades with their identity:

> "You want me to write an essay? I can't write essays." —A student who struggled on written portions of assessments

> "Hey, stupid, sit over here. We can both suck at this course." —An at-risk student inviting a friend to sit near him on the first day of the school year

> "I don't ever get good grades, but in this class, every once in a while, I can feel smart." —A student talking about her use of the retesting system

First, I think we could change some of these narratives if educators decided that all grades, including zeros, should reflect student learning and understanding of the standards. Second, our misuse of zeros may act as a confusing "mixed message" in our attempts to have our students understand the purpose of grading. Unfortunately for our most disengaged students, some educators contend that a zero should be used to represent an absence of all evidence; *nothing was handed in, so therefore it's a zero.* When a zero is used in this situation, the grade ceases to reflect understanding and instead shifts to compliance. Although it's possible a student might have no understanding whatsoever of the material, I'd suggest such cases are rare and often the result of abysmal attendance. On the contrary, if a student has been in class and has taken part in conversations or demonstrated at least *some* understanding of the material, isn't a zero an unreasonable score to report? I recall believing that a zero *was* an appropriate score for a student, despite that student having been in my class, present for my instruction. I now consider using a zero in this circumstance to be a rather brutal indictment of my own teaching.

The "Minimum 50" Solution. A few years ago, I received a call from a school administrator who was in crisis. In an attempt to deal with the devastating effects of zeros and still maintain a percentage grading system, her school had implemented a "minimum 50" policy. Teachers had returned from the winter holiday to find out that instead of using a zero as the lowest score possible, they were to use 50 instead. This led to a virtual riot, which we will address in a moment.

The idea behind the "minimum 50," *when used within a percentage-based system,* actually makes a lot of sense when people calm down long enough to try to understand it. Consider the logic of the following points:

- In many jurisdictions, the difference between an *A* and a *B* is around 10 percentage points, and so it is for *B* to *C* and *C* to *D*.
- If 60 is the passing grade, then both 0 and 50 are scores in the failing range.
- Using a 50 instead of a 0 means that the difference between an *F* (failing) and a *D* (passing score) is also 10 percentage points, just as it is for the other letter ranges.
- A 50 factored into a student's grade will have a far less devastating effect than a 0.

One can begin to see that the intention of the "minimum 50" is not to award a score of 50 for doing nothing, but rather to bring consistency to all the major increments on the grading scale. However, the virtual riot developed at this school as an underlying assertion among teachers, parents, and students became *Do nothing and get a 50!* If our goal is to empower students by welcoming them into the assessment arena, slogans like this are not helpful.

In hindsight, this confusion resulted from a few factors, not least of which was the attempt to marry a letter-grade scale and a percentage scale while knowing that "torpedo to the hull" zeros were being used in many classes. As Guskey (2013) so aptly states, "the true culprit in this matter is not minimum grades or the zero—it's the percentage grading system" (p. 71). To reiterate, when incorporating a "minimum 50" system, the floor, or zero, has been raised to 50. Considering Guskey's point, I would argue that if we wish to use numbers to represent levels of student understanding, we might rather keep the zero as the floor but lower the ceiling from 100 to a number ranging between 3 and 8.

Considering the arguments thus far, benefits to shifting to a performance scale include the following:

- We have one level that represents failing, not 60 different levels.
- Zero can appropriately represent a situation in which a student has attempted but been unable to demonstrate understanding on a narrow band of learning.
- Increments between levels are consistent and understandable.

- A more accurate form of averaging can be used as a piece of evidence if desired.
- In rare cases, a zero can be included in determining an average without the disproportionate power of the zero swaying the data. There's no longer a "zero torpedo" to the bow.

The Conversion Game

A few years ago, a local radio station played a fun translation game. The morning show hosts would take one or two lines from a popular song and, using a foreign language translation app, convert the lyrics to, say, Russian. They would then use the same app to translate the Russian words into another language such as Mandarin. The final step involved translating the Mandarin back into English. After this final translation was completed, they would read it to a caller and see if the person could name the popular song.

I tried to replicate this activity recently, but with modern translation algorithms, it seems that the computers cannot be fooled. I suppose this game was fun while it lasted. The idea behind it reminds me of something that we often do in schools but that's less entertaining.

In countless schools around the world, students receive scores on quizzes, tests, assignments, and projects in the form of fractions, which are then converted to percentages. At first glance, this system seems to make sense. Seldom are there exactly 100 points available on any one of these assessments, so a fraction is used to indicate the points scored out of a possible perfect score. Once the fraction is obtained, then a percentage can be calculated. I've seen it a million times. Here's how it played out in my grade 6 class back in 1997.

I enter the class holding a stack of tests that I've finally finished grading. I know from experience that students will listen intently as long as I'm holding the tests, and many will cease to care after I hand them back. Therefore, I speak as long as possible, about things students *should* have done differently, as my faithful subjects pretend to be interested. When Jimmy finally gets his test back, he sees that he scored 38 points out of a possible 48. Wanting to convert this score to a language that seemingly makes sense, he lunges for the nearest calculator, punches in the data, presses the equal sign, and sees "0.79166."

Dismayed and confused, he holds the calculator at a slight angle between his thumb and forefinger and begins to wander around the classroom mumbling "0.79166, 0.79166, 0.79166." If Jimmy is lucky enough to bump into the kid who knows the next and final step, and if that kid cares enough and is paying him any attention, Jimmy is given the keys to the castle.

"Multiply that by 100!" says the other kid.

"What?" Jimmy cries out, not sure of what he heard in the "just got the tests back" din of the grade 6 mob.

As a Coast Guard officer might yell while tossing the lifeline to a stranded sailor, the kid calls out again, *"Multiply that by 100!"*

The light bulb illuminates above Jimmy's head as he realizes he's so close to knowing how he did. Talking himself across the finish line, he speaks while he types, "times… one… hundred… equals…." Finally, the percentage appears.

"I got 79 percent!" Jimmy exclaims. No sooner are the words out of his mouth when a different look washes over his face. He scours the test for some way he can convince me to make it an 80. As he leans on my desk arguing that he meant to write such and such, or that I unfairly scored a question as 4 points when it really should've been a 5, he and I both realize we wouldn't be having this conversation to turn an 81 into an 82. Sand in my molars.

Back to our propensity to convert, convert, convert. Once this scenario plays itself out repeatedly throughout a reporting period and each student has accumulated a collection of scores, it's time to send home a report card. And what do we so often do? Convert. The overall percentage is converted to one of *five* letter grades on a report card—A, B, C, D, F.

This raises the question: *Why are so many individual educators, schools, or entire districts married to a percentage system when in the end they intend to report on one of five levels?*

Seriously, why are we seemingly addicted to converting the symbols used to convey student learning? Instead of playing the grading conversion equivalent of the radio game, why not correlate our day-to-day grading language with the language we intend to use to report it? This point was one of the best elements of the six-level proficiency scale we adopted at Summerland Secondary School. For the first time in my career, *the same language* could be used to grade, assess, and report.

Rethinking the Value of Learning Ceilings

I think it's OK for us to sometimes dream in education—to imagine what things could look like if we truly pursued learning and worried less about grading systems and numbers. As our standards continue to invite students to *analyze, predict, model,* and *create* using the content knowledge of our curricular areas, is it possibly time to question the limits or ceiling we might place on this learning?

In a percentage system, perhaps unfortunately, the ultimate goal is 100 percent. I've often heard students proudly report, "I got 100 percent on that!" or dream aloud, "I hope I get 100 percent." When listening to such statements, I increasingly hear them as a potential limit to learning instead of a measure to be proud of. Seldom have I seen a student wanting to pursue learning beyond her 100 percent score. Just watch the body language of a student who gloats over a score of 100 percent. If they're sitting, they'll often cross their arms, sit back, revel—all indications that the learning is over. Watching and listening to this student, I'm overcome with the realization that the material was likely too easy.

Come to think of it, as a current high school volleyball coach, I regularly overhear my players talk about their academic standing in terms of percentages, but *never* do they use this language in framing their volleyball skills. It would simply be unheard of, and absurd, for any player to refer to their athletic ability as 100 percent. As jurisdictions around the world incorporate descriptions of learning that use neither letter grades nor percentages, I see the potential in truly shifting how we talk about deeper learning with our students.

The American School Foundation of Monterrey (ASFM) in Mexico has largely moved away from the use of numbers to report student achievement, and instead has designed language like that shown in Figure 5.3. Melanie Henning is a middle and high school instructional coach at ASFM, and she's seen a number of positive results in shifting to this type of language:

> [This framework] allows us to focus more on the feedback, less on the final number. A score of 100 percent is never really attainable, and if it is accomplished, may encourage a student to think they're done. We know learning is never finished. This new language allows for dialogue around specifics for where students are at in their learning and what they might need to do to move forward. It helps them focus not on the number but on growth.
>
> For example, it has also encouraged productive dialogue between educators to discuss what are we looking for when we see a student meeting a standard. When there are only four indicators, there is a more focused conversation around the skills students will be demonstrating at each level. Perhaps most important, this information tells the teacher and student what is needed to move forward on that skill. This supports a more profound learning process, and less of a final ceiling of accomplishment. (personal communication, April, 22, 2020)

Figure 5.3
Student Rating Scale

Beginning	Approaching	Meeting	Extending
Student is in the process of acquiring and developing the basic knowledge and skills toward the standard.	Student demonstrates basic knowledge and skills according to the standard.	Student demonstrates understanding of concepts, knowledge, and skills according to the standard.	Student demonstrates transferable understanding of concepts, knowledge, and skills according to the standard.

Source: Courtesy American School Foundation of Monterrey (ASFM), Monterrey, Mexico. Used with permission.

I asked if Melanie could speak to any challenges related to this shift, and if teachers were seeing a change in student achievement, learning, or disposition. She responded:

> There have been some struggles with shifting away from a traditional grading system. We've had to support both parents and students in their understanding of each level. Overall, however, there have been very positive outcomes. (personal communication, April 22, 2020)

She mentioned a few teachers specifically, including Josh Almoite, a 7th and 8th grade science teacher/middle school science coordinator:

> Shifting to levels of achievement has helped students in his class take more ownership over the process, as they are much more aware of what they specifically have to do to reach the learning targets. Mr. Almoite now uses student trackers in his class [see Figure 5.4, p. 126]. Students use diagnostic evidence at the beginning of each unit to set personalized learning goals, rather than focusing on a grade. For example, when working on a concept or phenomenon in science, he will initially utilize formative assessment avenues to ascertain what his students understand. Students then use this information to set a goal of Approaching (A), Meeting (M), or Extending (E). Obviously the student is not given the option to set the lowest level, Beginning (B), as a goal.
>
> With those personalized goals and the evidence, students are able to make informed choices about the activities they should engage with to support them where they are in the process.
>
> The students are now able to speak of themselves as leading the process, selecting activities that will support their learning and the evidence that will show they have met expectations. Students use their trackers, formative feedback from their teacher, and the activities they engage in to determine what level of assessment they need to start with in the assessment process. As they collect evidence from different assessment processes, they fill in the "progress" boxes. They own it, feel more confident, and have much more concrete evidence of their needs as learners.
>
> Mr. Almoite was laughing the other day as he started a new unit. A student brought to his attention that he had forgotten to share out the tracker. The student wanted to make sure he could guide his learning through the unit. If that's not a positive example of ownership, I'm not sure what is!
>
> Removing the cap has also allowed students to extend far beyond 100 percent. Joelle Hernandez and Elizabeth Salinas, business teachers at ASFM, have seen students take risks and stretch their learning far beyond the classroom. A number of students have taken products developed for their classes and turned them into real businesses. One student turned an initial product of cauliflower rice into multiple iterations, added flavors, and eventually struck a deal with local restaurants. Another group of students who had already met expectations for their Marketing class ended up designing the logo for the school's conference, "Live Curious and Go Beyond," and were a part of the marketing team for the event. One student took her learning to levels never imagined and was actually hired by Disney Mexico based on her portfolio! These are a few of the many examples we have of students taking skills they've learned and transferring them beyond the classroom. Thankfully, 100

Figure 5.4

ASFM Student Self-Progress Tracker

Unit Topic: Artificial selection	Goal:	Progress 1	Progress 2	Revisit Goal:	Progress 3	Final
	I need to analyze more precisely how artificial selection modifies the pheno-type, and evaluate whether or not it's a good thing.			My goal is to evaluate whether the tech-nique is positive or negative and restate with evidence.		E
E						M
M						A
A						B
				Conversations happen here.		

Pieces of Evidence of Learning

Notes on articles of cases						
All tasks				Track and give feedback.		
Presentation on genetically modified tomatoes						
Notes on others' presentations				Never give a summative.		
Vaccines and diabetes activity and notes						
Debate research and participation						

Source: Courtesy American School Foundation of Monterrey (ASFM), Monterrey, Mexico. Used with permission.

percent is no longer the goal—deeper learning is. (personal communication, April 22, 2020)

Emboldened by experiences like that of ASFM, I'm eager to see whether terms such as *transfer* or *sophistication* may one day alter how our students describe their learning journey and define their ultimate learning goals. I allow myself to wonder if one day our goal will be to have all our students continually stretching their learning rather than reaching the supposed pinnacle of it. I'm currently listening to the audiobook version of James Donovan's *Shoot for the Moon* (2019), and I'm fascinated with the account of how, in the 1960s, NASA's scientists were struggling with an endless number of challenges. Imagine if they had adhered to a learning standard such as this:

Design a model and *develop* tools for landing people on the moon and getting them back to Earth.

Based on Donovan's account, I think that NASA's brightest would have often reported feeling like beginners on the Monterrey scale. Throughout history, the best scientists in the world have found themselves at the "emerging" or "beginning" level of any vexing situation. The COVID-19 pandemic we are experiencing as I write this serves as a poignant contemporary example, as around the world, our best researchers are frantically seeking a vaccine. New challenges, inquiry, and solutions to problems once thought unsolvable have a natural way of making everyone feel like a novice.

Perhaps getting rid of the ceilings of A+ and 100 percent would be an important step in helping our students reframe what it means to learn and a "giant leap" in communicating it. If nothing else, it would help our next generation of scientists prepare for that fascinating place, the "real world."

Innovation at the University Level

If you visit the Registrar's Office page of the Massachusetts Institute of Technology (MIT) website, you may find something interesting under the tab titled "Classes, Grades, and Evaluations." Under the "Grades" tab on the left side is a link called "Experimental Grading Policy." Clicking on this tab reveals something quite remarkable. Similar to our focus on purpose, or the elevator pitch, MIT seems to have adjusted its grading scale with purpose in mind. The wording on the site is as follows:

First-year grading is designed to ease your transition to MIT by giving you time to adjust to factors like increased workloads and variations in academic preparation and teaching methods. (MIT Registrar's Office, n.d.)

How exactly is MIT attempting to ease the transition for students? Well, upon arriving at MIT, a freshman will find that only two grading levels exist: Pass or No Record.

Yup, that's right. While we thought we were really adventurous at Summerland Secondary piloting a six-level scale, and Roseville City middle schools took the daring plunge to four, MIT has chosen two levels—including *one that doesn't really count.*

In part, MIT's shift may be a response to the high dropout rates experienced at many top universities—especially among first-year students. More than half of all college students will drop out within six years of first enrolling (Selingo, 2018). A contributing factor for some is the shock and stigma of seeing their first-year grades well below the level of their high school scores. As Malcolm Gladwell writes in *David and Goliath,* "What matters, in determining the likelihood of getting a science degree, is not just how smart you are. It's how smart you *feel* relative to the other people in your classroom" (2013, p. 84). A student accustomed to having the top score among her peers at Glenbard High School in Chicago might not *feel* confident once she's surrounded by other big fish at MIT. With her confidence already rattled, a *B* or two sends her into panic.

There's no question that grades often fall once a student reaches postsecondary education. Childs, Finnie, and Martinello (2017) have found that more than half of first-year university students in Canada experience a drop of at least one letter grade, with nearly a quarter seeing a drop of two. Only one-quarter of first-year students are able to maintain their high school grade levels, and a mere 2.5 percent increase them. Furthermore, we might be surprised to find out who's most at risk. Data suggest that students with the highest grades in high school are likely to see the biggest drop in their grades after their first year of college (Jerema, 2010). Universities such as MIT have high academic entrance requirements and therefore enroll first-year students who've been at the top of their classes in high school. This creates a perfect storm of frustration, embarrassment, confusion, and depression for students accustomed to high grades. Many drop out.

Changes like the ones at MIT will be an interesting trend to observe, especially in light of the conversation I had with Rayman, as recounted at the start of this chapter. High school students accustomed to expressing their learning in terms of "98 percent" may sustain quite a jolt when they encounter "Pass/No Record" structures at universities such as MIT. Classes for our youngest students—those in preK and kindergarten—have simple grading scales (if they have any at all), and universities such as MIT are adopting similar ones. Perhaps it's time for the educators in the middle to reconsider theirs.

Closing Thoughts

If we choose *to sit beside* our students and talk about learning, the language and symbols we select are going to have a big impact on the nature of that conversation. As our standards shift toward more complex applications of knowledge, and students are asked to *develop, model,* and *create,* perhaps there's good reason to look for language to match this more sophisticated approach to learning. In addition, as we invite students to self-report on their learning, research suggests that the accuracy of these reports will increase if students *really* understand the scale being used (Rosen, Porter, & Rogers, 2017). Percentages have long been a cornerstone for both grading and reporting, but fewer categories matched to meaningful descriptions may prove more effective when inviting students to the assessment realm. Just ask Rayman.

STUDENT SELF-REPORTING: "IT'S MORE THAN NUMBERS"

How can we allow students to effectively and purposefully report on all aspects of their learning experience?

It's tough to predict which players will be successful in the National Football League—just look at Tom Brady. By all accounts, when he showed up to the NFL Scouting Combine in 2000, he was, well, dreadful. For those not familiar with the NFL draft process, the combine is a series of athletic tests that are intended to help teams compare and rank players who are heading into the draft. One of those tests is the 40-yard dash. Back in 2000, Brady lumbered through this event to post a time of 5.28 seconds, which ranks as the slowest time ever among active quarterbacks in the NFL (Breech, 2015). When it came to testing his vertical jump, it seemed the Earth's gravitational pull was hardest on Brady, as he could get only 24.5 inches into the air (Breech, 2015). To provide some context, it's not uncommon for quarterbacks to leap well over 30 inches. Following the tests, Brady received an overall ranking of *F*, and his aggregate score of 12 out of 100 was one of the worst.

Websites like MockDraftable.com offer an interesting visual perspective of a player's combine results. Often referred to as a "spider chart" for its resemblance to the creature's web, this chart plots each player's results along a line emanating from the center (0 percentile) to the outside of the chart (100th percentile). For each item in the chart, a dot is plotted on the line to represent a player's percentile score compared with other players who play the same position. Once a dot is posted on each line, the dots are connected to form a unique shape for each player. Like a fingerprint, finding two players with identical spider charts would be next to impossible.

This enclosed area of the spider chart is then shaded to give an overall impression of that player's ability. A really strong spider chart would be mostly shaded in, whereas a weak chart would have very little of the area shaded. Tom Brady's 2000 spider chart is one of the worst ever, as only his height contributes to shading that stretches beyond the 50th percentile (see Figure 6.1). Three of his measures fall below the 5th percentile! In addition to scoring in the 4th percentile in the broad jump (the number near the center of the chart), he's in the 2nd percentile for vertical jump and the 1st percentile for the 40-yard dash (numbers that are obscured in the chart).

Figure 6.1
Tom Brady's NFL Combine Spider Chart

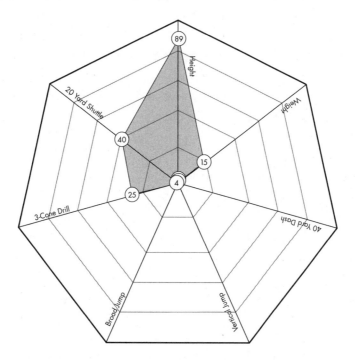

Source: Copyright Marcus Armstrong, MockDraftable.com. Adapted with permission.

Now, if you've paid any attention to professional football in the last decade, you'll realize that Tom Brady is a rather interesting case study. Drafted 199th overall in the sixth round of the 2000 draft, Brady played for 20 seasons with the New England Patriots—his entire career, until shifting to the Tampa Bay Buccaneers in 2020. Arguably, he's had a fairly successful stint as an NFL quarterback—or should we say, perhaps he's been the best ever (Bruton, 2017; Ruiz, 2019)! A mere sampling of his 54 NFL records as of 2020 include

- Most career wins by a starting quarterback (including playoffs): 245
- Most touchdown passes in NFL history (including playoffs): 603
- All-time leader in total yards (including playoffs): 85,151
- Most Super Bowl starts of all time: 9
- Most Super Bowl victories of any player: 6
- Most comebacks by a quarterback after trailing by 10 or more points since 2000: 32 (McArdle, 2019)

Perhaps Tom Brady's initial ranking during the combines best exemplifies Elliot Eisner's (2012) contention that when measuring a person, "it's more than numbers" (p. 14).

Apparently, Brady is not the only player to defy the NFL Combine stats. In 2014, wide receiver Jarvis Landry of Louisiana State University was drafted 63rd overall, seeing 12 other wide receivers drafted ahead of him. Although Landry had notable successes in college, many doubted his ability to succeed in the NFL. Hank Joness (2014) noted Landry's shortcomings as follows: "Landry has a very limited catch radius, due to short length and height. Landry lacks ideal explosion from the position as well… he lacks suddenness and lateral quickness…:. I think he is limited in how many yards after the catch he can create on his own" (p. 1).

Reporting on Landry at the NFL Combine, *Sports Illustrated*'s Doug Farrar focused on the same event that plagued Brady—the 40-yard dash. Predicting a second- or even third-round selection for Landry, Farrar (2014) wrote, "Landry's combine performance wasn't anything to write home about—he posted the slowest official 40 time among all receivers at 4.77 [seconds]." When it came to his combine tests, they were a complete disaster (Davenport, 2014; Farrar, 2014; Joness, 2014; Sobleski, 2014). In fact, given his own wretched spider chart, it's a wonder anyone picked him at all.

Yet, in an article written before the 2014 draft titled "Jarvis Landry Is More Than His NFL Combine Performance," Carter Bryant makes the case that Landry is a game player, and his array of experiences on the field mattered more than his NFL Combine test scores. He wrote of Landry's natural feel for the game, his creativity and "fearlessness." He quoted Landry's interview with the *Indianapolis*

Advocate around the time of the tests. Landry predicted his own NFL success by saying, "I'm going to play special teams, I'm (hard to bring down) across the middle, I'm going to block linebackers, safeties... (and do) just the little things that people forget" (Bryant, 2014, para. 12). Bryant was one of the few people to go on record predicting success for Landry, writing, "whoever drafts him in May will strike gold" (para. 24). Perhaps most appropriate was Bryant's contention: "Landry is more than just numbers" (para. 8).

Like Tom Brady, Jarvis Landry has gone on to prove how rankings, test scores, and pools of data fail to predict the success of an NFL player. Landry has appeared in five Pro Bowls and tallied more receptions in his first five seasons than any player in NFL history. Upon retirement, most players can only dream of having their jersey hanging in the Pro Football Hall of Fame. At age 27, Landry's is already there (Gribble, 2018). Clearly, his potential amounted to "more than just numbers" on a combine test.

When trying to decide whom to draft, the scouts and coaching personnel of NFL teams have a mountain of stats, digital footage, and game-play observations. You could say they are swimming in performance data. But despite this plethora of information, predicting who will be better than others in actual NFL games is still somewhat of an enigma. This observation should give educators reason to pause when relegating students to a single letter or percentage score. The NFL Combine is an attempt to describe a player using 15 numbers, compiled using stopwatches and other precise measurement tools, and in many cases, this process still fails to encompass the individual. Similarly, although grades *can* serve as predictors of student performance, we should be careful not to confuse a predictor with what it is predicting. For instance, I've noticed that many high school graduates who have gone on to become successful entrepreneurs were nowhere close to being top achievers in high school.

If we're going to welcome each student into the world of assessment, it's critical that we understand just who this student is, and why a single number, letter, or comment is not an accurate representation. As well, let's not forget that the person who was arguably the most accurate in predicting Jarvis Landry's success was Landry himself.

The Impact of Context

The Wediko Summer Program is a 45-day residential treatment program for students ages 8 through 19 who have social, emotional, and behavioral challenges. Children visiting this 450-acre lakefront camp in New Hampshire are generally referred by schools, educational consultants, and clinicians who believe that a "fresh-air, therapeutic experience can create positive change" (Wediko Children's Services, para. 1). This camp was the location for an interesting study done by Yuichi Shoda and his colleagues. Their study involved 84 male campers and examined the contextual factors that might affect their social interactions. Researchers structured the data collection by first separating the campers' interpersonal interactions with peers from those that involved adults. They further divided these interactions into two categories: those that were positive in nature, such as the camper getting praise or support, and those that were negative, such as teasing from a peer or punishment from an adult (Mayer, 2017; Shoda, Mischel, & Wright, 1994).

Researchers then spent more than 160 hours observing each of the 84 campers in the study (Rose, 2016). The 77 camp counselors and staff spent well over 14,000 hours looking for instances that elicited verbally aggressive behavior, such as uttering threats or name-calling (Mayer, 2017; Shoda et al., 1994). What researchers discovered was that individual campers acted very differently depending on the situation. Although two boys might have been referred to the camp for "aggressive behavior," whether they were aggressive or not in any situation depended on… the situation. For some boys it depended on whether the interaction involved an adult or a peer, and then it was further dependent on the positive or negative nature of the interaction. Essentially, whether or not the camper was aggressive was not solely determined by behavior traits but, rather, depended largely on the "micro-situation," or surrounding context (Mayer, 2017; Rose, 2016; Shoda et al., 1994).

There's a long history of studies that try to determine how and why children make certain decisions. Many readers will remember the "marshmallow study." The basic steps involved placing a marshmallow in front of individual children, typically ages 3 to 5, and promising the young subjects that they would receive a second marshmallow if they could wait 15 minutes before eating the first one. The adult making the promise would then leave the room, and the time it took for the child to eat all or part of the first marshmallow was used as a singular measure of self-control (Rose, 2016). Devised by Columbia University psychologist Walter Mischel in the 1960s, the marshmallow study sought to prove that a child's ability to delay gratification through willpower or self-control could pay off later in life and lead to success in education, the workplace, and beyond. When Mischel and others caught up with the participants much later in life, those who had appeared to exhibit the highest level of self-control, on average, were more socially adjusted and enjoyed greater academic success (Shoda, Mischel, & Peake, 1990).

Predictably, these findings set off something of a self-control craze. The problem with heading off on this tangent, however, was that people assumed self-control to be a trait in need of development, rather than suggesting that children could develop strategies to better handle situational pressures (Rose, 2016). Situational pressures, or the contexts in which kids make decisions, prompted some researchers to ask more questions. Celeste Kidd, then a graduate student of brain and cognitive sciences at the University of Rochester, wondered if anyone had looked into the children's experience with adults—specifically around issues of predictability and trust. In my conversations with Kidd, she spoke of her experiences working with children in a homeless shelter and thinking, "There's no way the kids I work with would wait 15 minutes—based on their past experiences they'd eat the first marshmallow right away!" (personal communication, December 11, 2018).

Kidd performed her own "marshmallow study," introducing a few elements to explore the potential influences of context. In the weeks leading up to the marshmallow moment, one control group of children spent time with a "reliable adult," and a second group was assigned an "unreliable" one. When I asked Kidd how exactly one can establish "unreliability," she described how fancy art supplies might be promised to the group, only to have the adult fail to bring them in. On the "reliable" side of the coin, the adult fulfilled the promises. After the children had spent time with these adults, Kidd and colleagues put each group through the marshmallow test.

Kidd found that the story involved much more than inherent self-control. Instead, past experiences loomed large in shaping the children's decision making. In their subsequent article, Kidd, Palmeri, and Aslin (2013) write that "children engage in rational decision-making about whether to wait for the second marshmallow. This implicit process of making rational decisions is based upon beliefs that the child acquired before entering the testing room" (p. 2). During my conversations with Kidd for the production of ASCD's *Ask Them* video series, she summarized her findings and provided a powerful lens through which all educators might want to view student decisions: "All of the decisions that we make, all of the behaviors that we exhibit, hinge very heavily on our expectations, and our expectations depend upon our life experiences, which are all different" (ASCD, 2019).

Kidd is not alone in revisiting the marshmallow study and explicitly investigating contextual variables over inherent traits. Tyler Watts, Greg Duncan, and Haonan Quan performed their own rendition of the study, greatly expanding the number of participants compared with Mischel's or Kidd's study. Watts and his colleagues put more than 900 participants through the study and controlled for factors such as economic and social disadvantages (Watts et al., 2018). In her *Atlantic* article "Why Rich Kids Are So Good at the Marshmallow Test," Jessica Calarco (2018) looks at the conclusions of the Watts study and writes, "[T]he capacity to hold out for a second marshmallow is shaped in large part by a child's social and economic background—and, in turn, that background, not the ability to delay gratification, is what's behind kids' long-term success" (para. 4). In other words, the environment in which you grew up, and literally how full your food pantry was, may have far more to do with your decisions than any supposed self-control trait. Writes Calarco, "A second marshmallow seems irrelevant when a child has reason to believe that the first one might vanish" (para. 9).

After a long and enlightening conversation with Celeste Kidd, I found myself reflecting on my two decades of interactions with students in the classroom setting—in particular, the countless times I acted on my assumptions about student behaviors based on my *perception* of reality. Many times I consciously, or unconsciously, attached a label to a student who seemed checked out or who failed to hand in assignments: *lazy, apathetic, disorganized,* or *disinterested.* Near the end of our interview, I hesitantly asked Kidd, "Is this kind of where you're going with the conversation—that we need to be careful with our assumptions?"

"Absolutely," she responded. "And it's not just relevant in the classroom context, but in life at large" (ASCD, 2019).

Every student brings a separate combination of life experiences and builds expectations based on their recollection of those events. Therefore, we need to look for avenues and opportunities to get more of the story. If we as humans are jagged in our profiles and affected greatly by our individual contexts, there must be inherent implications for assessment. This idea makes me pause to consider the following questions:

- *Could we report on the learning and development of a student with more than one letter, or number, and brief commentary—often computer-generated?*
- *How could we provide students the opportunity to explain factors in their personal and academic lives that may affect their learning?*
- *How can we foster learning environments that are sensitive to student experiences, perspectives and contexts, socioeconomic differences, race, and gender identity?*
- *How do we adhere to learning standards while demonstrating that building caring relationships is paramount?*
- *Can we build assessment tools and provide self-reporting opportunities that allow students to have a voice in reporting their own learning journey?*

The Power of Individual Perspective

Who was arguably most accurate in the assessment of Jarvis Landry before the 2014 draft? The answer: Jarvis Landry. He told the *Advocate* reporter that he could play special teams, was hard to tackle, and could face off against multiple positions. He declared that he could do "just the little things that people forget." It's worth pointing out that none of the so-called experts, with the exception of Carter Bryant, were even close to matching Landry's accuracy concerning *his own abilities*. Looking at the follow-up marshmallow studies of Kidd and Watts, who might be in the best position to comment on whether they believe adults, or whether they've learned to eat food based on availability over promise? Probably the kid staring at the marshmallow.

In my interview with John Hattie for the ASCD video series *Ask Them* (ASCD, 2019), he cites the meta-data analysis showing that students are remarkably accurate in predicting their own success. His blunt advice to teachers is to literally "shut up and listen. And it really comes down to that—listen to how they are interpreting." Further in the interview, Hattie contends that student self-reporting does not mean we should throw out all that we've done in assessment but, rather, that we should be deliberate in creating space for student voice and meaningful self-evaluation, and that we should work on common language to facilitate this process.

Accuracy: The Elephant in the Room

Many teachers have expressed concern over the accuracy of student self-reporting, and indeed there are circumstances in which students may not be accurate in their self-evaluation. Has every young athlete who's proclaimed, "I'm going to play in the NFL!" later found himself waving to Mom via the television camera lens? Of course not, and there's research to suggest that accuracy can be a mixed bag in schools. Some studies have suggested that students may often misrepresent their grades (Cassady, 2000; Maxwell & Lopus, 1994; Mayer et al., 2007; Teye & Peaslee, 2015). But other research has concluded that students can be accurate in their self-reporting (Kuncel, Credé, & Thomas, 2005).

If we're going to invite students to self-assess and self-report, it's imperative that we address the issue of accuracy. Thankfully, some guidelines are emerging in this area of study. Rosen, Porter, and Rogers (2017) suggest that a self-reporting structure has four components, and an error in any of these can render the entire report inaccurate. The four components are

- *Comprehension*—Does the student understand what is being asked?
- *Retrieval*—Does the student recall a balanced and representative collection of events in order to make an accurate report? Studies suggest that we tend to remember events that are most distinctive (Rosen et al., 2017), and these can form the basis of our memories.

- *Judgment*—Is a final conclusion based on sufficient data? If memories are incomplete, so, too, will be a judgment based on these memories.
- *Response*—Two issues can compromise accuracy in student responses to self-reported grades: (1) the student may not understand the scale used in the response, and (2) social factors such as embarrassment may alter the student's report.

I've witnessed each of these potential accuracy potholes while developing and implementing student self-reporting structures. The self-reporting form I used in my Leadership class provided a portal for students to self-report every three to four weeks, as well as being used as a final report. As part of this process, I would collect the forms and carefully read my students' responses. I soon learned that the forms' value was not necessarily in the accuracy of the report but, rather, the window it provided for better understanding the student's perspective and context.

I would be concerned the moment I read a self-report such as the one shown in Figure 6.2, which I have closely modeled after a real one. For one, the student grossly underreported her achievement. Therefore, this document is likely inaccurate in terms of both *retrieval* and *judgment*. She chose to report mainly on negative traits, and I would suggest she exaggerated them considerably. Comments such as "I didn't contribute to anything" and her decision to check off every available area in need of improvement suggested she was choosing only to report on negative events, and her *judgment* was based solely on these points.

On the other hand, I'd consider a report like this to be potentially accurate concerning her current social-emotional state. Upon reading comments like these, I could discreetly take this information to one of our counselors, who may have concerns similar to mine. On a few occasions, these self-reporting templates prompted me to coordinate with school counseling staff to provide support for students who might need it.

This example illustrates an important point: a student self-report can be inaccurate in some respects but accurate in others. I was visiting a large high school in the U.S. Midwest when I was approached by a teacher concerned over the accuracy of student self-reporting. He was wearing a basketball coaching shirt, so I asked if he was involved in school sports. He replied that he was the coach of the varsity girls basketball team. The following is my recollection of our conversation.

After he started our chat by expressing his concerns, I responded with a question: "Do you ever ask your athletes to evaluate their own performance?"

"I'd say so, yes. We look at game tape and I ask players to discuss their decisions and game-play," he responded.

Figure 6.2

Self-Report Form for Leadership Class

Name: _____   Date: _____January 30_____

Leadership Evaluation   1   2   3   Potential Grade:

6	Expert
5	
4	Apprentice
3	
(2)	Novice
1	

Grade 9/10   Leadership

"I am a   (NOVICE)   APPRENTICE   EXPERT   in Leadership."

Strengths/Challenges:

| Game-changer |

I come to class most of the time.

| Middle player |

I don't create distractions or talk to others during class.

—I don't participate in class discussions.
—I have zero enthusiasm.

| Follower |

—I have a hard time focusing in class.
—I didn't contribute to anything.
—I didn't do a final project.
—I'm not good at remembering or understanding.

Areas to improve:

☑ Homework/self-study

☑ Group work—tasks, communication, etc.

☑ Journal—depth

☑ Journal—completion

☑ Class discussions/debate

☑ Organization—project work

☑ Quizzes (study)

☑ Unit tests

☑ Retesting

Notes:

I knew nothing of his team or athletes, so my next question might've seemed strange. "Is your starting point guard the best in your league, or for that matter the conference, or even the state?"

Appearing a little surprised by the nature of my question, he laughed and said, "No, she is new to the position at varsity and is struggling at the moment."

I continued, "OK, so what if you asked her to evaluate herself, and she reported that she was the best point guard in the league, citing specific reasons she thought that to be true. Would you consider her self-report to be accurate?"

"Absolutely not," he replied. "She's nowhere close to being the best in the league. Her account would certainly be an inflated view of her ability."

"So as her coach, would you render her inflated self-report to be totally useless?"

At that question he paused for a few moments.

"No," he said hesitantly. "As a coach I could find her appraisal useful. Perhaps it would give me a better understanding as to why she makes certain decisions."

"What kinds of decisions?" I asked.

"Players who have inaccurate views of their ability may be prone to taking unnecessary risks. Like, say, you're up by four points with less than a minute left in the game, and she makes a risky pass."

I then shifted the conversation to the classroom. "Besides coaching at your high school, what else do you teach?

"Biology."

"So, imagine you asked your biology students to self-report. And suppose you had a student contend that she was doing great in her understanding of biology, and that her tendency to do homework with her two friends was working out just fine. If you disagreed with her self-report, would it not be inaccurate but still useful in better understanding the student?"

"I suppose so."

For the remainder of this chapter, we'll explore tools, methods, and structures that encourage student voice and engagement through self-assessment. Some of these ideas involve using innovative and emerging technology. Considering the four potential accuracy obstacles listed by Rosen and colleagues (2017)—comprehension, retrieval, judgment, and response—I encourage you to take note of ways to increase accuracy, including

- Being clear about questions and prompts.
- Providing structures that remind students of the various aspects of the report.
- Using scales and measures that make sense and avoid ambiguity.
- Creating safe and supportive environments for students to self-report.

- Looking at all dimensions of the process, aware that a report can be both accurate and inaccurate depending on the nature of the data and how they're used.

Above all, we want to explore various ways that our students can report on their own understanding and learning.

Sharing Circles: Opening the Door to Student Self-Reporting

When I started writing this book, I never imagined I'd include a sharing circle strategy as an essential component of student self-reporting. However, since experiencing various sharing circles in the past two years, both with my class and with adults, I couldn't imagine starting any other way. What I've come to realize is that people's willingness to self-report, and the depth and quality of those assessments, is directly related to the safety and stability they sense in the environment. Learning, and the successes and struggles we experience in pursuing it, is inherently personal. We cannot expect everyone to immediately self-report on something this sensitive. Rather, we need to develop a sense of community—one in which sharing is natural, healthy, and even fun. Be reminded of Kidd's contention: how students act in any situation depends a lot on their expectations of the environment.

A sharing circle is *one* way to greatly affect our students' self-reporting behavior by establishing a positive expectation of the learning environment. I want to be really clear, however: my initial attempts at a sharing circle were a total disaster.

Getting Started with Sharing Circles

It was just before my initial grade 9/10 Leadership class of the year at Summerland Secondary, and I was searching frantically for an "object." Never before in my nearly 20 years of teaching had I needed an "object" to start the year, but this time was different. Two colleagues, Naryn Searcy and Judith King, had encouraged me to introduce a sharing circle protocol to my classroom routines—and apparently this activity required an "object."

A few factors had converged to push me out of my teacher-centered comfort zone and start this class differently. I had just attended a fantastic professional learning day put on by Judy Halbert and Linda Kaser, currently the co-directors of Networks of Inquiry and Indigenous Education in British Columbia. They had begun by splitting the large group of adults into two sharing circles and giving them the following prompts:

- Share with the group one highlight from your summer.
- What's something you are looking forward to in the year to come?

As an object was passed from person to person (in our case, a tree branch), the holder of the object could answer one or both questions, or simply pass.

It was a powerful and unique way to start a day of professional development. First, rather than the presenter owning the conversation, we started by *giving everyone a voice.* Second, instead of just talking about the value of self-reporting, Judy and Linda had participants *experience* and *feel* it. During our debrief of the activity, Linda commented that sharing circles have been a part of human existence for thousands of years, present in a variety of Indigenous and non-Indigenous cultures, and were a powerful tool to aid in our communication and understanding of one another. Judy and Linda reminded the group to exercise great care and respect when adopting any type of Indigenous practice in the class-room. Indigenous practices can vary by place, and teachers wanting to introduce something like a sharing circle may wish to contact local Indigenous leaders for support and guidance.

Back to my Leadership class.

Nearly a week had passed since our adult sharing circle, and I was excited to replicate the success with my class on the first day of school. Naryn, one of the two colleagues who had encouraged me to introduce sharing circles, was incredibly helpful in sending me a link to her own blogging page, which included background information on "Indigenous Peoples' Sharing Circles" and a set of protocols to con-sider. In consultation with local Indigenous community leaders, Naryn used a set of 8–10 protocols, which included the following:

- Only the holder of the object may speak; all others listen respectfully.
- No one is forced to share when they receive the object; everyone has the right to pass.
- Once the sharing starts, no one may join or leave the circle.
- What is said in the circle stays in the circle.

As I was new to sharing circles, this information was invaluable.

So, about that object. Planning has never been my forte, so it came as little surprise that I did not have an appropriate object ready for class. Ten minutes before we were set to begin, I was frantically combing the school grounds in search of a fallen branch or stick. I first looked on the ground, but maintenance had just swept all fallen foliage. Quickly looking both ways to determine a moment with the fewest witnesses, in sheer desperation I removed a small appendage from a tree closest to the school entrance. Just as a slight snapping sound signaled my acquisition of the needed object, a student passing by asked what I was doing. I mumbled something about needing it for class and reentered the school. As fate would have it, this inquisitive student was in my Leadership class.

Slightly out of breath, perspiring just a touch, and with branch in hand, I was starting the school year in uncharted waters. In my nervous state, I felt a little better seeing that only 14 students had registered for the course. Understandably, the student who had witnessed my pruning thievery looked at me suspiciously. After moving the desks to the sides of the room and arranging the chairs in a circle, I introduced the activity. I decided to go first, using the same two questions Judy and Linda had used. Soon, my students knew that I had visited Atlanta with my son in August and that I was looking forward to coaching volleyball in the fall. As I passed the branch to the student beside me, things began to unravel.

The student holding the branch stared at it for a second, and with a dazed expression looked up at the group. The seconds seemed like hours until the silence was punctuated by her realization that she had an out, and she quickly uttered, "Pass!" The branch then raced through the hands of the next five students, held only long enough for each to say, "Pass!" As the object got to a boy sitting opposite me in the circle, he seemed to look upon me with pity and decided to share: "I had a boring summer, and I'm not looking forward to anything."

"Wonderful!" I declared, realizing that my elation over someone sharing eclipsed my ability to respond appropriately. Two girls glared at me, and one whispered that I did not have the branch and therefore I should not have spoken at all.

No sooner had I spoken out of turn when a knock at the door interrupted our circle. The door opened, and the school counselor entered along with two students who had just registered for the course. The boy holding the branch reminded me of a protocol: "What do we do now, Mr. Dueck? You said no one can join or leave once we've started."

In my haste to locate a branch, I had forgotten to post a "Do not disturb" sign on the door indicating that a sharing circle was under way. Not wanting the two new arrivals to feel any more out of place than they already did, we broke the rule, widened the circle by two more chairs, and I reintroduced the activity and reviewed the protocols. Once we resumed the sharing circle, the remaining students, including the two new arrivals, all chose to "pass." My first attempt at a sharing circle was a total disaster.

I called Naryn at the end of the day, adamant that I would never attempt another sharing circle. She reassured me that most first attempts weren't much better than mine. I suspected she was just trying to make me feel better. When she encouraged me to have another go at it, I told her I'd rather swim in shark-infested waters dressed as a seal. Ignoring my protests, Naryn suggested that I put the prompts up on the whiteboard *before* moving the desks and chairs, so students would have time to think about the questions and better prepare a response.

The next day I garnered the courage to try again. Before moving the furniture, I had taken Naryn's advice and had written on the board: "What's your favorite movie or book, and why?"

It seemed that with a little more time to think, a few students were willing to share a movie or book title and maybe a single sentence justifying their choice. Unfortunately, I again forgot to post "Do not disturb" on the door, and we must've been interrupted four or five times as new students entered the class. With each visit from the counselor, I gave him a death glare. The circle swelled from 16 at the start of class to 28 by the end. With each new arrival, we added more chairs to the circle and I repeated the protocols for the newcomers. And yes, we were breaking one of the protocols every time we restarted.

We were still far from calling this endeavor a success, but ever so slowly I saw the environment begin to change. As a few students found the courage to hold the branch and share their favorite movie or book choice, I could see other students around the circle react with silent gestures and expressions. Although one or two students reacted negatively to someone's book or movie choice, for the most part the facial expressions of their peers showed agreement or approval. (Note that some sharing circle protocols suggest that listeners not react at all to the feelings and opinions shared by the speaker [Pass The Feather, n.d.].)

As students began to share, I noticed that we all needed reminders that only the holder of the branch was allowed to speak. Rather than looking at this as a challenge, perhaps it was an opportunity. Seeing that students wanted to respond, I suggested we pass the branch around the circle again. This time the prompt was for students to respond to someone else's comment from the first round. One student started with "I can relate to [student name] as I too like that book series." This comment started a chain reaction of responses to one another's choices. As the branch went around the circle for the third and fourth time, I watched students reach across the circle with their words of agreement, support, and connection. Naryn and Judith were right: the learning environment was slowly taking on the feel of a community.

By the fifth week of the course, the circle protocol was established, and the pain of the first few attempts not nearly as acute. We started every Monday with a sharing circle, and sometimes we'd run one in the middle of the week. If a major event occurred in the news, our community, or school, the sharing circle provided a venue for us to discuss our thoughts and concerns openly and safely. Our topics varied widely, to include "scariest/funniest animal experience," "defend your favorite fruit," "if you had $1,000 to spend," and many others. Most students arrived on Monday mornings excited about the prospect of a circle.

I remember putting up a topic around week six, asking students to "tell us about something lost or something found." It was by far the most memorable sharing circle ever; the results were amazing. The branch must've circled the group six times or more. The stories told were funny, interesting, sad, and compelling. More than 50 minutes had passed, and students were still busy relating to one another. One student chose to "pass" the branch the first four times it came to her, only feeling comfortable on the fifth lap. She spoke of recently losing her grandpa and how especially difficult it was, as he was the family member to whom she felt most connected.

Considering how quickly students chose to "pass" on our first attempts at the circle, I was amazed how six weeks later they openly shared stories involving remarkably personal elements. One student mentioned that she hadn't seen her dad for a long time and hoped they'd reconnect in future years. Another boy commented on the closeness he felt with an older brother, coming to this realization only after his sibling moved to college. The story I'll never forget is a student's incredibly detailed account of being left behind at the Shanghai airport while her other seven family members flew on to India! And all this time I thought *Home Alone* was pure fiction! Throughout the remainder of the course, I had students often ask, "Can we do a sharing circle today?"

Sharing circles are not reserved only for courses such as Leadership. In "Building an Inclusive Culture in an Intermediate Classroom," grade 6/7 teacher Kim Ondrik (2011) describes her regular use of "talking circles" to solve classroom problems. Should you garner the courage to try a circle, visit www.myrondueck.com to find sharing circle links and resources. Some resources include sharing circle prompts to get you started and demonstrate the wide array of topics that circles can explore. Some of the prompts involve using the circle to introduce or support curricular targets. For instance, imagine a teacher is about to embark on a study of genetics by focusing on dog breeds. The opening activity of the unit could start with the circle prompt "If you could own any breed of dog, which one would you choose, and why?"

Looking back on my 20 years in the classroom, I wish I had started topics with this type of student voice and engagement activity. I can now imagine a different start to my World War II unit, using prompts such as these:

- What images first come to mind when you hear "World War II"?
- Do you know of a way that your family or our community was affected by World War II?

I did run a sharing circle asking my students about self-reporting, and their comments were helpful. Perhaps I could have considered a sharing circle on grades, upcoming report cards, or a change to performance scales. The opportunities are endless.

Considering some of the major issues confronting societies around the world, I suggest that in all areas of education we look for strategies and tools that support shared storytelling, acceptance, and tolerance. We all have a story but seldom have the opportunity to tell it. Halbert and Kaser (2013) suggest incorporating Indigenous peoples' principles of learning in all areas of education, with sharing circles being just one example. Here are a few of these principles:

- Learning is experiential and relational—focused on connectedness and a sense of place.
- Learning is embedded in memory, history, and story.
- Learning involves patience and time.

Benefits of Sharing Beyond the Circle

Despite the eventual unexpected success of the sharing circles, some of the greatest benefits surrounded what happened when my students and I *weren't* in the circle. Little did I know at the time that this activity would contribute to student self-reporting in profound ways, including

- A stronger cohesion among students in all activities.
- ESL students learning language skills in a new setting.
- A heightened willingness for people to speak up in regular classroom conversations.
- Increased acceptance among students of different races, cultures, orientations, and genders.
- Increased risk taking.
- Increased comfort and confidence with sharing personal thoughts and feelings.

As mentioned in Chapter 3, one of the self-reporting structures I introduced consisted of journals in which students would respond to class activities, speakers, or topics we encountered. These wire-bound paper diaries also served as a communication tool between the students and me. After a few weeks of classes, I asked my students how they felt about the sharing circle activity. International students commented that it was a chance to learn English in everyday conversations, and other students divulged that the sharing circle was the best part of the class. On a few occasions, students confessed to at first hating the sharing circle, only to really enjoy it weeks later.

It was more luck than strategy that my introduction of a sharing circle to my Leadership class coincided with the implementation of a student self-reporting structure. Although I cannot definitively conclude that the sharing circle contributed to student self-reporting and self-assessment, I strongly suspect that it did. The sharing circle helped establish community, safety, and a sense that it's OK to be honest about oneself. I'm so convinced of this connection that I would endure some of the initial difficulties of developing a sharing circle protocol, or something similar, to enjoy the later benefits to our classroom communication and culture.

Conversation-Based Grading

In my role as a high school administrator, I had many opportunities to chat with students. If I was talking to a student in my office about an issue, I'd often ask, "How are you doing in your classes?" Far too often, the student would shrug their shoulders and mumble something to the effect of "I don't know." This was not a good sign! Wouldn't it be strange if I asked my buddy how his kitchen renovation was progressing, and he just responded with a shrug, saying, "I'm not really sure"?

Combining our awareness that Hattie's top achievement indicator was "student self-reported grades" and our realization that many of our students seemed unable to conjure even the simplest self-report of their learning, our team responded with two goals:

- Increase students' self-reporting of their own learning.
- Decide on a language to facilitate this conversation.

We were certainly not the first educators in our province to open the doors to student self-reporting. The principal of my high school at the time, Chris Van Bergeyk, spoke of his brother Dave having developed a rather innovative conversation format for determining his students' grades. I was further intrigued to find out more, considering that Dave taught senior calculus! Members of our Summerland Secondary team met with Dave Van Bergeyk, and he summarized his grading system in surprisingly simple terms. Whenever final academic grades were required for reporting purposes, Dave would sit down with students, individually, and ask *the students* what they thought their final grade should be. The greatest departure from the norm was that the students needed to come up with a grade and supporting evidence *before* the teacher did.

The students' determination of their grade was not arbitrary. Dave would encourage his students to keep track of their quiz, test, and assignment scores and use these data points to form an educated opinion. He recounted that in most cases, the student would arrive at a grade very similar to what he would've determined, but not always. If a student reported a score significantly higher or lower than what Dave had determined, he'd ask the student to provide supportive evidence. Often when faced with a potentially inaccurate self-report, he'd ask the student, "Help me understand why you think...."

Our visit with Dave felt a bit like we had entered the Twilight Zone. I recall hardly believing what I was hearing. I'd never imagined a grading conversation, led by the student, being used to determine a final grade for a report card. Maybe I could've envisioned this in my grade 6 art class or grade 9 Leadership, but senior calculus? Absurd!

As Dave finished describing his system, it appeared to be built on a few basic foundations:

- Students were quite accurate in describing their progress and abilities.
- Students were generally honest about their overall standing in the course.
- There was greater student buy-in to the reporting process when the conversation was led by the student.
- Whatever grade students believed they had earned needed to be backed up with evidence (assessment results from the course).
- Student performance was better described in a range of scores than in one "precise" number, and generally the teacher and student could agree on this range.
- A final course standing in the form of a percentage score was required by law and could generally be agreed upon once a range was established.

Considering our Hattie book study and the research we'd examined, we felt that an approach similar to Dave Van Bergeyk's might be feasible at our school. We wanted our students to speak about their learning in a way that was similar to how we talk in everyday life. We imagined that this shift might better facilitate understanding the learning goals and what students could do to improve learning after receiving feedback. Our language went through many changes and iterations, and with help from teachers such as Shona Becker, Ben Arcuri, Marnie Mennell, Nick Kast, Troy Stubbert, and Rachel Stubbert, it evolved over time into a usable framework. Each of these teachers sought feedback from their students, seeking a better way for students to evaluate their own learning. You'll notice our framework expanded to include both "teacher speak" and "student lingo" (see Figure 6.3).

We asked students to look for evidence and examples from their own journals, assignments, quizzes, tests, and projects, and present a case for how *they* thought they were doing. *Conversation-based grading* was all about us *sitting beside the student* and letting students talk about their learning. Using an approach similar to the one taken by Dave Van Bergeyk, we developed the mental model shown in Figure 6.4 (p. 150) to guide the conversation. We encouraged students to consider numerous "sources of evidence" when deciding what to self-report.

Figure 6.3

Proficiency Scale with Teacher and Student Language

		"Teacher Speak"	**"Student Lingo"**
Expert	6	Near perfect demonstration of understanding/skill; high confidence; mastery of learning standard	"You could teach this!"
	5	Strong demonstration of understanding/skill; high confidence; slight error involved	"Almost perfect; just one little error!"
Apprentice	4	Good demonstration of understanding/skill; confidence evident; a few errors	"Good understanding, with just a few errors."
	3	Satisfactory demonstration of understanding/basic skills; key concepts are lacking; errors common	"You are on the right track, but understanding is lacking on a key concept."
Novice	2	Basic understanding of key concepts and rudimentary demonstration of basic skills; many errors	"You showed just enough evidence to pass this."
	1	Needs better understanding of key concepts and demonstration of basic skills; many errors	"You have some more learning to do on this outcome or skill."

Source: Courtesy Ben Arcuri, Shona Becker, and Myron Dueck. Used with permission.

As we welcomed students to talk about their own learning and to report on themselves, the results were incredible. We literally saw the assessment process shift from being entirely in the teacher's sphere of influence to being appropriately shared with the student. Although we deliberately did not include behaviors such as attendance, effort, and participation in the grade, we found that, invariably, these factors had a place in the learning conversation. Take the issue of poor attendance, for example. Conversation-based grading helped many students realize that missing classes was negatively affecting their overall understanding of the learning outcomes.

I've come to accept that we will not transform the world of percentages and grading overnight, and it's important to include students in a conversation on when and why we might still use percentages—particularly for high schools and in light of reporting requirements and postsecondary application considerations. In Figure 6.5, Ben Arcuri makes this point clear with his chemistry students. Ben can attach one of three percentage scores to any of the proficiency levels. For instance, a student completing the term or course with a 6 would have 95, 97, or 100 as their posted percentage.

Figure 6.4
Sources of Evidence

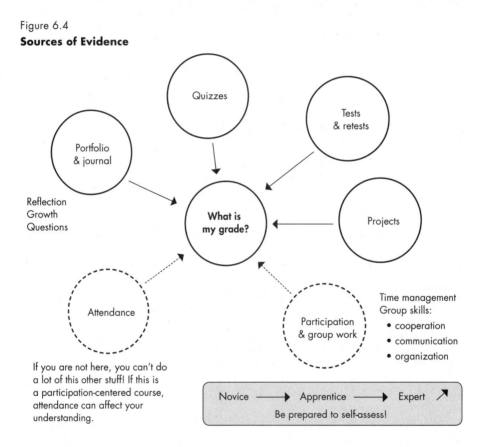

Source: © 2016 Myron Dueck. Used with permission.

Teachers in our pilot study came up with their own self-reporting templates. Figure 6.6 (p. 152) was designed by Shona Becker. She not only included clear learning targets for her students but also allowed them to see the grading scale we were using and self-report on their work habits. Note that Shona decided that for some of the more broad-ranging learning outcomes, three categories was sufficient, whereas the precision of six levels was appropriate for others. It's also important to note that our educational jurisdiction still requires us to report a percentage at the conclusion of the course. Considering this requirement, we have established percentage scores that correlate to each of the proficiency levels.

Figure 6.5

Percentages as Related to Rubric Categories and Levels

Category	Ranking	This section is *only* used at the end of each semester to determine a percentage for your report card.		
Extending	6	95	97	100
Proficient	5	86	90	94
	4	73	80	85
Developing	3	60	66	72
	2	50	56	59
Beginning	1	30	40	45

Source: Courtesy Ben Arcuri. Used with permission.

Marnie Mennell and I created the "Drive-Thru Evaluation" shown in Figure 6.7 (p. 154), so named because the efficient exchange of the student-teacher assessment conversation is reminiscent of that at a drive-thru restaurant—plus, the name fit her Foods & Cafeteria course. After coming up with the tool, we introduced it to students, used it with them, and then entered a codesigning stage where we solicited student feedback and suggestions for design changes and improvements. About every three weeks or so, Marnie gives her students the opportunity to self-report on all aspects of their learning. She gives her students time in class to fill out the forms, then reads them when it's convenient. Marnie can then decide which student responses require a face-to-face conversation.

Inspired by the NFL spider charts, Tristan Mennell and I codesigned the student self-reporting template in Figure 6.8 (p. 155). On this one form, following a cooking project or menu design, students can plot how they believe they are doing on the six wider competencies of the course—taking risks, prototyping, testing, and so on. Once they decide if their work reflected a Sophisticated (S), Complete (C), Partial (P), or Beginning (B) approach to the competency, they plot it on the graph. Once all six tines of the web have a dot, the students can connect the dots and produce an impression of progress. Below the spider chart, students have space to further explain some of their choices for the chart, and the teacher

Figure 6.6
Self-Reporting Template for Learning Goals in Science 10

Name: _____

Learning Goals	Novice		Apprentice		Expert	
	1	2	3	4	5	6
1. I can *pose* questions and *formulate* scientific hypotheses.						
2. I can *plan* a scientific inquiry.						
3. I can safely *conduct* an experiment.						
4. I can *analyze* data.						
5. I can *evaluate* and *reflect* on my inquiry processes.						
6. I can *apply* my data and *explain* societal impact.						
7. I can *communicate* my scientific inquiry.						
8. I can *explain* DNA structure and its function.						
9. I can *explain* the principles of Mendelian genetics.						
10. I can *explain* the impact of mutations in diversity of life.						
11. I can *explain* the impact of natural and artificial selection.						
12. I can *explain* the application of genetics and ethical considerations.						
13. I can *explain* how atoms are rearranged in chemical reactions.						
14. I can *explain* the law of conservation of mass.						
15. I can *explain* the energy change during chemical reactions.						
16. I can *explain* the law of conservation of energy.						
17. I can *explain* the relationship between potential energy and kinetic energy.						
18. I can *explain* the role of thermal energy in a range of scenarios.						
19. I can *explain* energy transformation.						
20. I can *explain* energy production and energy use in the Okanagan.						
21. I can *explain* Aboriginal perspectives on energy.						
22. I can *explain* nuclear sources, technologies, and applications.						
23. I can *explain* how astronomical data is collected.						
24. I can *explain* the stages in the formation of the universe.						

My Letter Grade Assessment:

Learning Category	Classification	Percent (%)		
Expert	6	95	97	100
	5	86	90	94
Apprentice	4	73	80	85
	3	60	66	72
Novice	2	50	56	59
	1	30	40	45

My Work Ethic Assessment:

Work Ethic	Needs Improvement	Satisfactory	Good	Excellent
I hand in all assignments *on time*.				
I come in for extra help when it is needed.				
I am a positive class member and contributor to our learning environment.				
I arrive to class on time and with all necessary supplies.				
I ask questions and push the boundaries of my understanding.				

Source: Courtesy Shona Becker, Summerland Secondary School, British Columbia, Canada. Used with permission.

has room to respond. The "overall impression" section can be filled out solely by the teacher, or by the teacher in consultation with the student. To access other self-reporting templates and examples from various curricular areas, visit the Resources and Tools section of www.myrondueck.com.

For the filming of the video series titled *Ask Them* (ASCD, 2019), I had a conversation with John Hattie in Melbourne, Australia. He commented on the underlying power of student self-assessment:

> When you are involved, and you have to help explain it … it becomes yours, and you know, who's in a better position to do that than the student?

I'm confident that our efforts around student self-reporting are finally placing students in the driver's seat.

Figure 6.7
Drive-Thru Evaluation

Name: _____   Date: _____

Drive-Thru Evaluation	1	2	3	Potential Grade:

Grade 9/10   Foods & Nutrition

"I am a   NOVICE   APPRENTICE   EXPERT   in Foods/Nutrition."

6	Top
5	
4	Middle
3	
2	Crisper
1	

Top Shelf

Middle Shelf

Crisper

Areas to improve:
☐ Cleanup
☐ Group work—tasks, communication, etc.
☐ Journal—depth
☐ Journal—completion
☐ Organization—kitchen
☐ Organization—portfolio
☐ Quizzes (study)
☐ Safety—behavior
☐ Safety—food safety and sanitation
☐ Timing
☐ Initiation/effort

Notes:

Source: Courtesy Marnie Mennell and Myron Dueck. Used with permission.

Figure 6.8
Cafeteria Spider Chart

Name: _____   Date: _____

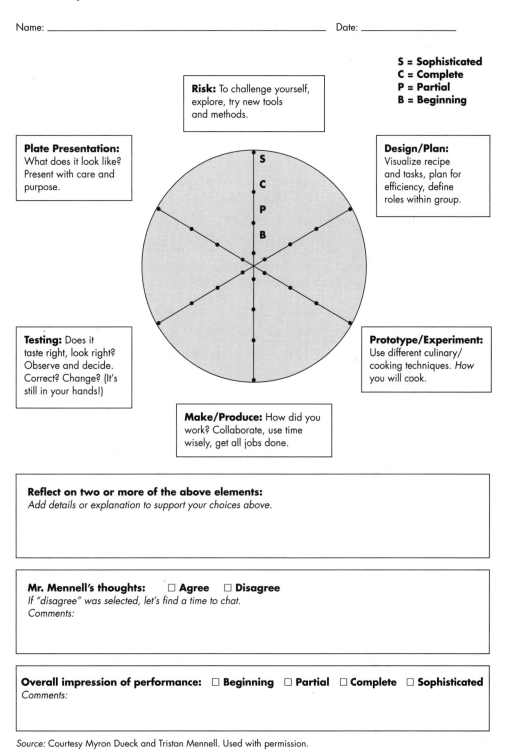

S = Sophisticated
C = Complete
P = Partial
B = Beginning

Risk: To challenge yourself, explore, try new tools and methods.

Plate Presentation: What does it look like? Present with care and purpose.

Design/Plan: Visualize recipe and tasks, plan for efficiency, define roles within group.

Testing: Does it taste right, look right? Observe and decide. Correct? Change? (It's still in your hands!)

Prototype/Experiment: Use different culinary/cooking techniques. *How* you will cook.

Make/Produce: How did you work? Collaborate, use time wisely, get all jobs done.

Reflect on two or more of the above elements:
Add details or explanation to support your choices above.

Mr. Mennell's thoughts: ☐ **Agree**   ☐ **Disagree**
If "disagree" was selected, let's find a time to chat.
Comments:

Overall impression of performance: ☐ **Beginning**   ☐ **Partial**   ☐ **Complete**   ☐ **Sophisticated**
Comments:

Source: Courtesy Myron Dueck and Tristan Mennell. Used with permission.

Getting Students to Embrace— and Talk About—Challenges

Having just returned from a conference in Melbourne, I'd been telling one of our math teachers, Paige Mullins, about a few interesting ideas I'd picked up while I was there. I wouldn't fault members of my staff if they cringed a little when I'd go to an international conference, as I'd come back all fired up about something new. I could imagine comments like, "He's back, everyone! Look out! Remember, just let him rant for a few days about the latest thing in education, and he'll soon calm down." Predictably, the first morning back I headed straight to Paige's classroom and probably talked far too excitedly about "desirable difficulties" and the impacts this idea could have on students who struggle in math. I shared Bjork and Bjork's (2014) definition. Here's a reminder from Chapter 4:

> Desirable difficulties, versus the array of undesirable difficulties, are desirable because they trigger encoding and retrieval processes that support learning, comprehension, and remembering. (p. 58)

Paige and I had been discussing how we might better support students who struggle in math, and specifically how we might increase resiliency. "Desirable difficulties" certainly applied to this conversation. We imagined how embracing challenges might change some students' perception of math and the inherent frustrations they experience.

Later that evening, Paige read more on Bjork and Bjork's work, and the following day we met again to discuss the concept. Paige admitted that in recent months she'd thought a lot about students' difficulties in math and how we might get them to recognize and articulate their struggles. "Desirable difficulties" provided a window through which students could approach challenges not from a deficit position, but rather as a tool to increase learning. She wondered aloud if getting students to journal in math might be a way to encourage this learning conversation. By the end of the week, we'd concocted a plan. I would visit her Foundations and Pre-Calculus Math class to help introduce the topic of "desirable difficulties," and immediately after, she would launch a weekly journaling routine.

During our introduction to her students, we branched well outside math to look at examples of risk taking. First, we looked at the Beatles, and how, despite their enormous success in the mid-1960s, they constantly dabbled with new ideas and directions, often forging ahead despite uncertainty. I played for them a clip from *Eight Days a Week: The Touring Years of the Beatles,* in which George Harrison states, "We were nervous with each step we went up the ladder—we didn't realize what was to come" (Howard, 2016). We explored how the Beatles continued to change their musical style, and how doing so resulted in an incredible transformation from 1964 to 1969. As a class, we discussed how risk may have been an essential ingredient in the Fab Four becoming arguably one of the greatest bands ever.

We also looked at Apple's creator, Steve Jobs, and his quote concerning artists such as Bob Dylan. Jobs once remarked,

> It always occurs to them at some point that they can do this one thing for the rest of their lives, and they can be really successful to the outside world but not really be successful to themselves. That's the moment that an artist really decides who he or she is. If they keep on risking failure, they're still artists. (Beahm, 2011, p. 91)

We speculated that Apple's enormous success was likely the result of tackling challenges, taking risks in the ever-changing tech space.

Next, Paige and I asked students to remember a time when a mistake or difficulty they personally experienced resulted in deeper learning. First in pairs and then as a class, students shared mistakes and pitfalls they'd experienced at work, during a basketball game, while snowboarding, and in other real-life examples. After collectively establishing the value of struggle *outside* school, we shifted the conversation to *inside* school. We reminded students that learning math comes with risk, and if learning is our ultimate goal, then *difficulties can be desirable*.

We concluded our conversation with her class by presenting Bjork and Bjork's (2014) four suggestions on how we can create desirable difficulties:

1. Vary the conditions of practice rather than keeping them constant and predictable.
2. Space study sessions on a given topic over time rather than massing or cramming.
3. Interleave instruction on separate topics rather than grouping or "blocking."
4. Use tests as learning events.

For the remainder of the course, Paige and her class revisited the theme of desirable difficulties through a weekly journal. The prompts included the following:

- What is a "desirable difficulty" you've experienced this week in math? What made it a desirable difficulty?
- How might you know when you have truly learned something, as opposed to just performing well on a test or quiz?

Students were remarkably candid in their discussion around these ideas. It was also interesting to see some of Bjork and Bjork's four suggestions represented in their responses.

One student wrote about learning by experiencing struggles and how being able to demonstrate his learning in different situations proved he was broadening his understanding. Another student wrote about learning through testing, and how being assessed over time and in multiple situations deepens her understanding. Of particular interest was a student who journaled about being able to demonstrate the understanding of a concept in the middle of learning something new. He noted that weeks had passed since covering the first topic, yet he still could retrieve the information when he most needed it. This observation reflects what Bjork and Bjork spoke of around spacing and interleaving topics.

Before this journaling exercise in Paige's class, I'd never have imagined how student voice and self-assessment could be used to venture this deep into the learning conversation. Based on our experience, I encourage teachers to delve into important learning questions *with* their students. I suspect that if we took Hattie's advice and just stopped more often to ask our students *about their learning*, we could use this insight to adapt our classroom routines. For instance, Paige was wondering about the effectiveness of her students' test preparation, so she crafted the following weekly journal prompt: "Explain what study strategies worked/ didn't work for a test you've recently written." One student replied as follows:

> I think that doing the homework questions from earlier learning targets was helpful later on so that I can retain the information. I think I should work on homework on a more stretched period of time instead of doing it in one night then forgetting the next week.

Paige considered this student's voice as reinforcing Bjork's research, but it also led her to question her own homework routines and expectations. Citing the above journal entry, Paige e-mailed me the following reflection:

> I thought it was great evidence to support what the research has said about retention and the recall of information. It's also interesting when you think about how many of us teachers do homework checks and expect everything completed for the next day. Is there really a point if they haven't had the time to retain? (personal communication, May 24, 2018)

Josh Eastwood, the IB math teacher mentioned in Chapter 4, has also been incorporating the topic of desirable difficulties into his classroom dialogue. He e-mailed me the following update:

> I've applied [Bjork's] research in my class by interleaving instruction and using tests as study events. I have actually revamped your test/retest model by testing

the students approximately every seven days, and then counting one out of every two. The tests have similar material but slightly different emphasis, and the kids have been enjoying it. I have also started quizzing every three days and instituted a system where the first quiz doesn't count, the second one does. The kids seem to be enjoying that as well.

The interleaving instruction has been fun. The course I am teaching has three major units (Calculus, Vectors, and Statistics), and I have been teaching these units by starting with one, then leaving and going to the next, then returning, and going to the next. It has been a fun exercise in long-term retention, and the kids have been responding. I have given them a survey and asked them to rate their experience as part of that, and overall, they are giving it 4/5 stars, so I'm encouraged. (personal communication, October 25, 2018)

Josh polled his students to get their opinions on a few changes he has made to his classroom routines. Here's a sampling of their responses:

I find I don't get frustrated if I do not understand it immediately, as I will come back to it and have time to get a firm foundation.

I've been using the studying tool of studying in multiple places randomly and it's working well.

It's helpful that I am practicing the material every so often. This is more effective than learning and practicing all at once.

Self-Reporting of Behaviors, Effort, and Work Habits

Many reporting processes, from report cards to parent-teacher interviews, involve some measure of *how* students arrived at their academic standing. We can certainly attempt to quantify effort, participation, and work habits, but I fear that over my classroom career I've failed to do so in an accurate and effective way. Effort is particularly interesting, as it's a very hard thing to observe, let alone measure. I think I was fairly naïve for much of my career, posting my *impression* of a student's effort to their report card. I now realize I cannot possibly determine the amount of effort being exerted by another human being; rather, I can only surmise or guess based on the behaviors I observe. Perhaps our attempts to report on effort and work habits would be far more effective—and accurate—if we actually asked the student.

I approached a grade 12 Summerland Secondary student, Xavier, and asked him if he'd be willing to share some of his opinions on student self-reporting. Although he seemed to me to be a fairly quiet student, often avoiding the limelight, he quickly agreed to the interview. He was incredibly candid on the topic of reporting "effort" and who should be responsible for reporting it: "Asking the student gives the teacher an understanding of what the student thinks about their work, whether they're putting in full effort or what the student thinks they can work on."

Later in the interview Xavier spoke of a reporting experience that had occurred years earlier. I was reminded of how personal reporting can be, as Xavier had no difficulty recalling the event. The situation involved him getting an *N* on his work habit score, which at our school represented "Needs Improvement." Here's what he told me:

> I remember I got an *N* on my report card, but, like, my buddy and I came in at lunch and after school for extra help. I think I got a mark that was barely passing, but what I really remember is that *N*. I guess the teacher thought I wasn't trying, but the thing is she never asked me. She never asked my part—why I wasn't putting in full effort, why I wasn't trying—but for my part I was. I was putting in full effort; it just wasn't paying off.
>
> You want to know how it is? I can have a report that says I'm putting in effort when really I'm not. Other times I'm putting in a lot of effort, maybe behind the scenes or whatever, but I'm told I'm not putting in effort. Why don't they just ask my opinion? (personal communication, May 9, 2018)

As I recorded his account, my mind drifted back over decades of my own reporting decisions—how I would classify student effort and participation based on *my perception* of the situation. I wondered just how often I had completely misinterpreted whether a student was trying or not. Xavier concluded his interview by saying, "I think it would be important to ask where I place myself, how I think I'm doing, what I think my mark should be."

I couldn't agree more. Thankfully, we're seeing more and more examples of how teachers are including student voice and self-assessment for nonacademic measures such as effort, participation, and work habits. The following are a few examples.

Grade 2 Math Self-Evaluation

Our district, through the work of Shona Becker, the Numeracy Helping Teacher at the time, sought to invite students to reflect on their learning goals. We've only just begun this work, but the template in Figure 6.9 gives an idea of how this information could be gathered and the data represented. You'll see that we're trying to devise a way to provide students with graphics, such as a bar chart, so that they can visualize how they are doing in different areas.

Figure 6.9
Math Grade 2 Report Summary

Math Grade 2

Learning Goals Self-Evaluation   Name: _____

Big Ideas:
1. **Numbers to 100** represent quantities that can be **decomposed into 10s and 1s.**
2. Development of computational fluency in **addition and subtraction with numbers to 100** requires an understanding of place value.
3. The regular change in **increasing patterns** can be identified and used to make generalizations.
4. **Objects and shapes have attributes** that can be described, measured, and compared.
5. **Concrete items** can be represented, compared, and interpreted pictorially in a graph.

Learning Goals	Fully Meeting	Meeting	Approaching	Curricular Competency (Put "X" where you are.)
1. I can use numbers 1–100.				**Reasoning** *I can estimate solutions.*
2. I can group numbers in groups of 25.				Strong To work on ◀———————————————▶
3. I can communicate and identify repeating patterns.				
4. I can add numbers to 100.				**Understanding** *I solve problems using multiple strategies.*
5. I can subtract numbers to 100.				Strong To work on ◀———————————————▶
6. I can symbolically show equality and inequality.				
7. I can demonstrate how to measure objects in metric units.				**Communication** *I can justify my thinking.*
8. I can compare 2D shapes.				Strong To work on ◀———————————————▶
9. I can compare 3D shapes.				
10. I can use the language of probability (*likely, unlikely*).				**Reflection** *I reflect on my learning.*
11. I can create different types of graphs.				Strong To work on ◀———————————————▶
12. I can demonstrate numerous ways (using coins) to make $1.00.				

(continued)

Figure 6.9—*(continued)*
Math Grade 2 Report Summary

Your Letter Grade Assessment: Create a **bar chart** of the above topics to visualize the trend in your overall achievement.

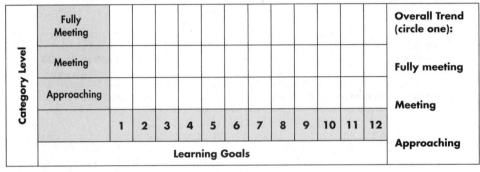

Source: Courtesy Shona Becker. Used with permission.

Secondary Student Self-Evaluation

Ben Arcuri developed a template that allows his senior chemistry students to do exactly what Xavier suggests—report on their own effort and behaviors (see Figure 6.10). On the form, the introduction underscores the importance of self-reflection and the value of monitoring one's own learning. Statements divided into sections for Personal Responsibility, Self-Regulation, Classroom Responsibility, Collaborative Actions, and Communication Skills allow students to self-assess by choosing from four options for each statement: *E* (Excellent), *G* (Good), *S* (Satisfactory), or *N* (Needs Improvement). The last section invites students to highlight two areas they wish to focus on for personal growth.

A strong message in this approach is that students control their own actions and have a voice in reporting them. Another strong theme is student empowerment. For example, in response to frustrations over cell phone use in class, Ben considered banning the devices. Upon further reflection, however, he realized that what he really wanted was for his students to learn to manage and regulate their own digital distractions. As Ben commented, "No one's going to ban their phones in university—they better learn to control this while they're in high school" (personal communication, January 2, 2020). A big step in shifting this responsibility to the student was including the following statement on the Self-Regulation portion of the form: "I only use my cell phone for school-based work."

The self-evaluation form can be given to students in a paper version or as a writable PDF that can then be e-mailed to parents. In his own work with other educators, Ben encourages them to consider customizing this template to suit

Figure 6.10

Student Self-Evaluation: Responsibility, Regulation, and Collaboration

Name: _____ Date: _____

A valuable aspect of the learning process involves students reflecting on their own actions and behaviors. To be successful lifelong learners, we all need to develop the ability to monitor, evaluate, and know what to do to improve our own outcomes. Please read the following list of descriptions and reflect on your behaviors, attitudes, and actions. Report on yourself as Excellent (E), Good (G), Satisfactory (S), or Needs Improvement (N).

General Category	Specific Elements	E	G	S	N
Personal Responsibility	I watch all suggested videos and complete the accompanying activities (e.g., Edpuzzle).	☐	☐	☐	☐
	I prepare for all quizzes and tests.	☐	☐	☐	☐
	I come to class with all necessary supplies.	☐	☐	☐	☐
	I arrive to class on time, ready to participate in learning activities.	☐	☐	☐	☐
	I stay on task during group and individual activities.	☐	☐	☐	☐
	I complete all assignments, labs, and projects on time.	☐	☐	☐	☐
		E	**G**	**S**	**N**
Self-Regulation	I can take ownership of my goals, learning, and behavior.	☐	☐	☐	☐
	I can solve most problems myself and can identify when to ask for help.	☐	☐	☐	☐
	I can persevere with challenging tasks—I try to embrace *desirable difficulties!*	☐	☐	☐	☐
	I take responsibility to be actively engaged in the lesson and class discussion.	☐	☐	☐	☐
		E	**G**	**S**	**N**
Classroom & Social Responsibility	I am focused and engaged during classroom discussions and activities.	☐	☐	☐	☐
	I encourage others and contribute to activities in a positive way.	☐	☐	☐	☐
	I do my part to keep the classroom safe, clean, and healthy.	☐	☐	☐	☐

(continued)

Figure 6.10—(continued)

Student Self-Evaluation: Responsibility, Regulation, and Collaboration

		E	G	S	N
Collaboration	I can work with others to achieve a common goal.	☐	☐	☐	☐
	I am kind to others, can work or participate cooperatively, and can build relationships with any of my fellow learners.	☐	☐	☐	☐
	I make contributions to my group and help others with what they are working on.	☐	☐	☐	☐
	I can identify when others need support and provide it.	☐	☐	☐	☐
My goal for this week/term:	Reflection... how did it go?				

Source: Courtesy Ben Arcuri. Used with permission.

their needs. For example, teachers might include prompts such as "I review for each requiz," "I watch all flip videos to prepare for class," or "I actively listen to my classmates when it is their turn to speak."

Self-Assessment Report Card Comments

Barry Morhart teaches social studies and planning at Similkameen Secondary School in Keremeos, British Columbia. When it's time to report on student work habits and participation, Barry invites his students to fill out a template titled "Student Self-Assessment Report Card Comments." It has the following four prompts:

1. Describe or explain your academic strengths in this class.
2. Describe or explain any areas in which you could improve.
3. Describe or explain how you could be supported in your learning.
4. Provide a brief description of your work habits and/or behavior in this class.

To help his students understand the prompts, as well as to improve the quality of the responses, Barry facilitates a class discussion *before* students fill out the template. They cover the four questions, their meaning, and possible examples students could draw on for their responses. Barry finds the student reports to be accurate, honest, and candid. In many cases, he uses a student's actual words on the reporting document and believes them to be more effective than if he had written his own version. For example, one student answered the question about work habits as follows: "I do most of my work, but the bottom line is I goof off a lot. But I'm improving in a lot of things." According to Barry,

> Students say things on their self-report that I cannot say. For instance, I would never comment on a formal report card that a student may "goof off a lot," but when I include that as the student's own words, it seems to resonate with the parents —it's more authentic. (personal communication, November 4, 2019)

Asking Students to Report on What's Not Obvious

Perhaps even more powerful than using student terminology for things we can see is asking students to self-report on things we can't. Barry cited a student who self-reported that she was shy in large-group situations, but not so much in small groups. She also commented that this was an area of her schooling life that she continues to work on. Another student self-reported that he needed to ask the teacher for more assistance and reduce the number of his "abrasive" comments toward others. This type of reporting, what Tolisano and Hale (2018) refer to as "below the surface" learning, is incredibly powerful. For too long we have focused the bulk of our reporting on what everyone can see—products such as projects, essays, and tests. Schools are just beginning to harness the power of allowing students to self-report what is not readily observable.

Influenced further by the work of Tolisano and Hale, our district is looking at structures that will deliberately provide students the opportunity to delve into reporting "below the surface" learning. The student-friendly template in Figure 6.11 (p. 166) can be used in paper or digital form. We were purposeful in letting the student describe elements that were obvious, but we then provided space for reporting the unseen. Note the inclusion of the core competencies that are required for students to self-report. I would encourage schools and districts to include desired or required self-reporting cues in this section.

A Final Word on Student Self-Reporting

Back to Jarvis Landry and the 2014 draft. Why was Carter Bryant one of few reporters to predict that Landry would be an NFL success? Did he have a stash of

Figure 6.11
My Learning: Above and Below the Surface

Name: _____

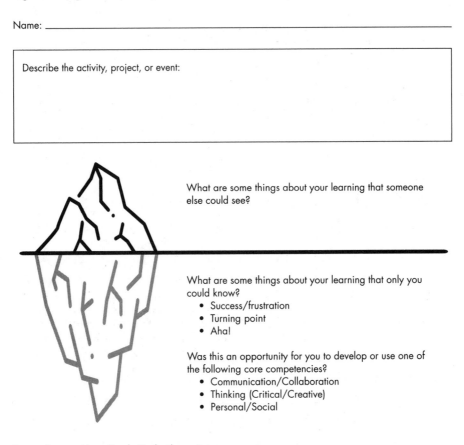

Describe the activity, project, or event:

What are some things about your learning that someone else could see?

What are some things about your learning that only you could know?
- Success/frustration
- Turning point
- Aha!

Was this an opportunity for you to develop or use one of the following core competencies?
- Communication/Collaboration
- Thinking (Critical/Creative)
- Personal/Social

Source: Courtesy Myron Dueck. Used with permission.

secret stats? Did he have a crystal ball? Was he clairvoyant? The more I thought about it, the more mystified I was by his isolated accuracy. Fed up with wondering, I decided to request an interview, and he readily agreed. On February 6, 2020, we chatted for more than an hour.

Bryant, an LSU alumnus like Landry, offered some context and confirmed a number of the things we've been discussing about self-reporting and the importance of looking beyond the statistics. Here's some of our conversation:

Carter: You know, I watched a game between LSU and Arkansas back in 2013, when Landry was a receiver at LSU. And while it's not a game that really mattered in the standings, and the stats from the game don't jump out at you, it confirmed for me that Landry was going to be an NFL Pro Bowler one day.

Myron: How did that single game convince you?

Carter: There were a few interesting things going on. It was a game near the end of the season, and a number of key players for LSU were sitting out, getting ready for the NFL draft.

Myron: Why were they sitting out? I don't understand.

Carter: Near the end of the season, with the NFL Combine tryouts coming up, some players don't want to risk an injury, so they sit out the game. Interestingly, even though he could've sat out, Jarvis Landry opted to play against Arkansas. Near the end of the game, with LSU's starting quarterback out with an injury and losing to the much lower seeded Arkansas, Landry made the most amazing catch I've ever seen, and likely ever will see. I mean, it was ridiculous. He reached around the back of the opposing player and literally caught the ball while pressing it against the other player's back. Seriously, there's a lot of people in football I've personally spoken to who say that's the best catch they ever saw. Then in the last minutes of the game, LSU completed a 99-yard drive to win, culminating in a play suggested by Landry, but one in which he didn't even get the ball! It was thrown to another player. In that moment Landry was not only a pure genius, but selfless.

Myron: Well, Carter, I guess I'm still confused. We could go back and look at that memorable catch, pore over the stats, be amazed by a 99-yard drive—but I'm still wondering how *you* were the only writer at the time predicting Landry's success in the NFL. In fact, in your December 2013 *Bleacher Report* article, summarizing the Arkansas game, you wrote, "If Arkansas was the last game Landry were to ever play in Tiger Stadium, it would be a fitting end to a stellar LSU career. He is ready to be a solid contributor on Sundays at the next level." Again, you are predicting him not only to make the pros, but to be successful there. That's what baffles me.

Carter: You know, Myron, here's the thing. There's a lot about Jarvis Landry that will not be shown in any statistics. He plays with a chip on his shoulder; he's more than just an athlete; he processes information incredibly fast—you can't measure those things. Only when you talk to these types of players do you appreciate things that 40-yard-dash statistics will never reveal: character, competitiveness, work ethic, or "Is he the kind of person I'd want to be around?" These things transcend statistics. In football, you can have the greatest arm or run the fastest 40-yard dash, but truthfully, what will matter most are the things you can't see.

Bryant went on to talk about the changing face of pro football—namely, how teams are expanding the nature and role of the coaching staff. Teams now have people looking beyond the statistics, trying to find and identify the next Tom Brady or Jarvis Landry.

Perhaps it's a similar predicament we find in our schools. We have lots of statistics and data—from test scores to GPAs—yet there's so much more to our students than the numbers. Perhaps our challenge is to take the advice of John Hattie and *make space for our students to tell us what's going on.* And perhaps paradoxically, by listening to our students, we'll find out more about ourselves as educators. As Hattie contends, as we listen to our students tell us what they understand, we are receiving the purest form of feedback—*for the teacher* (ASCD, 2019).

CONCLUSION

Of the many stories in Thomas Guskey's book *Benjamin S. Bloom: Portraits of an Educator* (2012), one in particular resonates with me. Elliot Eisner, former professor emeritus of education and art at Stanford University, and a student of Bloom's, recalls a powerful moment during one of his classes at the University of Chicago. After much preparation, it came time for Eisner to present in front of his peers the findings from pilot studies that would lead to his dissertation research. Eisner's data looked at interrater reliability among judges grading the artwork of 10- and 11-year-old students. Writes Eisner, "Despite my best efforts, the interrater reliability correlation coefficients turned out to be only .40 to .50—a point of some embarrassment to me" (Eisner, 2012, p. 14). In plain English, this meant that the "degree of relationship" among the judges' ratings was well below what most measurement people would find acceptable. Eisner was surrounded by aspiring educational measurement specialists, and a few of these students began to snicker. Noticing this, Bloom seized the opportunity to lead a discussion around the *complexity* of these types of judgments and the *purpose* of measurement. Eisner (2012) recounts two powerful lessons he learned that day:

> The first is the importance of supporting students in difficult times. Ben believed that nothing positive was ever gained by embarrassing a student. Embarrassment, he insisted, was a poor motivator and a worse teacher. The second lesson is the

value of always putting statistics in context. How one interprets a set of numbers depends not only on matters of measurement but also on the characteristics of the situation from which those numbers are derived. Both are lessons I never forgot. (p. 15)

As Guskey points out, "Bloom used what happened to help the other students understand that how well you measure something is important, but not nearly as important as what you are measuring and why you're measuring it" (personal communication, May 20, 2020). For most of my teaching career, I've graded tests, compiled scores, and filled out countless report cards. As Guskey challenges us to pause and think deeply about what we are measuring and why, I've only begun to appreciate the array of things that assessment data can reveal; next steps for students and my own effectiveness are just two of many.

The further we go down the path of engaging in authentic assessment *with* our students, the more I'm convinced that it's actually not that hard. That said, it does require a paradigm shift. When Steve Jobs asked John Sculley, "Do you want to sell sugar water for the rest of your life? Or do you want to come with me and change the world?" he probably jarred Sculley into thinking about his job differently. I suspect Sculley experienced a paradigm shift.

My first paradigm shift occurred about 10 years ago, when I came to a few critical conclusions that greatly affected how I designed the classroom learning environment for my students. I realized that although I *cannot* control the home environments of my students, I *can* control the design of our homework routines and expectations. Although I *cannot* control the present socioeconomic realities of my students, I *can* build assessment and grading structures that take into account diversity, equity, and fairness. Although I *cannot* control the rate at which different students learn and understand, I *can* design ongoing assessment structures that reflect the fluidity of learning. Last, although I *cannot* control the interactions that my students have with other adults, I *can* certainly control how I approach my interactions with them. I wrote extensively on this paradigm shift in my 2014 book, *Grading Smarter, Not Harder*. In the years since, however, I've realized that I have more work to do in changing my grading, assessment, and reporting systems. A piece was missing. I needed to ask the people who were in the best position to plan, engage in, assess, and report their own learning—my students! This has been my second paradigm shift.

In her book *The Gift of Failure*, Jessica Lahey (2015) contends that we must give students a voice. She writes, "From the very first day of kindergarten, it is vital that children learn to advocate for themselves" (p. 198). Lahey goes on to suggest that the level of responsibility should increase with age:

As children move into middle school, students should be responsible for dealing with the details of the education and scheduling, including planned absence forms, permission forms, and deadlines. Certainly, when students are in high school they should be completely in charge of their schedules and the requisite school obligations and details. (p. 199)

At first, I was a touch horrified by some of Lahey's suggestions, but the more I've adopted them in my own parenting, the better I've been feeling about some of my decision making. Sloane is in grade 9 this year, and Elijah in grade 11, and I've been trying to be less of a "helicopter parent." It's time for them to take more responsibility, make mistakes, and learn from those experiences. Recently Sloane called me in a panic and asked me to bring her gym clothes to her at school. She had forgotten them at home—again. I normally would've jumped in the truck and raced the clothing to her—confirming my superman status as a dad. Instead, leaning on Lahey's advice, I said, "That's too bad, Sloane. Perhaps you should start packing up your stuff the night before or make that checklist we've been talking about. In any event, I'm writing at the moment, and I'm sure you'll figure out a solution. You have your friends there to help if needed. See you when you get home!"

Sloane is not a big Jessica Lahey fan. (For the record, however, either Sloane has not forgotten anything since, or she has learned to navigate her own challenges.)

The more I think about it, Lahey's advice for parents should not be dissimilar from how we might navigate our paradigm shift in assessment. It's time our students had more of a voice, more control, more agency. As Celeste Kidd argues, we shape our expectations of our environment based on our past experiences, and these expectations will greatly affect our behavior (personal communication, December 11, 2018). If Sloane and Elijah's life experiences teach them that I will always be there to control the situation, pick them up when they fall, or make sure they avoid risks altogether, then they will likely behave accordingly. If our students continue to expect a school environment in which the realm of assessment is controlled solely by the teacher, they will continue to act as complacent passengers in the coverage of curriculum, never pilots of their own learning journey.

Thankfully, I do not feel alone on this second paradigm shift. Based on my work in my own school district and in districts and schools around the world—such as Roseville City School District in California and the American School Foundation of Monterrey in Mexico—I am seeing evidence that student empowerment in assessment is emerging as a powerful force in education.

I am most encouraged by receiving e-mails from the teachers who are experiencing these changes in the classroom, with their students, on a day-to-day basis. One such e-mail was from Mark Osborn, a middle school math teacher at ASFM.

Mark wrote about the trepidation he felt when his school moved away from traditional number grades to the new four-word descriptor grading system described in Chapter 5. He recalled feeling especially nervous handing back the first formative assessment of the term, as he believed his students were focused on the "numeric grade." Mark made one last attempt to cushion the blow by explaining that the true purpose of feedback was not a number but, rather, to know where students are in the learning progression and identify what they need to move forward in their learning.

It turned out that Mark's nervousness may have been misplaced. He didn't receive pushback; instead, he witnessed his students reading over his comments and asking a few clarifying questions. One student was an exception, however. Mark writes:

> After class, one of my students came up to see me. He proceeded to tell me that he understood the feedback I had provided him and the reason he had not been given a grade. However, he was curious about what grade he would have received if it had been graded. I told him that I would be happy to answer his question, but first I would like him to self-assess his grade. I instructed him to take the feedback and apply it to the assessment rubric and determine which indicators he had successfully showed evidence of. I asked him to come see me the next day and share with me what he discovered.
>
> The next morning, the student came in to see me before school. He told me that he had completed the self-assessment and thought that he was at the "Approaching" level. I asked him why he thought that, and he explained to me what he had done well and what content/skills he was missing to be at the "Meeting" level. He understood what he had to do to reach the "Meeting" level.
>
> In that moment, I saw before me a student who clearly understood where he was in the learning progression and what he needed to do to move forward. I truly believe that this process was powerful for both of us. (personal communication, October 1, 2019)

It's clear that Mark is also experiencing a paradigm shift. He's trying a new four-point scale in math. He's echoing Hattie's contention that the feedback he gives students is also feedback about his teaching. He's recognizing that it's through *progress* that we all achieve. He's building rubrics with clear objectives. He's handing back assignments to students without a grade. He's nervous.

Earlier, we discussed Michael Jordan's glowing review of failure and the role it has played in making him arguably the greatest basketball player of all time. Like Brady of the NFL, it's unlikely that Jordan's list of records will ever be matched. For example, he holds the NBA record for most consecutive games scoring in the double digits: 866 (Carley, 2009). Yes, that's right, 866 games *in a row!* In his career of more than 1,000 games, he averaged just over 30 points per game. It's little wonder he's been called "Superman." Along the road to six NBA championships, it would be safe to say that Jordan learned a thing or two about being nervous. On this topic, Jordan is widely quoted as commenting, "Being nervous isn't bad. It just means something important is happening."

Like every teacher I've mentioned in this book, I'd argue Mark is embarking on something important. Assessment is the lifeblood of learning, and it's time we gave students more control. As we hand over the joystick to our students, we can take solace in Amelia Earhart's adage, "There's more to life than being a passenger."

Speaking of being a passenger, back in the days when I occasionally found myself in a crowded elevator, I would look up at the ceiling, using the quiet, slightly uncomfortable moments to think. And every so often, I'd think about my purpose as an educator, a parent, a learner—you might say that I'd use elevator rides to continually hone my elevator pitch. As O'Reilly (2017) argues, a 30-second ride between floors should be enough time to summarize my purpose for assessment. Here's where it sits currently:

> In every aspect of assessment, we will engage and empower the student by offering opportunities for student voice, choice, self-assessment, and self-reporting.

This is my floor. See you next time.

REFERENCES

Alaska Arts Standards. (n.d.). *Dance: Artistic process; Create*. Retrieved from https://education
.alaska.gov/akstandards/Arts.pdf?v=2

Allain, R. (2012, November 12). Olympic physics: Diving and the moment of inertia. *Wired*.
Retrieved from https://www.wired.com/2012/08/diving-and-the-moment-of-inertia/

Arthur, C. (2014). *Digital wars: Apple, Google, Microsoft and the battle for the internet*. London: Kogan Page.

ASCD. (2019). *Ask them* [Video series]. Alexandria, VA: ASCD.

ASCD. (n.d.). *Smarter assessment in the secondary classroom* [Video]. Alexandria, VA: ASCD.

"Assess." (n.d.). In *Online etymology dictionary*. Retrieved from https://www.etymonline.com/
word/assess

Baseball-Reference.com. (n.d.). Retrieved from https://www.baseball-reference.com/leaders/
batting_avg_career.shtml

Beahm, G. (Ed.). (2011). *I, Steve: Steve Jobs in his own words*. Chicago: Agate Publishing.

Bennett, S., & Mulgrew, A. (2013). *Building better rubrics*. Edmonton, AB: Alberta Assessment
Consortium.

Bjork, R. A., & Bjork, E. L. (1992). A new theory of disuse and an old theory of stimulus fluctuation. In A. F. Healy, S. M. Kosslyn, & R. M. Shiffrin (Eds.), *Essays in honor of William K. Estes; Vol. 2: From learning processes to cognitive processes* (pp. 35–67). Hillsdale, NJ: Erlbaum.

Bjork, R. A., & Bjork, E. L. (2014). Making things hard on yourself, but in a good way: Creating desirable difficulties to enhance learning. In M. A. Gernsbacher & J. R. Pomerantz (Eds.), *Psychology and the real world: Essays illustrating fundamental contributions to society* (2nd ed., pp. 59–68). New York: Worth Publishers.

Breech, J. (2015). *LOOK: Tom Brady was really, really bad at the NFL combine in 2000.* Retrieved from https://www.cbssports.com/nfl/news/look-tom-brady-was-really-really-bad-at-the-nfl-combine-in-2000/

British Columbia Ministry of Education. (2019). *Draft K–9 student reporting policy (2019): Handbook for piloting schools and districts.* Retrieved from https://curriculum.gov.bc.ca/sites/curriculum.gov.bc.ca/files/student-reporting-policy-pilot-handbook.pdf

Brookhart, S. (2013). *How to create and use rubrics for formative assessment and grading.* Alexandria, VA: ASCD.

Brown, G. T. L. (2011). Self-regulation of assessment beliefs and attitudes: A review of the Students' Conceptions of Assessment inventory. *Educational Psychology, 31*(6), 731–748.

Brown, G. T. L., & Hattie, J. (2012). The benefits of regular standardized assessment in childhood education: Guiding improved instruction and learning. In S. Suggate & E. Reese (Eds.), *Contemporary debates in child development and education* (pp. 287–292). New York: Routledge.

Brown, G. T. L., Peterson, E. R., & Irving, S. E. (2009). Beliefs that make a difference: Adaptive and maladaptive self-regulation in students' conceptions of assessment. In D. M. McInerney, G. T. L. Brown, & G. A. D. Liem (Eds.), *Student perspectives on assessment: What students can tell us about assessment for learning* (pp. 159–186). Charlotte, NC: Information Age Publishing.

Brownell, M. D., Nickel, N. C., Chateau, D., Martens, P. J., Taylor, C., Crockett, L., et al. (2015). Long-term benefits of full-day kindergarten: A longitudinal population-based study. *Early Child Development and Care, 185*(2), 291–316.

Bruton, M. (2017). The top 10 quarterbacks of all time. *Bleacher Report.* Retrieved from https://bleacherreport.com/articles/2726739-the-top-10-quarterbacks-of-all-time#slide0

Bryant, C. (2014). LSU football: Jarvis Landry is more than his NFL combine performance. *Bleacher Report.* Retrieved from https://bleacherreport.com/articles/1971112-lsu-football-jarvis-landry-is-more-than-his-nfl-combine-performance

Calarco, J. M. (2018, June 1). Why rich kids are so good at the marshmallow test. *The Atlantic.* Retrieved from https://www.theatlantic.com/family/archive/2018/06/marshmallow-test/561779/

Canadian Wood Council (CWC). (n.d.). *Visual grading of dimension lumber.* Retrieved from http://cwc.ca/how-to-build-with-wood/wood-products/lumber/grades/

Carley, M. (2009). Four reasons Michael Jordan is, and will be, the greatest ever. *Bleacher Report.* Retrieved from https://bleacherreport.com/articles/153659-4-reasons-why-michael-jordan-still-is-and-will-be-the-greatest-ever

Cassady, J. C. (2000). Self-reported GPA and SAT: A methodological note. *Practical Assessment, Research, & Evaluation, 7*(12). Retrieved from https://scholarworks.umass.edu/pare/vol7/iss1/12/

Ceci, S. J. (1996). *On intelligence: A biological treatise on intellectual development* (Expanded ed.). Cambridge, MA: Harvard University Press.

Cepeda, N. J., Vul, E., Rohrer, D., Wixted, J. T., & Pashler, H. (2008). Spacing effects in learning. A temporal ridgeline of optimal retention. *Psychological Science, 19*(11), 1095–1102.

Chappuis, J., Stiggins, R. J., Chappuis, S., & Arter, J. A. (2012). *Classroom assessment for student learning: Doing it right, using it well* (2nd ed.). New York: Pearson.

Childs, S. E., Finnie, R., & Martinello, F. (2017). Postsecondary student persistence and pathways: Evidence from the YITS-A in Canada. *Research in Higher Education, 58,* 270–294.

Cornell University Center for Teaching Innovation. (n.d.). *Using rubrics.* Retrieved from https://teaching.cornell.edu/teaching-resources/assessment-evaluation/using-rubrics

Daspin, E. (2018). Why we remember. In *The science of memory: The story of our lives* (TIME Special Edition). New York: Time Inc. Books; Meredith Corporation.

Davenport, G. (2014). Poor workouts will cost WR Jarvis Landry dearly in loaded 2014 NFL draft. *Bleacher Report*. Retrieved from https://bleacherreport.com/articles/2023665-poor-workouts-will-cost-wr-jarvis-landry-dearly-in-loaded-2014-nfl-draft

Davies, A. (2000). *Making classroom assessment work*. London: Connections Publishing.

Deslauiers, L., Schelew, E., & Wieman, C. (2011). Improved learning in a large-enrollment physics class. *Science, 332*(6031), 862–864.

Donohoo, J. (2017a). *Collective efficacy: How educator's beliefs impact student learning*. Thousand Oaks, CA: Corwin.

Donohoo, J. (2017b). Collective teacher efficacy: The effect size research and six enabling conditions [Blog post]. *The Learning Exchange*. Retrieved from https://thelearning exchange.ca/collective-teacher-efficacy/

Donovan, J. (2019). *Shoot for the moon: The space race and the extraordinary voyage of Apollo 11*. New York: Little, Brown.

Dougherty, M. J. (1998). Why are we getting taller as a species? *Scientific American*. Retrieved from https://www.scientificamerican.com/article/why-are-we-getting-taller/

Dueck, M. (2014). *Grading smarter, not harder: Assessment strategies that motivate kids and help them learn*. Alexandria, VA: ASCD.

Dunlosky, J. (2013, Fall). Strengthening the student toolbox: Study strategies to boost learning. *American Educator*, 12–21.

Dunlosky, J., Rawson, K. A., Marsh, E. J., Nathan, M. J., & Willingham, D. T. (2013). Improving students' learning with effective learning techniques: Promising directions from cognitive and educational psychology. *Psychological Science in the Public Interest, 14*(1), 4–58.

Dupont, K. P. (2012). Vermont's "Death Race" a test of mental, physical strength. *Boston Globe Online*. Retrieved from https://www.bostonglobe.com/sports/2012/06/02/vermont-death-race-test-mental-and-physical-strength/6dnQG6jemw78wx3x8Mp3EK/story.html

Eberly Center for Teaching Excellence and Educational Innovation. (n.d.). *Creating and using rubrics*. Carnegie Mellon University. Retrieved from https://www.cmu.edu/teaching/assessment/assesslearning/rubrics.html

Eisner, E. W. (2012). It's more than numbers. In T. R. Guskey (Ed.), *Benjamin S. Bloom: Portraits of an educator* (pp. 14–15). Lanham, MD: Rowman & Littlefield.

Ericsson, A. K., & Pool, R. (2016). *Peak: How all of us can achieve extraordinary things*. Toronto, ON: Penguin.

Farrar, D. (2014, February 27). Receivers Odell Beckham Jr. and Jarvis Landry bring new level of LSU excellence to draft. *Sports Illustrated*. Retrieved from https://www.si.com/nfl/audibles/2014/02/27/odell-beckham-jr-jarvis-landry-lsu-2014-nfl-draft

Ferriss, T. (2017). *Tools of the titans: The tactics, routines, and habits of billionaires, icons, and world-class performers*. New York: Houghton Mifflin Harcourt.

From the Lab Bench. (2012). Olympic diving physics. Retrieved from http://www.fromthelabbench.com/from-the-lab-bench-science-blog/olympic-diving-physics

"g-Force." (n.d.). In *Formula 1 online dictionary*. Retrieved from http://www.formula1-dictionary.net/g_force.html

Gardner, H. (2006). *Multiple intelligences: New horizons in theory and practice* (Rev. ed.). New York: Basic Books.

Gernsbacher, M. A., & Pomerantz, J. R. (Eds.). (2014). *Psychology and the real world* (2nd ed.). New York: Worth.

Gladwell, M. (2013). *David and Goliath: Underdogs, misfits, and the art of battling giants*. Boston: Little, Brown.

Gregory, G., & Kaufeldt, M. (2015). *The motivated brain: Improving student attention, engagement, and perseverance*. Alexandria, VA: ASCD.

Gribble, A. (2018, October 8). Jarvis Landry's jersey headed to Pro Football Hall of Fame after smashing receptions record. *Cleveland Browns: News*. Retrieved from https://www.clevelandbrowns.com/news/jarvis-landry-s-jersey-headed-to-pro-football-hall-of-fame-after-smashing-recept

Guskey, T. R. (Ed.). (2012). *Benjamin S. Bloom: Portraits of an educator*. Lanham, MD: Rowman & Littlefield.

Guskey, T. (2013). The case against percentage grades. *Educational Leadership, 71*(1), 68–72.

Guskey, T. (2015). *On your mark: Challenging the conventions of grading and reporting*. Bloomington, IN: Solution Tree.

Guskey, T., & Brookhart, S. (2019). *What we know about grading: What works, what doesn't, and what's next*. Alexandria, VA: ASCD.

Halbert, J., & Kaser, L. (2013). *Spirals of inquiry for equity and quality*. Vancouver, BC: BC Principals' and Vice-Principals' Association.

Hardy, J. (2016). 23 Michael Jordan quotes that will immediately boost your confidence. *Inc.* Retrieved from https://www.inc.com/benjamin-p-hardy/23-michael-jordan-quotes-that-will-immediately-boost-your-confidence.html

Hattie, J. (2012). *Visible learning for teachers*. New York: Routledge.

Hierck, T., & Larson, G. L. (2018). *Grading for impact: Raising student achievement through a target-based assessment and learning system*. Thousand Oaks, CA: Corwin.

Howard, R. (Director). (2016). *The Beatles: Eight days a week: The touring years* [Film]. Apple Corps Imagine Entertainment, Whitehorse Pictures.

Jerema, C. (2010). Your grades will drop: How universities and high schools are setting students up for disappointment. *Maclean's*. Retrieved from https://www.macleans.ca/education/uniandcollege/your-grades-will-drop/

Joness, H. (2014, February 14). Jarvis Landry 2014 NFL draft profile. *SBNation*. Retrieved from https://www.bigcatcountry.com/2014/2/14/5409480/jarvis-landry-2014-nfl-draft-profile

Jordan, B. (2007). *Speaking the truth with eloquent thunder*. Austin, TX: University of Texas Press.

Kahneman, D. (2011). *Thinking, fast and slow*. Toronto, ON: Random House.

Kapur, M. (2015). Learning from productive failure. *Learning: Research and Practice, 1*(1), 51–65.

Kidd, C., Palmeri, H., & Aslin, R. N. (2013). Rational snacking: Young children's decision-making on the marshmallow task is moderated by beliefs about environmental reliability. *Cognition, 126*(1), 109–114. Retrieved from https://dx.doi.org/10.1016%2Fj.cognition.2012.08.004

Kornell, N., & Bjork, R. A. (2008). Learning concepts and categories: Is spacing the "enemy of induction"? *Psychological Science, 19*(6), 585–592.

Krathwohl, D. R. (2002). A revision of Bloom's taxonomy: An overview. *Theory into Practice, 41*(4), 212–218. Retrieved from https://doi.org/10.1207/s15430421tip4104_2

Kuncel, N. R., Credé, M., & Thomas, L. L. (2005). The validity of self-reported grade point averages, class ranks, and test scores: A meta-analysis and review of the literature. *Review of Educational Research, 75*(1), 63–82.

Lahey, J. (2015). *The gift of failure: How the best parents learn to let go so their children can succeed*. New York: HarperCollins.

Landauer, T. K., & Bjork, R. A. (1978). Optimum rehearsal patterns and name learning. In M. M. Gruneberg, P. E. Morris, & R. N. Sykes (Eds.), *Practical aspects of memory* (pp. 625–632). London: Academic Press.

Little, J. L., & Bjork, E. L. (2011). Pretesting with multiple-choice questions facilitates learning. In L. Carlson, C. Hölscher, & T. Shipley (Eds.), *Proceedings of the 33rd Annual Conference of the Cognitive Science Society* (pp. 294–299). Austin, TX: Cognitive Science Society.

Luros, M. (2015). Can I fire a chronically late employee? [Blog post]. Retrieved from https://www.hudsonluros.com/2015/01/can-i-fire-a-chronically-late-employee/

MacKillop, M., & Nieuwland, H. (2012). Firing for absenteeism and lateness [Blog post]. Retrieved from http://www.somlaw.ca/blog/blog-post/blog/2012/08/08/firing-for-absenteeism-and-lateness

Marzano, R. J. (2010). *Formative assessment and standards-based grading*. Bloomington, IN: Marzano Research Laboratory.

Marzano, R. J., & Haystead, M. W. (2008). *Making standards useful in the classroom*. Alexandria, VA: ASCD.

Maxwell, N. L., & Lopus, J. S. (1994). The Lake Wobegon effect in student self-reported data. *American Economic Review, 84*(2), 201–205.

Mayer, J. D. (2017). *Personality: A systems approach* (2nd ed.). Lanham, MD: Rowman & Littlefield.

Mayer, R. E., Stull, A. T., Campbell, J., Almeroth, K., Bimber, B., Chun, D., et al. (2007). Overestimation bias in self-reported SAT scores. *Educational Psychology Review, 19*, 443–454.

Mazarakis, A., & Shontell, A. (2017, August 10). Former Apple CEO John Sculley is working on a startup that he thinks could become bigger than Apple. *Business Insider*. Retrieved from http://www.businessinsider.com/john-sculley-interview-healthcare-pepsi-apple-steve-jobs-2017-8

McArdle, T. (2019). Tom Brady holds these 54 NFL records. *Boston.com*. Retrieved from https://www.boston.com/sports/new-england-patriots/2019/05/19/tom-brady-nfl-records

McDowell, M. (2017). *Rigorous PBL by design: Three shifts for developing confident and competent learners*. Thousand Oaks, CA: Corwin.

McKeown, G. (2014). *Essentialism: The disciplined pursuit of less*. New York: Crown Business.

Mervis, J. (2013). Transformation is possible if a university really cares. *Science, 340*(6130), 292–296.

Metcalfe, J., Butterfield, B., Habeck, C., & Stern, Y. (2012). Neural correlates of people's hypercorrection of their false beliefs. *Journal of Cognitive Neuroscience, 24*(7), 1571–1583.

MIT Registrar's Office. (n.d.). First year grading. Retrieved from https://registrar.mit.edu/classes-grades-evaluations/grades/grading-policies/first-year-grading

MockDraftable.com. (n.d.). Tom Brady: Measurables: Percentiles vs. quarterbacks. Retrieved from https://www.mockdraftable.com/player/tom-brady

Moss, C. M., & Brookhart, S. M. (2012). *Learning targets: Helping students aim for understanding in today's lesson*. Alexandria, VA: ASCD.

National Science Teaching Association (NSTA). (n.d.). 3rd grade: Weather and climate. Retrieved from https://ngss.nsta.org/DisplayStandard.aspx?view=topic&id=14

Newman, R. (1998). *African American quotes*. Phoenix, AZ: Oryx Press.

O'Connor, K. (2007). *A repair kit for grading: 15 fixes for broken grades*. Portland, OR: ETS.

O'Connor, K. (2018). *How to grade for learning: Linking grades to standards* (4th ed.). Thousand Oaks, CA: Corwin.

Ondrik, K. (2011). Building an inclusive culture in an intermediate classroom. In F. Brownlie & J. King (Eds.), *Learning in safe schools: Creating classrooms where all students belong* (2nd ed., pp. 68–79). Markham, ON: Pembroke.

O'Reilly, T. (2017). *This I know: Marketing lessons from Under the Influence*. Toronto, ON: Alfred A. Knopf.

Organisation for Economic Co-operation and Development (OECD). (2017). *The OECD handbook for innovative learning environments.* Retrieved from https://www.oecd.org/education/the-oecd-handbook-for-innovative-learning-environments-9789264277274-en.htm

Pass The Feather. (n.d.). *Talking feathers for sharing and restorative justice circles.* Retrieved from https://passthefeather.ca/sharing-circles/?v=e4b09f3f8402

Pollack, A. (1983, April 9). Apple gets president from Pepsi. *New York Times.* Retrieved from https://www.nytimes.com/1983/04/09/business/apple-gets-president-from-pepsi.html

Pyc, M. A., & Rawson, K. (2010). Why testing improves memory: Mediator effectiveness hypothesis. *Science, 330*(6002), 335.

Quaglia Institute for Student Aspirations. (2013). *My voice national student report 2013 (grades 6–12).* Retrieved from http://quagliainstitute.org/dmsView/MyVoice_NatReport2013

Quaglia Institute for Student Aspirations. (2018). *Student voice: A decade of data. Student voice grades 6–12.* Retrieved from http://quagliainstitute.org/dmsView/Student_Voice_Grades_6-12_Decade_of_Data_Report

Quaglia, R. J., & Corso, M. J. (2014). *Student voice: The instrument of change.* Thousand Oaks, CA: Corwin.

Queen's University. (n.d.). Rubrics. *onQ support.* Retrieved from https://www.queensu.ca/onqsupport/rubrics-new-experience

Reeves, D. B. (2010). *Standards, assessment, & accountability: Real questions from educators with real answers from Douglas B. Reeves, Ph.D.* Englewood, CA: Leadership and Learning Center.

Reinalda, R. (2014). Why you should never use absolutes. *HuffPost.* Retrieved from https://www.huffpost.com/entry/never-use-absolutes_b_4646420

Rohrer, D., & Taylor, K. (2007). The shuffling of mathematics practice problems improves learning. *Instructional Science, 35,* 481–498.

Rose, T. (2016). *The end of average: How we succeed in a world that values sameness.* New York: Harper Collins.

Rosen, J. A., Porter, S. R., & Rogers, J. (2017, April–June). Understanding student self-reports of academic performance and course-taking behavior. *AERA Open, 3*(2), 1–14. Retrieved from https://journals.sagepub.com/doi/pdf/10.1177/2332858417711427

Ruiz, S. (2019, September 12). The 100 best NFL quarterbacks of all time. *For the Win.* Retrieved from https://ftw.usatoday.com/2019/09/nfl-100-best-quarterbacks

Selingo, J. J. (2018, June 8). Why do so many students drop out of college? And what can be done about it? *Washington Post.* Retrieved from https://www.washingtonpost.com/news/grade-point/wp/2018/06/08/why-do-so-many-students-drop-out-of-college-and-what-can-be-done-about-it/

Shoda, Y., Mischel, W., & Peake, P. K. (1990). Predicting adolescent cognitive and self-regulatory competencies from preschool delay of gratification: Identifying diagnostic conditions. *Developmental Psychology, 26*(6), 978–986. Retrieved from https://depts.washington.edu/shodalab/wordpress/wp-content/uploads/2015/05/1990.Predicting Adolescent_Shoda.pdf

Shoda, Y., Mischel, W., & Wright, J. C. (1994). Intraindividual stability in the organization and patterning of behavior: Incorporating psychological situations into the idiographic analysis of personality. *Journal of Personality and Social Psychology, 67*(4), 674–687.

Simon, D., & Bjork, R. A. (2001). Metacognition in motor learning. *Journal of Experimental Psychology: Learning, Memory, and Cognition, 27*(4), 907–912.

Sinek, S. (2009). *Start with why.* New York: Penguin.

Smith, S. M., Glenberg, A. M., & Bjork, R. A. (1978). Environmental context and human memory. *Memory & Cognition, 6*(4), 342–353.

Sobleski, B. (2014). NFL combine 40-yard dash times. *SportsWire.* Retrieved from http://sportswire.usatoday.com/2014/02/23/nfl-combine-40-yard-dash-times-running-backs-quarterbacks-wide-receivers-johnny-manziel/

Swiss Education. (n.d.). Educational standards. Retrieved from https://swisseducation.educa.ch/en/educational-standards

TEKS Resource System. (n.d.). Instructional focus document: Grade 3 social studies. Retrieved from https://www.teksresourcesystem.net/module/standards/Tools/PDF Standard/237010/236812

Teye, A. C., & Peaslee, L. (2015). Measuring educational outcomes for at-risk children and youth: Issues with the validity of self-reported data. *Child & Youth Care Forum, 44*(6), 853–873.

Tolisano, S. R., & Hale, J. A. (2018). *A guide to documenting learning: Making thinking visible, meaningful, shareable, and amplified.* Thousand Oaks, CA: Corwin.

Tomlinson, C. A., & Moon, T. R. (2013). *Assessment and student success in a differentiated classroom.* Alexandria, VA: ASCD.

Waack, S. (2013). Glossary of Hattie's influences on student achievement. *Visible learning.* Retrieved from http://visible-learning.org/glossary/

Watts, T. W., Duncan, G. J., & Quan, H. (2018). Revisiting the marshmallow test: A conceptual replication investigating links between early delay of gratification and later outcomes. *Psychological Science, 29*(7), 1159–1177.

Wediko Children's Services. (n.d.). *Wediko Summer Program.* Retrieved from https://www.wediko.org/our-services/wediko-summer-program/overview

Western University Centre for Teaching and Learning. (n.d.). Grading with rubrics. Retrieved from https://teaching.uwo.ca/teaching/assessing/grading-rubrics.html

Wiliam, D. (2018). *Embedded formative assessment* (2nd ed.). Bloomington, IN: Solution Tree.

Willink, J., & Babin, L. (2015). *Extreme ownership—How U.S. Navy SEALs lead and win.* New York: St. Martin's Press.

Wisconsin Department of Public Instruction. (n.d.). *Academic standards.* Retrieved from https://dpi.wi.gov/standards

INDEX

Page references followed by an italicized *f* indicate information contained in figures.

ABOUT THE AUTHOR

Jeremy Hiebert

Myron Dueck has worked as both a teacher and an administrator for 23 years in Canada and New Zealand, with students in grades 4–12. In 2006, Myron began developing grading, assessment, and reporting systems with his classes that offer students an increased opportunity to show what they understand, adapt to the feedback they receive, and play a significant role in reporting their learning. Myron has been a part of administrative teams, district groups, school committees, and governmental bodies that have further broadened his access to innovative ideas. In recent years, Myron has served in an administrative role supporting assessment and innovation in his local school district, Okanagan-Skaha 67. Myron has shared his stories, tools, and firsthand experiences with public, charter, and international school educators throughout the world. Recently, his presentations have diverged to include global education trends and broader socioeconomic realities that affect learning.

Myron is the author of the best-selling ASCD book *Grading Smarter, Not Harder: Assessment Strategies That Motivate Kids and Help Them Learn* as well as an array of articles for *Educational Leadership*. In 2015, ASCD released a video project based in his school district titled *Smarter Assessment in the Secondary Classroom* and, in 2019, the first of a three-part online streaming series titled *Ask*

Them, hosted by Myron, looking at how we include students in assessment. The *Ask Them* series features John Hattie, Lorin Anderson, Celeste Kidd, and others.

Myron lives in Summerland, British Columbia, with his partner Tracey and their two children, Elijah and Sloane. You can reach Myron and learn more about his work through his website (www.myrondueck.com), e-mail (myrondueck@gmail.com), or Twitter (@myrondueck).

Related ASCD Resources: Assessment and Grading

At the time of publication, the following resources were available (ASCD stock numbers appear in parentheses).

Print Products

Advancing Formative Assessment in Every Classroom: A Guide for Instructional Leaders, 2nd Edition by Connie M. Moss and Susan M. Brookhart (#120005)

Assessment and Student Success in a Differentiated Classroom by Carol A. Tomlinson and Tonya R. Moon (#108028)

Changing the Grade: A Step-by-Step Guide to Grading for Student Growth by Jonathan Cornue (#118029)

Charting a Course to Standards-Based Grading: What to Stop, What to Start, and Why It Matters by Tim R. Westerberg (#117010)

Checking for Understanding: Formative Assessment Techniques for Your Classroom, 2nd Edition by Douglas Fisher and Nancy Frey (#115011)

Grading Smarter, Not Harder: Assessment Strategies That Motivate Kids and Help Them Learn by Myron Dueck (#114003)

How to Create and Use Rubrics for Formative Assessment and Grading by Susan M. Brookhart (#112001)

Learning Targets: Helping Students Aim for Understanding in Today's Lesson by Connie M. Moss and Susan M. Brookhart (#112002)

Making Standards Useful in the Classroom by Robert J. Marzano and Mark W. Haystead (#108006)

Mastering Formative Assessment Moves: 7 High-Leverage Practices to Advance Student Learning by Brent Duckor and Carrie Holmberg (#116011)

Peer Feedback in the Classroom: Empowering Students to Be the Experts by Starr Sackstein (#117020)

Rethinking Grading: Meaningful Assessment for Standards-Based Learning by Cathy Vatterott (#115001)

What We Know About Grading: What Works, What Doesn't, and What's Next by Thomas R. Guskey and Susan M. Brookhart (Eds.) (#118062)

For up-to-date information about ASCD resources, go to **www.ascd.org.** You can search the complete archives of *Educational Leadership* at **www.ascd.org/el.**

PD Online

Assessment: Designing Performance Assessments, 2nd Edition (PD11OC108S)

Assessment and Student Success in a Differentiated Classroom (#PD14OC019S)

Differentiated Instruction: Using Ongoing Assessment to Inform Instruction (#PD11OC117S)

Formative Assessment: Deepening Understanding (#PD11OC101S)

Grading Smarter, Not Harder (PD16OC005S)

ASCD myTeachSource®

Download resources from a professional learning platform with hundreds of research-based best practices and tools for your classroom at http://myteach source.ascd.org/.

For more information, send an e-mail to member@ascd.org; call 1-800-933-2723 or 703-578-9600; send a fax to 703-575-5400; or write to Information Services, ASCD, 1703 N. Beauregard St., Alexandria, VA 22311-1714 USA.

WHOLE CHILD
TENETS

HEALTHY
Each student enters school healthy and learns about and practices a healthy lifestyle.

SAFE
Each student learns in an environment that is physically and emotionally safe for students and adults.

ENGAGED
Each student is actively engaged in learning and is connected to the school and broader community.

SUPPORTED
Each student has access to personalized learning and is supported by qualified, caring adults.

CHALLENGED
Each student is challenged academically and prepared for success in college or further study and for employment and participation in a global environment.

THE **WHOLE CHILD**

The ASCD Whole Child approach is an effort to transition from a focus on narrowly defined academic achievement to one that promotes the long-term development and success of all children. Through this approach, ASCD supports educators, families, community members, and policymakers as they move from a vision about educating the whole child to sustainable, collaborative actions.

Giving Students a Say relates to the **engaged, supported,** and **challenged** tenets. *For more about the ASCD Whole Child approach, visit **www.ascd. org/wholechild**.*

Become an ASCD member today!
Go to www.ascd.org/joinascd
or call toll-free: 800-933-ASCD (2723)

LEARN. TEACH. LEAD.

DON'T MISS A SINGLE ISSUE OF ASCD'S AWARD-WINNING MAGAZINE,

EL EDUCATIONAL LEADERSHIP

If you belong to a Professional Learning Community, you may be looking for a way to get your fellow educators' minds around a complex topic. Why not delve into a relevant theme issue of *Educational Leadership*, the journal written by educators for educators.

Subscribe now, or buy back issues of ASCD's flagship publication at **www.ascd.org/ELbackissues.**

Single issues cost $7 (for issues dated September 2006–May 2013) or $8.95 (for issues dated September 2013 and later). Buy 10 or more of the same issue, and you'll save 10 percent. Buy 50 or more of the same issue, and you'll save 15 percent. For discounts on purchases of 200 or more copies, contact **programteam@ascd.org**; 1-800-933-2723, ext. 5773.

To see more details about these and other popular issues of *Educational Leadership*, visit **www.ascd.org/ ELarchive.**

LEARN. TEACH. LEAD.

1703 North Beauregard Street
Alexandria, VA 22311-1714 USA

www.ascd.org/el